The SOCIOLOGY of the INDIVIDUAL

To my Son, Husband and Father
who showed me new ways to consider
Life, Love and Loss

Athanasia Chalari

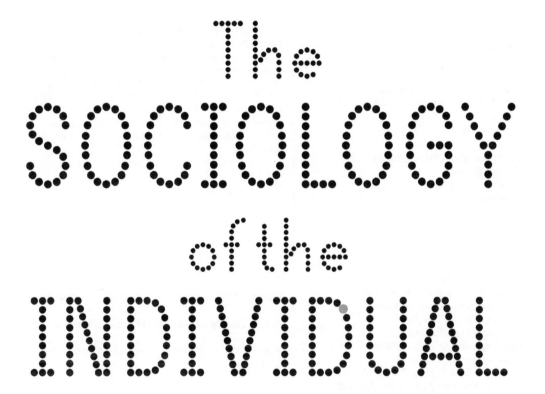

The SOCIOLOGY of the INDIVIDUAL

Relating Self and Society

Los Angeles | London | New Delhi
Singapore | Washington DC | Melbourne

Los Angeles | London | New Delhi
Singapore | Washington DC | Melbourne

SAGE Publications Ltd
1 Oliver's Yard
55 City Road
London EC1Y 1SP

SAGE Publications Inc.
2455 Teller Road
Thousand Oaks, California 91320

SAGE Publications India Pvt Ltd
B 1/I 1 Mohan Cooperative Industrial Area
Mathura Road
New Delhi 110 044

SAGE Publications Asia-Pacific Pte Ltd
3 Church Street
#10-04 Samsung Hub
Singapore 049483

Editor: Natalie Aguilera
Editorial assistant: Delayna Spencer
Production editor: Katherine Haw
Copyeditor: Bryan Campbell
Proofreader: Rebecca Storr
Marketing manager: Sally Ransom
Cover design: Shaun Mercier
Typeset by: C&M Digitals (P) Ltd, Chennai, India
Printed and bound by CPI Group (UK) Ltd,
    Croydon, CR0 4YY

© Athanasia Chalari 2017

First published 2017

Library of Congress Control Number: 2016936395

British Library Cataloguing in Publication data

A catalogue record for this book is available from the British
Library

ISBN 978-1-4462-7202-2
ISBN 978-1-4462-7204-6 (pbk)

At SAGE we take sustainability seriously. Most of our products are printed in the UK using FSC papers and boards.
When we print overseas we ensure sustainable papers are used as measured by the PREPS grading system.
We undertake an annual audit to monitor our sustainability.

Contents

About the Author

Dr Athanasia Chalari is a Principal Lecturer in Sociology at the University of Northampton and Research Associate at the Hellenic Observatory, LSE. She has worked as a Lecturer in Sociology at the University of Manchester, as a Postdoctoral Research Fellow at the Hellenic Observatory at LSE and as Senior Lecturer in Sociology at Worcester University. She has also conducted research at Harvard University as Visiting Fellow in Sociology and more recently at Toronto University, Canada as Visiting Professor. In Sociology her research focuses upon current and classic Social Theory and Modern Greek Society.

Introduction

Why the 'Sociology of the Individual'?

The title of this book might seem rather 'provocative', or maybe too ambitious, or perhaps even naïve. Why should and how could sociology be concerned with the individual? And perhaps more importantly, why should such an area of investigation merit a distinct place within sociology? If we could agree that sociology refers to the scientific study of human life, social groups, whole societies and the human world, then why should there be a separate concern about the sociological investigation of the individual? Shouldn't this be a psychological rather than sociological area of investigation?

Such questions are certainly legitimate and there is indeed valid ground for them to be raised. Inevitably the sociological exploration of the individual refers to the ongoing social-theoretical exploration of the relationship between the individual and society (or the relationship between structure and agency). It therefore seems that there is a fundamental need in current sociology to offer a distinct and well defined sociological 'space' to allow the novel exploration of what this book terms 'individual' or others may call 'self' or 'selfhood' or 'ego' or 'agency' or 'identity' or 'human being' or 'person' or 'subjectivity'.

Such exploration is by no means a new innovation. To the contrary, this book reveals in detail, how systematically, sociology (as well as psychology) has been concerned with the exploration, analysis and explanation of such terms and the ways they may be related to society. It seems though, that as far as sociology is concerned, there is some kind of restriction regarding 'how much' sociology should be involved in terms of the exploration of the individual as such. And perhaps this might be the fundamental criticism that this book may receive. Sociology is not about one 'individual'; rather it is about at least two related individuals. Therefore the minimum level of sociological analysis is a 'dyad' (in Simmel's terms). In fact, I couldn't agree more. Sociology is about at least two individuals relating to one another, or else, exchanging some short of action between them (interaction).

As accurate as this approach might be, this book is about to explain that sociological investigation is *also* about the ways (any) individual is relating to oneself. And for such relation to occur, the individual, or any form of human existence, should be in relation to someone else, as well as oneself. This book is written in an attempt to further support existing literature (primarily related to the exploration of the relationship between structure and agency) that promotes the urgency of continued sociological exploration of the ways the individual exchanges action with oneself, or in other words, the sociological significance of intra-action.

Why Individual?

This book aims in exploring through a variety of relevant concepts views and ideas, what could be sociologically defined as 'individual'. The first question one would inevitably ask is why 'individual' and not 'self' or 'selfhood' or 'ego' or 'agency' or 'identity' or 'human being' or 'person' or 'subjectivity'?

The reason why this book was not titled 'The Sociology of the Self' or 'Self and Society', following similar attempts by distinguished colleagues (May, 2013; Elliott, 2009; Burkitt, 2008; Adams, 2007; Harre and Moghaddam, 2003; Hewitt, 1997), is because this book is not interested in exploring a rather abstract connection between society and the notion of 'self'. Chapters 5 and 6 discuss and explain why the idea of self cannot be a concept that enables the exploration of the relationship between the individual and society (or structure and agency). Self is supported to be an over-researched area of exploration by both sociology and psychology, but it still remains a vague and unclear concept which could be, and has been, used in a rather free and certainly not consistent way.

Similarly, associated terms, such as 'selfhood', 'subjectivity' and 'person' entail the exact same uncertainty. In the same vein, and as discussed in Chapter 4, the idea of 'identity' (often confused with the notion of self) involves a similarly rich and fruitful plurality of sociological and psychological approaches and views, that it becomes impossible to be restricted in a specific and concrete definition. The concept of 'ego' is certainly related to psychoanalytic explanations (discussed in Chapter 6) which would inevitably restrict the purpose of this book.

Equally, analogous limitations are related to the usage of the concepts 'human being' and 'agency'. The former was not used because, the systematic usage of the term 'human being' requires a sophisticated engagement with philosophical principles and theorizations which could alter the content of this book to a rather philosophical enterprise. The latter, 'agency', is certainly a pertinent and appropriate concept, and indeed several established scholars have used it systematically (Kogler, 2012; Elder-Vass, 2010; Archer, 2003; Bratman, 2007; Fleetwood, 2008; Wang, 2008; Hitlin and Elder, 2007; Apter and Garnsey, 1994). Agency is a term usually used in relation to structure as the core sociological question regarding the relationship between these two spheres of analysis remains a vivid sociological area of exploration. The reason why the concept of agency is not used in the title of this book is because this concept is primarily involved in this particular debate and although this book is profoundly engaged with this problematization, the term 'agency' might denote certain levels of theoretical argumentation that could prove to be beyond the purpose of this book.

However, the usage of the term 'individual' implies the involvement of a rather modest, ordinary and at the same time equally valid and intellectually relevant term which has not been extensively analysed or even used by sociological or psychological literature. In this sense, it might be appropriate to use this term as it allows some scope of novel sociological conceptualization.

The notion of the individual is then used as an umbrella term as it allows the parallel usage of two central conceptualizations that allow the examination of the relationship between structure and agency on a rather 'simplified' basis which could be viewed as the connection between interaction and intra-action. The 'Sociology of the Individual' can then be perceived as an attempt to open up to a wider public the opportunity to engage with a fundamental and continuous sociological discussion about the ways the individual is connected to society.

And the way this is done is by explaining how and why prominent sociological (as well as psychological) conceptualizations (interaction, symbolic interaction, socialization, identity, self, unconscious and conscious self) used repeatedly in literature could be viewed through (or in relation to) an additional perception which synthesizes characteristics of innovative social-theoretical and psychological theorizations: that of intra-action. Thus, this book reviews a certain range of sociological and psychological concepts, views, ideas and perceptions which have contributed towards the suggestion of this book, namely to explain the distinction (along with the connection) between interaction and what this book terms intra-action.

Sociological and Psychological Approaches

Although the title of this book clearly indicates its sociological content and purpose, a plurality of psychological approaches, theorizations and explanations have been incorporated. The reason is that the exploration of the idea of the individual (or any of the associated concepts mentioned above), cannot be examined in a holistic manner by excluding either of those disciplines (although admittedly, in this attempt even more disciplines could be added). Furthermore, the additional reason why both disciplines were involved relates to the anticipation that each of them can contribute distinct explanations and evaluations which should be brought together while trying to approach a more inclusive understanding of intra-action as well as interaction (and all supplementary terms and ideas discussed in the following chapters).

Various publications, particularly relating to the exploration of self or identity, follow explicit sociological or psychological approaches as there seems to be a hesitant tendency regarding synergies between the two disciplines. However, this book aims at bridging possible conflicting perspectives by the focusing of synthesizing rather than contradictory tendencies. There are various sections in certain chapters, where sociological and psychological perspectives are so closely interrelated that it may become impossible to provide a clear distinction between them. This book is structured in a way to promote the prospect of fruitful interdisciplinary synergies that sociology and psychology could offer regarding the exploration of the individual.

What is the Purpose of this Book?

These are the main objectives of this book:

- This book aims at offering thorough, critical and simplified overviews of key sociological and psychological concepts related to the sociological exploration of the individual.

- To be able to explain the limitations related to each conceptualization regarding its ability to provide a concrete definition of what the individual is.

- To try to combine in a balanced way, sociological and psychological explanations of the approaches that will be employed, in a complementary rather than contradictory way.

- To offer a rather simplified opportunity to a wider public to get engaged with fairly complex sociological and psychological intellectual discussions regarding the ways the individual is connected to society.

- To inspire, through everyday examples, a more comprehensive understanding of applicable sociological and psychological theorizations related to the individual.

- To combine, in a critical and synthesized manner, sociological and psychological views towards the construction of a meaningful, comprehensible and applicable sociological theorization of intra-action.

- Finally, to make clear that the relationship between the individual and society or between structure and agency can be approached through the combined as well as distinct examination of the concepts of interaction and intra-action.

Structure of the Book

This book will try to meet the targets of this enterprise by using a wide variety of tailored everyday examples (at the beginning and end of each chapter) and by focusing on the following areas: Chapter 1 will introduce the initial definitions of the main concepts used in this book, namely those of interaction and intra-action. The sociological examination of the idea of interaction will be provided by incorporating one of the first sociological approaches employed by Georg Simmel, who has been focusing on the study of the distinction between interaction and inner life. A number of associated theories and perspectives will be discussed whereas the size of interaction will be analysed according to Simmel's works (dyad, triad). Furthermore, contemporary sociological and psychological views on group interactions will also be discussed.

Chapter 2 introduces the school of thought of symbolic interactionism by providing an overview of its origins and the main concepts associated to its content (thinking, meaning, symbols and socialization). Intra-action is also discussed in relation to this theoretical perspective. Separate psychological views deriving from symbolic interactionism and related to the individual are also considered whereas distinct concepts promoted through this school of thought are also analysed (self, the 'I' and the 'Me' as well as dramaturgy). A brief discussion regarding the sociology of emotions is also presented as well as an indicative overview of the methods and methodology of symbolic interactionism.

Chapter 3 is involved with the concept of socialization as an ongoing form of interaction. Socialization is then defined through sociological classic and current theorizations whereas psychological perspectives are also discussed thoroughly. Furthermore, intra-action is discussed in relation to the process of socialization. Childhood socialization is extensively discussed through sociological and psychological perspectives whereas specific socialization processes are separately discussed (family, school, peers, gender, media, socialization through the life course).

The following three chapters of this book are devoted to two central and interrelated sociological and psychological notions directly related to the idea of the individual: that of identity and the self. Chapter 4 introduces identity by incorporating a plurality of sociological and psychological perspectives primarily focused on the aspects of personal, social/relational and collective identity. An attempt to bring the idea of intra-action closer to the notion of identity has also been incorporated. Certain identity theories have also been discussed thoroughly (role identity theory, identity theory, act control theory and queer theory). Also, certain forms of indicative as well as prevailed identities have been considered (stigmatized, gender, sexual, race and ethnic identity).

Chapter 5 explores sociological and psychological approaches of the self by focusing on classic social theory and the work of Simmel, the school of thought of American Pragmatism, symbolic interactionism as well as current approaches, including reflexive self. Psychological perspectives associated to self exploration are reviewed by providing a broad definition, followed by separate discussions regarding self-concept, self-awareness and self-consciousness as well as selfhood. Certain synthesized approaches are then considered, like those of the association between self and identity, social cognition and the self, and finally the association between intra-action and the self.

Chapter 6 further explores the notion of self, only this time primarily psychoanalytic and psychotherapeutic views are used in relation to the ideas of conscious and unconscious self. Self, if thus defined through Freudian psychoanalytic tradition, followed by neo-Freudian views, the Frankfurt school perspectives, post-Freudian evaluations and Lacanian psychoanalytic accounts regarding the idea of the self. The following section is related to person-centred perspectives of the self which are related to Rogers' relevant theory and practice. Pertinent psychotherapeutic techniques are then employed in the exploration of the notion of self by focusing on psychoanalytic psychotherapy and client-centred psychotherapy. Limitations of psychotherapeutic discourse are considered and intra-action is also evaluated in relation to the psychotherapeutic techniques discussed.

Finally, Chapter 7 investigates the concept of intra-action as a way to reveal a term that might be used as a concrete explanation of how the individual experiences exchange of action within oneself. The relationship between intra-action and interaction is initially defined as a dualism and then as a duality. The origins of intra-action are traced in the work of Simmel, the school of thought of American Pragmatism and the works of Vygotsky and Piaget. Intra-action is then further explained as a form dualism through theories and studies associated to dialogic perspectives. Following that, intra-action is defined as a form of duality through theories and applications associated to the idea of inner speech and internal conversation. External conversation is also discussed as a form of interaction. The concept of reflexivity (again through dualism and duality) is then analysed as an applied form of intra-action whereas applied intra-action is finally simplified through the idea of mediation.

Acknowledgements

This book was written in an attempt to explain possible ways individuals may relate to society while living their everyday lives. Such an attempt is by no means new, however, it might be one of the first endeavours to become an accessible companion to undergraduate and postgraduate sociology and social sciences students while they try to understand how people are connected to society, to other people but more importantly to oneself. The purpose of this book is to navigate through fundamental sociological and psychological concepts that could explain the ways people relate to one another, while they relate to themselves and how individuals exchange action between them, while they exchange action within oneself. To do that, a number of topical examples have been discussed while a rather creative side of sociological imagination has been employed.

This book is the outcome of endless silent conversations the author had within her mind with herself as well as a number of new and old colleagues, family members, close friends, loved ones who are no longer with us, treasured ones who were recently born, trusted ones who are no longer friends and strangers who became companions. Therefore, this book is about the life one can live inside her/his own mind while trying to share the same life with others. As will be explained in the pages of this book, this is not an easily maintained endeavour, but somehow most individuals end up 'finding their ways through the world',[1] partly privately and partly publically. Such an ongoing accomplishment remains constantly incomplete, unpredictably fragile and inevitably unstable. Therefore, it embodies a first class example of sociological investigation.

It would have been impossible to envision this book without reading and considering all the books and journal articles mentioned in it and without trying to expand on my previous monograph, which although it was published in 2009, has remained an unlimited source of unanswered questions. Equally, I owe a particular debt of gratitude to my PhD supervisor Professor Margaret Archer, who without realizing it, became one of my constant and continuing internal conversation partners. In mentioning her name I do not in any way presume upon her endorsement or willingness to underwrite the views and interpretations discussed in this book. To the contrary, as she knew nothing about this publication, I only wish to thank her for her support and guidance ever since I had the privilege of meeting her.

I should also like to thank some colleagues I had the pleasure to share my thoughts with while considering this project. First, I would like to thank Professor Nicos Mouzelis who has always been one of the most influential and inspiring social theorists that I had the honour to encounter. I should express my gratitude to Professor Erik Schneiderhan, at the University of Toronto, Canada and Professor Philip Walsh, at the University of York, Toronto, who both facilitated my research for one year by enabling me to use the magnificent resources offered by both universities. I should also thank my colleagues Mike Webb and Lesley Spiers for their continuous support and also Drs Daniel Nehring and Stavros Emmanuil for their valuable comments and encouragement. Additionally, I would like to thank Dr Alina Tryphonidou for her empathetic understanding. Finally, I need to thank my mother and family for their support but above all, my father, my son and my husband who unintentionally inspired extraordinary internal conversations that I never thought I could even consider.

Note

1   To use one of Archer's (2007) famous book titles.

1

Interaction

Society is the sum of interactions among its members. (Simmel, 1908a)

Why is Interaction Important?

Social interaction is the most basic unit of sociological analysis and exploration; if we want to understand how the social world works, we first need to understand what social interaction is. Any form of social interaction involves and entails at least two human beings. The way these individuals connect, relate and associate may reveal aspects of how society is organized. Social interaction is perhaps the most ephemeral unit of social analysis; at the same time it might become one of the most fruitful sources of sociological and psychological knowledge. Social interactions are formed, re-formed, ceased, recreated, negotiated, reinvented, reconsidered and ultimately reproduced, through an unconceivable plurality of potential combinations. Interaction is what makes society possible. But, then again, where does interaction derive from? Is it sufficient to discuss interaction without involving the way individuals produce intra-action? Can we start exploring the social world without realizing the source of their action?

This chapter explores what we actually mean by interaction in providing definitions and relating the concepts of interaction and intra-action. Simmel's analytical exploration on interaction is then provided by linking interaction with socialization and explaining the distinction between: a) content and form of social interaction, and the concepts of; b) domination and conflict. A wide variety of additional approaches are also discussed in this chapter by providing brief overviews of the importance of social interaction in the thought of critical theory and exchange theory, functionalism and feminism as well as approaches related to micro-sociology and social networks research. Group formation and group size in the work of Simmel are then considered, followed by sociological and psychological perspectives on inter-group and intra-group relations.

EXAMPLE

A member of a national government in a high position receives a phone call from his fellow colleague in the United Nations announcing that his country is about to be attacked by a neighbouring country. What will this person do? Will he try to confirm the validity of the information he received? Will he follow the required national protocol? Will he inform the other members of the government and possibly the parliament? Will he inform his family and maybe some friends? Will he try to get in contact with the neighbouring country? Will he alert the Ministry of Defence? Or perhaps will he just book a ticket to an unknown destination? Therefore, the question is: What kind(s) of possible interaction(s) will this person follow? Will he act on his own? Will he act as a member of a group? Will he follow the appropriate and required forms of action? Will he follow his personal principles or perhaps will he run to save his life? This extreme and hopefully rare example, outlines the potential complexity of an initial interaction between two people (receiver and sender of a specific message). The interaction produced during the phone call in this example, is not the primary unit of analysis. The potential interaction(s) that this individual is about to produce, is exactly what both sociological and psychological research might try to explore. But is this example exclusively about how one individual might interact with other individual(s), or groups, or even nations? Or is it also (if not mainly) about how this individual might get in contact with oneself?

What Do We Mean by Interaction?

Sociological perspectives on interaction

Interaction refers to exchange of action between at least two individuals or groups of individuals (Chalari, 2009). There are uncountable ways that people can exchange action and some of them refer to face-to-face relationships or ways of connection between people; for example: an intense look, a gesture, flirting, money transaction, class attendance, specific kinds of dressing, ways of talking, body language, expression of emotions (crying, smiling) or even children's games. In current societies, interaction can be mediated by smartphones, social media for example forms of interaction may include: a phone text, a voice message, a video message, a Facebook profile statement. All kinds of interactions require a 'sender' of action and a 'receiver' of action. Some kinds of interaction require the usage of language or symbols (symbolic interactionism will be discussed separately in the following chapter) (Ritzer and Stepnisky, 2014). Many forms of interaction may be completely silent (e.g. flirting through eye contact) some others may involve power (arguing) or physical involvement (fighting), abuse (manipulation), structural reproduction (wedding), role playing (acting as a professional), order (following the letter

of the law), automatic responses (giving way to the car ahead), reflexive deliberations (deciding to have a family), oppression (living in authoritarian regimes),
learning (toddler learning to eat on her own), teaching (teaching an older person
how to use the Internet) and endless more forms of action exchange. Social interaction may concern trivial daily routines (shopping) or can have profound
consequences (family planning). Even seemingly private actions may derive from
some form of social interaction (reading a book, writing an essay).

Interaction is experienced by all individuals, in our everyday lives, in various
forms, for various purposes and in amazingly complicated combinations. Still, interaction remains a very specific and well-defined unit of social research and one of
the most useful concepts sociology and psychology use to understand how the
social world works. Interaction or social engagement according to Vom Lehn (2007)
involves two or more individuals who perceive and orient their actions to one
another. But as interaction is about human contact, then where does it derive from?
How can we approach the source of this social phenomenon?

What do we mean by intra-action?

Interaction derives from the exchange of human action experienced between individuals. However, human action is not only perceived as interaction between
individuals but interaction within the individual (Charon, 2011). Intra-action is a
recent and not fully-established concept used in sociology and psychology to
describe the exchange of action within the individual (Chalari, 2009). Following
the definition of interaction, intra-action concerns the exchange of linguistic, or
non-linguistic forms of action between the sender and the receiver, who is the
same person. The individual acts towards others but also acts towards oneself
(Charon, 2011). Although this concept will be analytically discussed in Chapter 7,
it is vital to explain how this notion is related to interaction, and actually to clarify
that interaction might not even be possible without intra-action. Intra-action refers
to subjectivity and inner life. It refers to thoughts, concerns, dialogues, hopes,
anticipations, needs, feelings, plans and intentions that each individual experiences
within oneself; others may or may not know about these experiences. This book,
perceives intra-action primarily through the concept of internal conversation proposed by Archer (2003, 2007). Although Archer uses the term internal conversation
she does not refer exclusively to communicative means of conversation. She refers
to all those ways that individuals use to become reflexive about themselves and
about the social world. Therefore, internal conversation and intra-action may be
perceived in similar (if not identical) terms. The reason why the term intra-action
is used in this book is because this term may be used in a broader way to describe
the ability of the individuals to experience action internally (inside their minds)
without necessarily being understood by others. A characteristic example would be
that of 'resistance' as individuals can experience internal resistance as something

completely different compared to the conventional understanding of resistance as a social act of opposition (Chalari, 2012).

The idea of intra-action, relates to Vygotky's work on inner speech, where he introduced the idea of intra-psychological properties and processes (further discussed in Chapters 3 and 7). At the same time this term has been used in current psychological literature primarily involved with developmental aspects and learning processes. Intra-action is then defined as the communication with oneself through the use of external tools. Psychological research has used specific ways to investigate such processes as: note-taking, annotation, diary-keeping and bookmarking; such methods involve repeated passing of meaningful messages, both informative and emotional, and hence could be regarded as communication (Hwang et al., 2009; Davies, 2014). Extensive discussion on related concepts will be presented in later chapters (particularly Chapter 7); indicatively, some similar terms used in sociological and psychological literature include: inner speech, self-talk, intrapersonal communication, egocentric speech, dialogical self. As can be seen, related terms involve communicational aspects, which will be explained later. For now, we need to make clear that intra-action relates to interaction in the sense that, as individuals are able to exchange action between them (in both verbal and non-verbal manners), similarly, each individual is equally able to experience exchange of action within oneself (in both linguistic or non-linguistic forms).

Interaction and intra-action

This chapter explores interaction as the way that individuals associate to one another and form relationships between them. As will be extensively discussed in the following chapters, in order for individuals to be able to form connections and relationships with other individuals and therefore produce interaction, they first need to produce intra-action. As Mouzelis explains, 'It is considered necessary to see how an actor deals not only with other actors during but also interaction (while interacting) with himself/herself' (2008). Current social theorists are trying to explore this connection more closely by, for instance, focusing on encounters and looking into the interface between interaction and intra-action since encounters both shape and are shaped by the exercise of our reflexivity (Carrigan, 2015). Both interaction and intra-action will be explored in sociological and psychological ways. The sociology of the individual concerns exactly this kind of exploration: how is the individual connected to society? One way to find out is to explore why individuals are concerned in relating to one another. Perhaps it might be helpful to first realize that individuals are predominantly concerned in finding ways to connect with themselves. Simmel very characteristically stated that, if we want to understand how society works, we need to study the people that created society (Simmel, 1908a). This chapter is focused on the exploration of interaction rather than intra-action but it has to be made clear that this book perceives interaction through intra-action, meaning that in order for interaction to be produced, some sort of intra-action should be experienced first.

Simmel's Exploration of Interaction

Although a wide variety of scholars have been concerned with the study of interaction over the last two centuries, Simmel is one of the first to provide systematic and analytic accounts of interaction as a way to comprehend social reality. Simmel was the only one out of the four founding fathers of sociology (Durkheim, Marx, Weber, Simmel), to investigate society primarily through social interaction. His work influenced sociological (and psychological) thought on both sides of the Atlantic and his exploration of the concept of interaction remains one of the most systematic elucidations regarding the ways people exchange action. Perhaps even more importantly, Simmel is one of the first social theorists (if not the first) to distinguish between interaction and some sort of inner life (or intra-action, although he never used this term) as he was concerned with the exploration of the exchange of action between, as well as within, individuals. It therefore seems appropriate to begin the discussion of this sociological concept by concentrating on Simmel's fundamental, as well as controversial, perspective.

Defining interaction

For Simmel (1908a), social interaction refers to the creation of bonds between individuals; social interaction unifies people into larger groups and societies. Individuals form groups when they interact or associate and therefore influence one another. Simmel perceived society as a way of describing the ways people associate and instead of referring to groups or societies he preferred to refer to social interactions that form groups and societies. For Simmel, society is based on creative social interaction; society exists only in the minds of individuals who participate in relationships with others and he believed that even if society is invisible, it forms the ways that people tie together in social relationships; therefore, if we want to understand how society works, we need to study the people that created society. Bougle (1905), while reviewing Simmel's masterpiece 'Soziologie' (Simmel, 1950), explained that the analysis of interaction for Simmel reveals the essence of sociology. Interaction has to concern institutions that dominate individuals (church, political power). However, the most important element regards the significance of 'association', referring to the relations between individuals and the effect they exert upon each other.

Interaction and sociation (socialization)

For Simmel (1908a), any form of interaction, as insignificant as it might seem, allows social beings to become fortified and accomplish the prospect of personal development and fulfilment. He explained that as individuals interact, they actually form/produce 'sociation' (socialization). As will be further explained in Chapter 3, socialization constitutes the basis of society and it is the outcome of the endless ways that individuals relate to one another. The phenomenon of sociability (Geselligkeit) regards the spontaneous generation of social relationships for whatever purposes. While individuals interact, they create (even ephemerally) social units (groups, associations, partnerships, intimate relations). These social units relate/interact with other social units (relations between partnerships, between families, couples, peer groups) in various forms (in conflicting, contradictory, complementary or even competitive ways) and this is exactly the way through which they are becoming vivid and active parts of society. Day after day, this is how society is recreated. The ways individuals within a group interact may vary tremendously (consider how differently families are shaped and function). In many cases individuals are not even conscious of the ways they interact (the ways children follow the parents' prohibitions/encouragements). Therefore, in turn, forms of socialization may vary enormously according to the degree of consciousness or realization of the formal ties that unite participants (Pampel, 2000). For example, a child might automatically follow its parents' instructions whereas in a workplace an individual might question the authority of a colleague.

Form and content of interaction

Simmel (1908a) explains that it is vital to distinguish between the content and form of people's interactions (and ultimately socialization). Content of interaction refers to the psychological drives of individuals like trust, loyalty, gratitude, devotion or in more general terms, the instincts, interests or tendencies of interaction whereas form describes the social form in which individuals interact (Watier, 2008). Pampel (2000) explains that for Simmel, content of interactions consists of all elements that bring people together in social interaction (if two individuals meet for the first time, the content of interaction might involve mutual attraction or indifference). In this context it might be appropriate to relate Simmel's understanding of content with what this chapter refers to as intra-action, as both concepts describe the individual's inner state of being during interaction. Form of interaction on the other hand, reflects common patterns and routines of behaviour that organize social interaction (in the above-mentioned case, the form of interaction would involve certain kinds of greetings, handshake, standard verbal expressions). Therefore, content of interaction has to do with the ways specific individuals interact on different occasions, whereas social form of interaction has to do with the ways interaction is socially organized on different occasions.

Indeed, in everyday life individuals follow specific patterns (forms) of behaviour to interact: the way we do money transactions, the way we smile, nod, kiss, say 'goodbye'. Naturally, different cultures follow different patterns, but there is a general understanding of what kind of behaviour is expected to be followed on certain occasions. Also, children follow different (perhaps in freer ways) patterns of interaction according to their age. As they move on to adulthood they learn to follow socially expected forms of interaction. It might also be notable that children's forms of interaction vary while they interact with same-aged peers and may be different when they interact with adults. Although individuals do follow patterns and forms of social interaction, the actual interaction on each occasion may vary tremendously. Although we may meet the same people every day, discuss the same issues in similar settings (in the workplace) it is not difficult to realize that each interaction will be completely different and unique. Therefore, the content of each interaction will be different as it depends on the individuals who conduct the actual interaction. Simmel uses the example of language to explain that social form is like grammar and syntax in a sentence. We might not be able to identify the exact grammatical and syntactic rules we follow every time we produce an utterance, but we have all learned this through school education and we are able to use them, usually fairly successfully. However, the meanings of each phrase we produce vary according to the content of each conversation. For Simmel, the role of sociology is to study social forms of interaction rather than explain the content of social interaction (Pampel, 2000).

Domination and conflict in social interaction

For Simmel (1908b) two significant components of social interaction are those of domination and conflict. Although both characteristics have been understood as negative forms of socialization and interaction, Simmel explains that actually, both of them might entail individual freedom and positive integration.

Domination

Craib (1997) explains that for Simmel, even the most tyrannical form of domination constitutes a form of interaction. For Simmel domination is not merely a matter of prestige or power; it can become a matter of mutual exchange of influence of both participants, which may involve considerable degrees of personal freedom. Even the followers may have choice in how they act (they can respond to domination with apathy, enthusiasm or they could resist and oppose the power of the leader or submit fully to his/her control). Perhaps what could be added here is that in any of the above-mentioned options, the individual who accepts or suffers the relevant consequences and acts accordingly, usually uses certain ways of appropriate compromise and adjustments (Chalari, 2009: 176–96). Social interactions where domination is profound could be seen in the relations between: child and parents, student and teacher, bureaucrats and clients or any other kind of individuals' interaction involving partners of unequal power. The nature and degree of mutual influence depends of the social circumstances of each occasion.

Simmel proposes three types of domination (Craib, 1997: 161): a) domination by an individual which could be accepted or opposed by the followers. This primary form of domination can be found in authoritarian regimes (where individual freedom is limited), in cases of political leadership (where the actions of the leader may be significantly influenced by the followers) or in classrooms between the teacher and the students (where order, rather than strict power, is imposed). b) Domination by a plurality or a group (a government, a church, the British Empire). Such domination may seem impersonal, unemotional and distant. The rights of the individuals in the dominant group are not necessarily extended to those in the subordinate group or crowd. c) Domination by an impersonal principle or law (after the French revolution, people took pride in obeying the principle of 'freedom' – as was then perceived). Modern societies are usually dominated by objective rules, norms and principles rather than by single persons. For Simmel, domination describes a specific kind of interaction between individuals which also includes power as well as freedom (even if it might be limited).

Conflict

Several social interactions are characterized by conflict. Intimate relationships, friendships, parent and children interactions, business partnerships, government negotiations and economic transactions are just some examples. Craib (1997) explains that for Simmel conflict may be an attempt to resolve divergences and restore unity even if it is through the elimination of one of the parties (divorce, break up, even breach of contract). For Simmel (1908b), conflict entails both positive and negative aspects; conflict might be destructive on an individual level (divorce) but could turn out to become a form of integration on a social level (feminist wave). Conflict can correct the harmful behaviour of leaders or dominating groups (conflicting public discussions about gay rights). Conflict between groups can generate solidarity within groups (conflict between nations usually increases nationalism within nations). In any event, domination and conflict are fundamental characteristics of social interactions as they can occur during the exchange of action between at least two individuals. As will be analytically discussed in later chapters, conflict in particular, is one of those characteristics of social interaction, that can also be experienced even if only one individual is concerned; this constitutes a form of intra-action.

Additional Approaches to Interaction

Various social-theoretical approaches have used social interaction in different ways to explore social reality. Each perspective provides alternative understandings of how individuals interact, by emphasizing specific aspects and concepts. The most influential explanations of social interaction are offered by the school of thought of symbolic interactionism, which will be discussed separately, in Chapter 2. In the following sections, some indicative theories and perspectives will be discussed; however, the rationale of this chapter concerns a wide and rather general overview of relevant approaches rather than the presentation of a complete and detailed discussion of any possible sociological view on social interaction.

Critical theory

Critical theory is a product of German Neo-Marxists who were dissatisfied with the state of Marxian theory (for further discussion see Agger, 1998). Habermas (1971) in particular, focused his criticism on Marx's failure to distinguish his analysis on work or labour (purposive rational action) and social interaction (communicative action). Habermas' work is based on the distinction between work and interaction (Habermas, 1970: 91) and he explains that the actions of people are coordinated through acts of reaching understanding rather than acts of egocentric calculations. Communicative action enables individuals to pursue their individual goals under the condition that they harmonize their plans of action on the basis of common situation definitions (Habermas, 1984: 286). As Stryker (1998) explains, the object of communicative action is to achieve communicative understanding although Habermas (1984: 278) refers to speech acts as well as non-verbal expressions. The communicative importance of interaction will be further analysed in the following chapter on symbolic interactionism. Critical theory, highlighted the omission of a clear distinction between the significance of work and interaction in Marx's work.

Exchange theory

Blau (1964) was one of the sociologists who were primarily interested in understanding the structures that govern social interactions rather than explore social interactions as such. He was mainly concerned with a specific form of interaction, that of exchange, and tried to study it by connecting personal exchange transactions between people with the ways differentiation and status are formed. He explained that people are attracted to one another for a wide variety of reasons. The outcome of this attraction is the formation of social associations (social interactions). The maintenance of the bonds between the individuals that form any given social association/interaction related to the rewards each person offers and receives (two individuals falling in love and both offer intimate feelings). Insufficient rewards may break the anticipated bonds (insufficient caring in a relationship). Such rewards may be intrinsic (love, affection, caring) or extrinsic (money, physical labour). Usually, inequality in exchange of rewards occurs, and then, difference in power is inevitably involved (in a family were only the father is working, the mother usually tries to balance her contribution by offering intrinsic rewards which are not evaluated as being equally important to the husband's extrinsic rewards, i.e. his salary). Blau (1964) explains that in cases that one member of the association is unable to offer adequate rewards then four options are possible: i) people can force other people to help them; ii) they can replace one person with another; iii) people can try to get along without receiving what they need from others; or iv) people can subordinate themselves to others and give the other the 'generalized credit' in their relationship. Power, in this case, is inevitably involved. This is how exchange theory analyses social interaction. This approach can be used in many cases of imbalance between the people who maintain an established social interaction, varying from the relationship of two lovers, to the relationship between nations. Unlike Simmel, for Blau social interactions cannot be analysed separately from social structures that surround them. Social structures have a separate existence that affects the process of interaction. Furthermore, Blau (1994) proposed specific explanations regarding group formations, which will be discussed in the following sections. Blau's explanation of how individuals interact within groups, reveals the significance of exchange and competition during interaction.

Structural functionalism

Functionalism (or structural functionalism) is one of the most influential social theories that tried to explain how the social world works. Despite its hegemony in the two decades after the World War II, structural functionalism has declined in importance as sociological theory. Although this school of thought takes various forms, societal functionalism is the most dominant approach and is concerned with the large-scale social structures and institutions. One of the main arguments of this school of thought regards social stratification, which is seen as universal and necessary (Ritzer and Stepnisky, 2014). Talcot Parsons' (1951) representative work briefly discusses social interaction while developing his theory of social systems. For Parsons, the most elementary form of social system is the interaction between the ego and the alter ego. This basic form of interaction is present in the more complex forms taken by the social system. The social system, for Parsons (1951: 5–6) is defined as the result of the interactions between the pluralities of individuals. Actors, while interacting within a particular cultural environment, have a tendency of 'optimization of gratification'. Interaction is therefore formed according to a 'system of cultured and shared symbols'. Therefore, although social system constitutes a system of interaction, Parsons clarifies that interaction is not the fundamental unit of analysis. Actually, he used the status-role complex as the basic unit of system. Status, ultimately refers to structural positions within a system and role is what the actor does in this position, which corresponds to the functional significance for the larger system. Therefore, the individual is perceived as nothing more than a bundle of statuses and roles (Ritzer and Stepnisky, 2014).

Feminist theory

Feminist theory perceives social interaction through a different perspective, which is based on the symbolic interactionism's (discussed in the following chapter) fundamental presumption that interaction is the construction of shared understandings and meanings. However, feminists clarify and emphasize that any shared understandings and meanings are ultimately shaped by dominant structures. As men are dominant at interaction, women end up following established meanings and understandings, which are not necessarily in agreement with their everyday life experience (promotions in the workplace are offered according to merit of performance whereas stereotypically it is more likely for a white, middle class, married, straight man to receive it). Feminist research indicates that the established social association of marriage is actually formed on the connection of two strangers who inhabit separate worlds of meanings. Women have access to a men's world as they have to conform to it, but men do not necessarily need to do the same (Smith, 1979). For feminists the only form of social interaction that allows women to experience equality and freedom is that of intimate relationships between women, as shared understandings and meanings are more feasible (Ritzer and Stepnisky, 2014).

Micro-sociology

Micro-sociology is the part of sociology that focuses on smaller-scale social phenomena. Social interaction is one of the central concepts micro-sociological approaches investigate. Collins (1981), as one of the most passionate supporters of micro-sociology (he is using the term radical microsociology) explains that the focus of radical micro-sociology is the 'interaction ritual chains' or bundles of 'individual chains of interactional experience, criss-crossing each other in space as they flow along in time' (1981: 998). For Collins, the emphasis is placed on the study of interactions, chains of interactions and the 'market place' of these interactions (Ritzer and Stepnisky, 2014). Collins was opposed to functionalism and structuralism as he was very critical of the idea of dominant structures. Similarly, he was very sceptical towards critical and exchange theory as he ultimately believed that it is only people who do anything: structures, organization, classes and societies cannot produce action, as it is because of the causal action of real individuals that anything can be done (Collins, 1975). In contradiction to Collins, Cicourel (1981) believed that it might be more useful to link the micro to the macro level of analysis whereas Collins stated that macro-structure is nothing more than large numbers of repeated micro-encounters. Notably, Collins did not use the term intra-action although he clearly prioritized individuals' contribution to the formation of interaction.

Social networking

As already discussed, interaction refers to the exchange of action between at least two individuals. In modern societies, technology has enabled individuals to interact through means and ways that the previous generations would perceive unconceivable. Today, the meaning of social interaction has been expanded, as physical presence during interaction is no longer required. In fact, people can produce intense and meaningful forms of interaction through social networking sites without ever meeting in person. Without even knowing what the other person looks like. The investigation into forms of interaction through social networking sites has attracted increasing attention in sociological research (Chriss, 2007; Kadushin, 2012). Social networking sites are analysed in order to understand how network interactions are organized and the implications of their organization in everyday life. Relevant research has tried to investigate how participants of specific social networking sites are connected by exploring possible combinations of connections and by evaluating the low- or high-centrality of the network (e.g. Facebook, Twitter) and by comparing strong and weak ties between participants. Social networking sites are used heavily in job search (LinkedIn, YouTube) and employers search for information about their potential employees through social networking sites (Pfeffer and Parra, 2009). According to Wortham (2013) increasing numbers of social networking users prefer to use Snapchat (an application that allows traces like photos to disappear after a given period of time). Also, social networking sites like Skype or Facetime have been facilitating the sustentation and continuation of long distance relationships even among family members, friendships and business partnerships.

Geometry of Interaction

Simmel (1908c) was perhaps the first to point out the importance of small group interactions and to study the specific characteristics of such interactions. As explained above, the forms of interactions refer to specific patterns of behaviour individuals follow while they interact. Although individuals may choose a pattern to adopt, they cannot choose not to adopt a pattern (Poggi, 2005). Simmel explained that there is a difference in terms of how people interact when the numbers of individuals or groups involved in a context of interaction are either two or three. Further sociological and psychological research has expanded Simmel's initial contributions on group investigation.

Dyad

According to Simmel (1908c), a dyad is the smallest form of a group and consists of two individuals. This kind of group is particularly fragile, as it will no longer exist if one of the partners decides to leave. Each member must commit fully to the group through trust and sharing in order for it to survive. Partners of this group usually share personal feelings, thoughts and goals, for example, a romantic relationship between two individuals. In the case of a more formal kind of relationship (e.g. marriage), certain rights and responsibilities may encourage further duration and stability of the relationship. Still, the primary purpose of any dyad regards the equally satisfactory participation of each member of the group (formal or not). If the interaction or connection between the two individuals is not as satisfactory as initially anticipated, then the group disappears (Pampel, 2000; Poggi, 2005).

Triad

A triad is a three-person group. Simmel (1908c) explains that unlike a dyad, when three units are involved and one of them leaves, the relationship is not dissolved but leaves open the possibility of its continuing between the two remaining units (e.g. a family consisting of two parents and a child will not disappear if the parents get a divorce). Alternatively, the group can recruit a replacement unit and re-form a triad (one parent may get married again and raise the child of the first marriage with a new partner). As soon as a third member joins a two-person group, there is a clear and rapid change in the relationship and form of interaction between the members of the group (a couple having a baby, two best friends come closer to a third person). The group may dominate over the individual, as the exit of one member cannot destroy the group. Each member of the group should follow the goals and plans of the group (families follow specific economic plans and raise their children according to specific principles). Also, coalitions between two members of the group may take place and marginalize the third, or one member of the group might try to manipulate the other two, or mediate between the two in the case of a conflict between them (Poggi, 2005).

Group size

What is important for Simmel is the structure/form of interaction deriving from a specific group size. Such structures emerge regardless of the specific individuals that compose the group. This means that specific forms of interaction emerging within, for example, a family, business partnership, or between co-workers or friends, follow specific patterns formed by each group separately and followed by each member. Each group however, forms different kinds of interactions, as the individuals comprising each group are different. Different people with different personalities will make one triad different from another but it is not the personalities of the people that make the triad itself possible (Webster and Sell, 2012). Simmel's logic of dyads and triads also applies to interactions between groups, for example, nations, corporations, political parties, etc. (Pampel, 2000). Furthermore, the study of interpersonal relationships, namely the relationships (and therefore interactions) between people, derive from the initial studies on Simmel's concepts of dyad and triad.

Interaction Within and Between Groups

A group is defined as a social unit of a relatively small number of people who over time develop a patterned relationship based on interaction with one another. Groups can vary between smaller or bigger families, peer groups, working groups, research groups or even groups of companies (Johnson & Johnson), of political parties (European socialist parties) or even nations (United Nations, European Union). Both sociology and psychology have been concerned with this specific social unit as it constitutes one of the smaller social units of analysis for sociologists and a unit of manageable size for social psychologists. Naturally, the size of groups varies however, as sociologists are not primarily interested in the exploration of the individual as a monad (as psychologists are), similarly, psychologists are not interested in the exploration of society as a whole. The concept of group (as a unit of analysis) is one of the areas that both psychological and sociological research has been investigating. However, interestingly enough, sociology and psychology follow completely different approaches while trying to explain how individuals interact within or between groups.

Sociological perspectives

Following Simmel's initial studies on groups and group size, Cooley (1909), proposed the initial distinction between 'primary' and 'secondary' groups. Primary are small groups that enable members to engage in face-to-face intimate interaction (family). Such interactions form personal relationships and the members of the group identify strongly with it (peer group). Primary groups may become exclusive and class and race may create stronger bonds between the members (Jerolmack, 2009). Secondary groups are bigger in size, the relations between the members are impersonal and the impact of each member is not particularly powerful (tennis club). Primary and secondary groups can be formed in the same social context (Siebold, 2007). For example, a group of close friends and a literature-reading group could both be formed at school. Blau (1964) explained that social interaction exists first within social groups. He proposed that people are attracted to specific groups when they feel that the relationships offered by these specific groups are greater compared to other groups (teenagers changing peer groups). As individuals are attracted to a group, naturally, they want to be accepted and for that reason they must offer rewards to the group and impress the older members (new members offer to a peer group concert tickets or the latest track of a music group). Blau explains that newcomers' efforts to join the new group may lead to group cohesion but could also involve competition and social differentiation. Leadership is a central issue in group formation for Blau (1964), as he explains that the members who are more able to offer impressive rewards have better chances to become more accepted (leaders in political parties are usually those who have promised to offer the best rewards). As soon as a leader is recognized by the members of the group, then the structure of the group alters as the followers are differentiated from the leader. Then, the followers reveal more openly their weaknesses as they are not interested any more to become leaders and this might become a way of integration between the followers. The elements of power and control are central in Blau's analysis of group formation.

A different approach on group formation processes is offered by Merton and Kitt (1950). They concentrate on the significance of 'reference groups', which are defined as groups that people take into consideration when they evaluate themselves. Individuals may belong to this group or they may compare themselves to a group to which they would have liked to belong (Ajrouch, 2007). An academic for example, might consider her/his academic value by comparing oneself to other colleagues within the university where s/he works, or s/he might compare her/his progress in relation to colleagues working in better or not as good universities. Reference groups reveal useful information about the ways individuals interact with others as they may influence possible plans, targets and ways of achieving desired outcomes.

Another area of sociological investigation on groups, which is influenced by psychological experiments, relates with conformity to the group. Individuals/members of the group generally have the tendency to conform with aspects of the group to which they belong (a student will probably follow the dressing style of her/his peer group, prefer the eating patterns of her/his family, adjust to the increasingly demanding school workload). A number of studies have actually supported that there are often cases that individuals will blindly conform to authority figures (Milgram, 1974; Zimbardo, 1973). Asch (1952), through his famous experiments, supported that the power of the group is so great that it may override an individual's own judgements and perceptions (Kinney, 2007). Conformity to a group is a repeatedly observed phenomenon especially when the demands come from someone in authority in the group (parent, teacher, line manager). This does not mean, however, that in modern societies people can be easily or massively manipulated although the power of authority might become notably controlling. Wolfson (2005), supports that many people are still willing to obey authorities such as the police, even when they are asked to engage in actions at odds with their own values.

Social psychological perspectives

Having introduced the principal ideas associated to social interaction, we can now consider specific concepts associated to the ways people connect and shape relationships. Social psychology has been systematically studying group dynamics since the 1980s. As discussed, the significance of groups in terms of how individuals interact is enormous. Social psychological perspectives have been proposing various definitions of what a group is (McGrath, 1984), but Shaw (1981) has concluded to the rather sociological explanation that all groups have something in common: their members interact with one another. Group refers to the interaction and influence between two or more people. A fundamental question social psychology asks has to do with the ways people are affected by the presence of others. According to the concept of 'social facilitation', people have the tendency to follow dominant (prevalent, likely) responses in the presence of others. Following Zajonc's (1965) experiments on how people get aroused by the presence of others, Mullen et al. (1997) explained that if individuals perform a task within a group, then there is a tendency to boost performance in easy tasks and hurt performance on difficult tasks. According to Aiello and Douthitt (2001) the reasons why people react in such ways is because of: a) evaluation appreciation, we are concerned about how others evaluate us; b) mere presence of others still influencing us; and c) destruction from the rest of the members of the group.

Social psychology has been primarily interested in people's behaviour within a group rather than the exact ways that individuals interact within a group. Extensive research has been concerned with the ways individuals work within teams or groups by suggesting that individuals pool efforts and work towards a common goal without individual accountability. The term 'social loafing' is used here to refer to the tendency for people to exert less effort when they pool their efforts towards a common goal than when they are individually accountable (Harkins, 1981; Hardy and Latane, 1986). Relevant research indicates that group members often work less hard when performing such 'additive' tasks and this finding also applies in everyday life settings (e.g. 'neighbourhood watch' agreements between home owners). In cases that people are benefiting from the group but giving little in return, the term 'free-rider' is used. However, it has to be noted that social loafing is predominantly observed in cultures where an independent self is endorsed (Karau and Williams, 1993; Kugihara, 1999). On the contrary, if the goal is important and the rewards are significant, then group members may work harder, for example, championship for a national football team (Shepperd and Taylor, 1999; Hoigaard et al., 2006). There are a variety of behaviour patterns social psychology explores within group settings like group polarization (Chen et al., 2000; Abrams et al., 2006), group thinking (Janis, 1971, 1982; Nemeth et al., 2004), group problem solving (Rietzschel et al., 2006) and group minority influence (Martin et al., 2008).

Sociology and psychology

Most of the above-mentioned approaches are based on experimental psychology and laboratory settings. Unlike sociology, specialized areas of psychology (like social psychology) may relate to experimental exploration of social circumstances and human behaviour. However, the sociological exploration of social interaction is almost exclusively concerned with naturally occurring occasions of human contact and as will be further discussed, language and conversation is one of the most characteristic cases of social interactions. Sociology and psychology follow different ways to explore similar phenomena. The combination and synthesis of such separate approaches might become fruitful in the attempt to produce a more systematic explanation of the ways individuals interact. As will be discussed in the following chapter symbolic interactionism has influenced both disciplines, and more detailed explorations of social interaction have been produced through this specific epistemological path.

Summary

This first chapter of the book introduced the sociological concept of interaction by explaining that this concerns the exchange of action between individuals. The interrelated concept of intra-action was briefly mentioned and defined as the exchange of action within individuals. Simmel's analytical exploration on interaction was then discussed as he was one of the first to systematically explore the meaning and significance of interaction by relating it to various social concepts. Simmel explained the explicit link between interaction and socialization, as well as the distinction between: a) content and form of social interaction and the concepts of; b) domination and conflict. A wide variety of additional approaches to the concept of social interaction were also discussed, by providing brief overviews of the importance of social interaction in the thought of critical theory and exchange theory, functionalism and feminism as well as approaches related to micro-sociology and social networking sites research. Interaction has also been related to group formation and group size (in the work of Simmel), followed by a number of sociological and psychological perspectives of interaction related to inter-groups and intra-group relations.

• •

Concepts in Context

Mary has just changed schools and joined her new peer group which is primarily interested in the new underground music trend of Manchester. Mary feels accepted and she is enthusiastic about being a member of this group, particularly after she got into a romantic relationship with Josh, the good-looking leader of this group. Unfortunately, her parents are not as thrilled, since their daughter's boyfriend dresses in very provocative ways and they think his influence on her is destructive. The girl is puzzled as she never had to disobey her parents' expectations but at the same time she really enjoys being in an intimate relationship with her boyfriend. She is also considering that if she breaks up with him she will additionally lose her privileged status in the peer group, but if she stays in this relationship her parents will certainly disapprove of her choice and will probably impose restrictive measures.

This example describes a typical synthesis of different social interactions that any individual can experience on a daily basis. In this example, the central character is Mary who is trying to figure out how to combine and synchronize different and potentially conflicting social interactions. All forms of interaction she is considering (smaller or bigger) concern her relationship with specific other individuals (her boyfriend, her parents, her friends). At the same time, she is trying to find a way to combine the above-mentioned units' interactions in a way that satisfies not only others but also herself.

• •

—— **SELF-REFLECTIVE QUESTIONS** ——————————

1. How can we study this specific case of interconnected interactions?
2. Why is Mary struggling?
3. Why are these particular forms of interactions conflicting?
4. Could such interactions be different within different social circumstances?

Possible ways of exploring the questions offered in this chapter and Further Readings:

Simmel's exploration of interaction may provide a good explanation of how these interactions are formed: a) in terms of size (the dominance of the triad group of the family, the significance and fragility of the dyad consisting the girl's intimate relationship; b) in terms of form (the domination of family forms of interaction, the influence of the peer group, the conflict between different groups, the socialization process the girl is going through).

Further Reading:

Craib, I. (1997) *Classic Social Theory: An Introduction to the Thought of Marx, Weber, Durkheim and Simmel.* Oxford: Oxford University Press.

1. The aspect of intra-action may reveal the importance of what this girl is considering and how significant the outcome of this personal experience of intra-action may be for the continuation and future of the social interactions she is involved with. Mary is struggling between what she has to do and what she wants to do.

Further Reading:

Chalari, A. (2012) 'The causal impact of resistance: mediating between resistance and internal conversation about resistance'. *Journal for the Theory of Social Behaviour*, 43(1): 66–86.

2. Exchange theory can explain the significance of the rewards this girl has been enjoying since she joined this specific peer group. Feminist theory may outline the reasons behind the girl's excitement to conform with the dominant structure of privilege offered by being the leader's girlfriend. Social networking sites' views may also be relevant here as the younger generation communicate their concerns and thoughts through technology (probably Mary has been texting her boyfriend secretly in the presence of her parents).

Further Reading:

Ritzer, G. and Stepnisky, J. (2014) *Sociological Theory* (9th ed.). New York: McGraw-Hill.

3. Psychological and sociological perspectives may analyse in more detail how inter-group and intra-group relations between the girl, her parents and her friends are formed, which relation is more possible to prevail and how this girl may interact with the members of the groups she belongs to.

Further Reading:

Brandstatter, H., Davis, J.H. and Stocker-Kreichgauer, G. (1982) *Group Decision Making*. New York: Academic Press.

This example describes one out of the endless possible combinations of different social interactions any individual may experience in everyday life. It is quite rare for any individual to be concerned with only one kind of interaction at any given time. Usually, different forms of interactions are combined in conflicting or complementary ways and individuals try to find the best possible way(s) to maintain or resolve forms, aspects or outcomes of continued interactions. What might be helpful to highlight in this example, is that, no matter what this girl might end up doing, the actual way that she has followed to produce these particular forms of interaction, derive primarily from intra-action. Namely, it is up to Mary to decide what she will do, how and when she will do it and why. Probably the criterion of her decision will be what is more important to her. This is how intra-action is connected or even blended to interaction. The following chapters will explore this connection even further.

2

Symbolic Interactionism

[Symbolic Interactionism is based on] deliberately constructed vagueness [and] resistance to systematisation. (Rock, 1979: 18–19)

Why is Symbolic Interactionism Important?

The previous chapter explored a wide variety of approaches regarding how social interactions are formed and shaped. However, within sociology and social psychology, there is a distinct and notably influential school of thought that it is exclusively concerned with social interaction. Symbolic interactionism studies social interaction by suggesting that the way people interact is shaped according to the symbolic exchange of meaning which is experienced at almost every level in our everyday lives. The significance of symbolic interactionism in modern sociological and psychological thought is unquestionable. It proposed a novel empirical way of studying interaction between individuals, which at the time, pioneered an enthusiastic group of empirical social scientists to open up a fresh look at how people construct social reality. Symbolic interactionism explored the individual in relation to society by proposing a specific kind of relationship shaped during symbolic interaction and exchange of shared meanings.

This chapter explores what we mean by symbolic interactionism, by revealing the origins of this school of thought and by providing an analytical definition of its content. The fundamental concepts of interaction, thinking, socialization, meaning and symbols will be analytically discussed. Following the rationale of the first chapter, the essence of intra-action will be also considered. The social-psychological components of symbolic interactionism will be discussed whereas the key sociological and psychological concepts associated with symbolic interactionism will be further elaborated: the concept of self will be introduced and particular emphasis will be placed on Mead's and Goffman's contributions. The separate discipline of the sociology of emotions will be briefly discussed as well as the methodological perspective of ethnography and the method of ethnomethodology.

EXAMPLE

A girl visits a friend in Toronto, Canada, for the first time. Her friend lives in a flat in one of the recently-developed skyscrapers in the city centre. As the friends enter the building's elevator the girl who is visiting Toronto notices that there are some floor numbers missing from the series of buttons. The floors '4' and '13', as well as the floors '14', '24', '34' and so on. The girl tried to make sense of this omission and she thought it might be accidental. But during her stay, she noticed that in most skyscrapers' elevators these specific floor numbers are missing. Any visitor in Toronto might find this omission strange, but it makes perfect sense when the reason is explained: in some Western cultures the number 13 represents bad luck whereas in China this is a completely indifferent number. However, in China, the number 4 represents bad luck whereas in Western cultures it is just another number. Interestingly, in the multicultural city of Toronto many skyscrapers are designed and build by Chinese and Canadian engineers who have deliberately omitted numbering floors in levels '4' and '13' or floors entailing the number '4'. Therefore, in many Canadian elevators these numbers are not included. According to symbolic interactionism this omission makes perfect sense to the engineers who designed the buildings and those who know the specific meaning given to those numbers/symbols. For any visitor who is unfamiliar with such interpretations the omission of these numbers/signs would seem odd and incomprehensible. This example outlines the significance of a learned common set of meanings through the usage of signs and symbols in every day life.

What Do We Mean by Symbolic Interactionism?

Origins

Symbolic interactionism is one of the most influential schools of thought in modern sociology and social psychology. It originated in the school of thought of American Pragmatism (George Herbert Mead, John Dewey, William James and Charles Peirce; more on this follows in later chapters), but primarily in the work of Mead (1863–1931). It might be worth mentioning though that none of the American pragmatists perceived themselves as symbolic interactionists. American Pragmatism is the first (out of two) American traditions that symbolic interactionism originates from. The second American tradition that formed the school of thought of symbolic interactionism is called the 'First Chicago School' which was a group of researchers organized by William Thomas and Robert Park and focused on the empirical investigation of the rapidly altering urban city of Chicago. Blumer, one of Mead's students at the University of Chicago, systematically engaged with Mead's theory and along with William Thomas and Charles Cooley were perceived as the pioneers of symbolic interactionism (Charon, 2011). Empirical studies conducted at the so-called 'Second Chicago School' during the 1920s–1940s by Blumer, Hughes and their students, formed the foundations of symbolic interactionism, as an extremely dynamic sociological school of thought that stood in sharp contrast to the functionalism of Harvard and Columbia Universities at that time (Fine, 1995).

Definition

The term 'symbolic interactionism' was first coined by Herbert Blumer in 1937. However, a description of a concrete definition of symbolic interaction- ism might not be an easy task, as Rock (1979: 18–19) explains, this school of thought is based on 'deliberately constructed vagueness' and a 'resistance to systematization'. The term symbolic interactionism is generally used to describe the work done at Chicago, including some of the most famous researchers like Goffman and Becker (although both resisted the label's application) (Dennis et al., 2013).

Waskul (2009) explains that symbolic interactionism is a diverse perspective that has been defined in various ways. There is an agreement regarding the fact that symbolic interactionism is a distinct conceptual and methodological framework for doing sociology. Waskul (2009: 110) defines symbolic interactionism as an approach that, among other things, emphasizes the active process by which people craft social worlds, create meaning, accomplish self, define situations and engage in cooperative, situated and structured joint action.

The central ideas in symbolic interactionism can be summarized in the following core principles (Charon, 2011; Ritzer and Stepnisky, 2014; Waskul, 2009):

- Human beings are perceived as social persons whose actions are led by con- stant lifelong *social interaction*. Therefore, social interaction is the basic unit of the study of individuals, as well as society, which are both created through interaction. The intertwined patterns of action and interaction make up groups and society. Therefore, every single form of people's action is perceived as social interaction rather than human personal behaviour (as psychology would have it) or outcome of structural action (as functionalism would suggest).

- Human beings are thinking beings. The capacity of *thought* is shaped by social interaction. Human action is not only interaction between individuals but interaction within the individual (Charon, 2011). Therefore, exchange of action within oneself produces thought, which allows individuals to evaluate, and choose appropriate forms of action. Thought is organized according to forms of social interaction.

- In social interaction people learn the *meanings* and the *symbols* that allow them to exercise their distinctive capacity of thought. Individuals define the situation they are in and they act according to their own understanding of the social world. Individuals' definitions and understandings are produced through social interaction.

- Meaning and symbols enable individuals to produce *shared understandings* and comprehensible *definitions*. Meanings and symbols can be used differently according to the specific situation and circumstance. Individuals are therefore perceived as active, rather than passive, agents although freedom is never complete.

- The cause of individual action is the result of what is occurring in our *present situation*. The reason why people act as they do can be found in people's present interaction with others, present thinking and present definitions. Social interaction is ephemeral and is constantly recreated and reinvented. Therefore, any kind of understanding of an individual's action is related to what is happening in the present rather than what has happened in the past or what might happen in the future.

Social interaction, thought socialization, meaning and symbols

The first and most important principle of symbolic interactionism is that meaning is derived from social interaction. In order for interaction to have meaning, Mead (1934) explained that individuals need to exchange symbols which share common meanings. Then, any act can be 'symbolic' if it produces similar outcomes for two or more people. Language refers to a series of symbols that can be combined in various ways and provide new meanings. Symbols and language can be verbal or non-verbal (say 'hello' or wave 'hello') (Hewitt, 2003). The process(es) by which we use symbols and language to give meaning and values to objects and people, is known as the '*social construction of reality*' (Berger and Luckman, 1967). The way people understand their everyday reality is achieved through day-to-day activities. Language enables us to communicate our own understanding with the understandings and experiences of others. This is how the social world is constructed. Notably, symbolic interactionism rejects the notion of structural determinism (the idea that social structures shape and organize human behaviour) but symbolic interactionists did not reject the notion of social structure. Structures for symbolic interactionists are the product of social interaction (Dennis et al., 2013).

Thinking

As discussed in the first chapter, interaction is defined in this book, as the exchange of action between individuals. Simmel was perhaps the first to explain that social

interaction consists of the basis of society and it is through interaction that individuals and society are ultimately formed. Symbolic interactionism used these
fundamental ideas and further elaborated on them. Simmel's work is proven to be
deeply influential in the thought of symbolic interactionism. Symbolic interactionism was also influenced by American Pragmatism and especially Cooley and
Mead. Mead (1982) in particular, promoted the reflexive abilities of individuals
and their active (rather than passive) role in society. Individuals are seen as active
agents because they are able to think; individuals produce actions (and interactions) as the outcome of reflexive deliberations in contradiction to functionalism
that perceives agents as passive receivers of structures programmed to reproduce
social norms and behaviours. Thinking is what allows individuals to conduct
unique and meaningful interactions. At the same time, thinking is organized by
social interaction, which consists of exchange and continuous recreation of symbols, meaning forms of socialization and even society. As can be seen, the
connections between social interaction, socialization, meaning and symbols are
interdependent and inter-related.

Socialization

The term 'socialization' (extensive analysis follows in Chapter 3) is used to
describe the specific ways social interaction is taking place. Meltzer (1978) explains
that socialization for symbolic interactionism is a dynamic process which allows
people the ability to think and to develop and therefore become unique human
beings. Interaction for Blumer (1969) is the process through which socialization is
developed and exercised (Ritzer and Stepnisky, 2014). Therefore, thinking shapes
and is shaped by interaction. For example, a school girl, is dressed in specific ways,
following the music and fashion trend shared in the peer group to which she
belongs. She dates a guy from the same peer group and her choices of friends,
clothing and lifestyle is in contradiction to her parents' expectations. According to
symbolic interactionism, the way this girl thinks and acts has to do with this girl's
specific chains of interactions, with her family, peer group, intimate relations and
the school.

Meaning

According to Blumer (1969) the process of interaction is built through the individual's learning of meaning(s) during socialization. The way individuals define the
social world and interpret reality is connected with the meaning they give to any
object (physical, social or abstract objects as Blumer categorizes them). Different
individuals may define common objects (or situations) completely differently. As
will be further discussed, symbolic interactionists focus on the symbolic interpretations of the shared meaning, which are shaped through language. Kailoglou (2010)
in his study of how Greeks use the slang word 'malakas' explained that there are
two meanings associated with this word: the first means 'wanker' and the second

means 'mate'. The meaning given in each occasion is understood and shared by the participants of each related linguistic encounter and depends on the context of the discussion. Therefore, the usage of the word 'malakas' could entail an insulting or friendly meaning, depending on the way it is used during verbal interactions and socialization.

Symbols

According to symbolic interactionism, people learn meaning along with symbols in social interaction. Individuals respond to signs automatically (stop when the light is red). Symbols on the other hand, are perceived as '*social objects*'. Social objects (in contradiction to physical objects) are pointed out, isolated, interpreted and given meaning through social interaction. Not all social objects are symbols but all symbols are social objects. Symbols are created socially, they are objects intentionally used in many different situations and they are understood in common ways by their users (Charon, 2011). A characteristic example would be that of the Christian symbol of the cross. The cross, as a sign, constitutes a specific kind of intersection of two measured lines. However, the cross as a symbol is created socially (through the meaning given by Christians) and represents the cross on which Jesus was sacrificed. This meaning was given intentionally as it represents the beliefs of a specific religion. All individuals who use this symbol, and perhaps many non-users, understand the meaning of this religious symbol. In most Western cultures for example, it is perfectly acceptable for people to wear jewels in the shape of the Christian cross. However, if a person who wears such jewellery travels to Middle East, it might be perceived as an insult if this jewellery is displayed publicly.

Intra-action?

Intra-action is a term introduced in the first chapter to explain the exchange of action within an individual. Symbolic interactionism did not use the term intra-action as such, but on many occasions, symbolic interactionists clarified that individuals are interacting with others as well as with themselves. Mead (1934) was one of the first to state that we act towards ourselves as objects in the same way as we act towards others. Perhaps the most detailed discussion on intra-action derives from Blumer (1962) as he was explaining the importance of the concept of self. Blumer explains that the individual can act towards oneself like s/he acts towards other people. Very characteristically, Blumer explains that as we can judge others, we can judge ourselves and characterize an idea as smart or stupid; he suggests that as we can talk to others we can also talk to ourselves. Indeed, how often do we talk to ourselves about literally anything that is going on in our lives? He also explains that as we can point things to others, we can do the same to ourselves; we can point things to ourselves about ourselves and about others (we make sure to dress properly before an interview, just as we would suggest our best friend should do).

Blumer further explains that we can get angry with ourselves as we get angry with others (because we have forgotten something), we tell ourselves what to do or what not to do as (as we give instructions to our children). We also set goals for ourselves (to pass the exams) and compromise with ourselves (readjust our lives to salary reductions). For Blumer (1962: 181) 'to recognise that the human being can act toward him/herself is not mystical conjuration' (Charon, 2011).

How is this kind of intra-action exercised? According to symbolic interactionists one way to understand the self is to look back on what we do; we can see, recognize and try to understand what is taking place within us: I am angry, I am sad, I am in love, I am worried, I am excited. People are able to view themselves as objects and therefore we are able to see what we are and what we do and how we feel (Turner and Stets, 2005; Charon, 2011). Charon explains that there are three categories of action associated to self: a) *Self-Communication*: thinking, for symbolic interactionists, is the individual's ability to talk to oneself with symbols. Thinking enables individuals to communicate with the others and ourselves. Thinking for Blumer (1966) is a mechanism of self-interaction through which individuals meet the social world. For Mead (1934), thinking is the internalized conversation of gestures that enables individuals to be reflexive. b) *Self-Perception*: our ability to see ourselves in situations as the object of our attention. As we are able to see and evaluate our interactions and connections with others, we are also able to understand and assess our own actions within a situation and develop a self-concept, self-judgement and identity (these concepts will be further discussed later in this book). c) *Self-Control*: our ability to instruct and direct ourselves what to do in situations. This is how we control our actions. These are forms of intra-action, as this book defines this term. Although symbolic interactionism clearly prioritizes the significance on social interaction over any form of personal or private characteristics and properties, it is significant to point out that some form of intra-action is indeed recognized by this school of thought. It might be helpful though to clarify that for symbolic interactionism, interaction pre-exists and even shapes intra-action (extensive discussion follows in Chapter 7).

Psychological Perspectives

The founding fathers of symbolic interactionism perceived themselves as social psychologists (Mead, James, Blumer) although their work was primarily sociological. However, symbolic interactionists have been criticized for ignoring psychological factors such as needs, motives, intentions and aspirations (Meltzer et al., 1975) as well as emotions and the unconscious (Stryker, 1980). Still, symbolic interactionsim is one of the main theoretical orientations underlying the work of many social psychologists and it has been perceived primarily as a social-psychological perspective

(Stryker, 1990). In fact, the concepts discussed in this chapter may be well-per-ceived as sociological and/or psychological units of analysis, as symbolic interactionism explores areas of investigation that both sciences are concerned with. As explained by Stryker (1990), social psychology perceives symbolic inter-actionism as a form of small-scale explanations of relatively limited scope, focusing on social-psychological events. Hewitt (2003) further explains that the task of social psychology is to create a theory of action (such as symbolic interactionism) in order to study action and interaction and to show how people are influenced by culture and society. To do so, social psychologists need to concentrate on topics as socialization, the self and the actual formation of conduct in everyday life.

Although various symbolic interactionists were involved with the social-psychological explanation of interactions, certain thinkers were clearly concerned with the exploration of psychological properties through symbolic interactionism. The first would be William James (1890/1950), one of the founding fathers of American Pragmatism, who explained the importance of society as a source of constraints of behaviour. He perceived the concept of self as possessing both (but separately) personal and social properties (Chalari, 2009), and he focused on the sources of people's character and self-esteem through people's mutual influences during interactions. John Dewey (1940), another founding father of American Pragmatism, distinguished the individual's personality organization (as a matter of habit) from social organization (as a matter of collective habit or custom) through studying the intimate relation of persons and society. He believed that thinking occurs in the process of people's interaction. Cooley (1902), as will be further discussed, was primarily interested in the importance of mental and subjective social life. He coined the term 'sympathetic introspection' to explain the process through which individuals use sympathy to understand things as others might have imagined them. For Colley, society and the individual are two sides of the same coin (Stryker, 1990). Finally, Mead was perhaps the most distinctive as well as influential American pragmatist who shaped the thought of symbolic interaction-ism through his social-psychological perspectives. Mead's basic social-psychological approaches derive from evolutionary principles that view mind and people's sym-bolic communication as the basis of society. As will be further analysed, Mead (1934) believed that the relations among the interactions of mind, self and society become the subject matter of social psychology (Rohall et al., 2007; Myers et al., 2010). As will be discussed, symbolic interactionism studied and defined the con-nection between the individual and society in a distinct manner, which influenced (if not defined) a wide part of sociological and social-psychological thought. Stryker (1990: 16) summarizes that the contribution of symbolic interactionism to social psychology relates to the assumption that humans must be studied on their own level but the most fruitful approach to the study of human social behaviour is through an analysis of society. Therefore, the human being should be perceived as an actor as well as a reactor.

Key Sociological and Psychological Concepts in Symbolic Interactionism

This section will concentrate on the key psychological and sociological perspectives deriving from symbolic interactionism; generally, all concepts discussed in this chapter should be treated as possessing both sociological and psychological qualities.

The self

Symbolic interactionists' exploration of the self and the individual may seem to point away from sociology and point towards some form of psychology. Interactionist research has explored the concept of self in a wide variety of ways and therefore this concept has a wide variety of formulations (Jacobsen, 2009). As this school of thought was primarily focused on the study of interaction and the establishment of shared meanings and common symbols, the formation of self (further discussed in Chapter 5), was regarded as a fundamental element of investigation. For symbolic interactionists the self is the object of the actor's own action. It is not the individual that acts; it is the actor who acts and the actor is able to act back on self (intra-action) as well as on the social environment (interaction). The self is part of the actor's social world that the individual acts towards. Every individual is an actor and every individual is the object of his/her own actions. The self is the internal environment towards which the actor sees and acts. Above all, the self arises from social interaction (Charon, 2011: 71–2). The self is shaped, organized and structured through social interaction. As will be analytically discussed in the following sections, the actor performs specific kinds of roles, according to the form of social interaction in which s/he finds themself. Therefore, for symbolic interactionism the self is perceived exclusively in terms of social interaction rather than intra-action.

The early symbolic integrationist, Charles Horton Cooley (1864–1929), proposed one of the initial explanations regarding the self through his '*looking-glass self*' theory. Cooley (1909, 1970) explained that as individuals develop they produce a self-image that reflects how others see us. Therefore, the sense people have about their self is formed through the interactions people have with others from a very young age (more on that follows in Chapter 3 on socialization). More specifically, Cooley (1970) explained that: a) we imagine how we appear to others; b) we imagine what their judgement of this appearance might be; and c) we develop some self-feeling in response to our imagining judgements (guilt or pride).

Mead (1934: 140) like Cooley, clearly demonstrated that it is 'impossible to conceive of a self arising outside the social experience' and he proposed that self is the knower and the known at the same time because for Mead the self is something people 'have' but it is also something that people 'do' (I have the dream of becoming a doctor and therefore I study medicine). Self is acquired through socialization and for that reason is fluid and multiple. We have multiple selves and we are one (or more) things to some people, and perhaps someone else to others (Jacobsen, 2009). For her colleagues a woman may be a strict, passionate, hard working lawyer whereas for her family she may be a caring, loving and devoted mother and wife. Modern symbolic interactionists have set the foundations of the concept of self on Mead's and Cooley's ideas. Blumer (1969: 12) defined self as 'nothing esoteric'. Individuals for Blumer can be the object of their own action and are able to act towards and guide themselves in actions towards others. Self is perceived as a process that helps humans act rather than simply respond to external stimuli.

Weigert and Gecas (2003) have proposed three main ways that symbolic inter-actionists have approached the concept of self: a) *Self as Process*, which refers to the idea that self is a creating process which is formed through individuals' inter-actions. The self is created and recreated by taking the role of the other. This approach derives from Blumer's thinking. For example, according to symbolic interactionism, the processes that a child goes through as s/he grows primarily involve her/his interactions with others and her/his ability to take the role of the other, such as learning to use the toilet like grown-ups, follow a daily routine like parents do, play with her/his friends like other children do, go to school like her/his schoolmates. b) *Self as Producer* refers to the self as a character that results from enacted scenes, dramatic action, appearances, encounters and presentations. This approach derives from Goffman's approach on dramaturgy (detailed discussion follows) and the emphasis is on how things are done. Therefore, 'self as a process' emphasizes role taking, whereas 'self as producer' focuses on the result of what people do. Mead explains that children learn to see things from other people's perspective through play. Following the above-mentioned example, a child may be perceived as a favourable fellow student by her/his schoolmates and a demanding and needy son/daughter by her/his parents. c) *Self as a Product* refers to how roles both link people to social systems and bestow identity. This approach derives from the 'Iowa School' that represents a more structural and rather quan-titative approach to symbolic interactionism. An example would be that of a monk who has devoted his life and spirit to the word of God and any other understanding or approach to life does not make sense to him. Therefore, any-thing that this person does derives from his passionate engagement with his role as a 'monk'.

Mead's 'I', 'Me' and the 'generalized other'

Mead's (1934) definitions of the 'I', the 'Me' and the 'generalized other' shaped sym-bolic interactionism's theorizing of the ways the individual is connected to society. Mead attempted to investigate the self by introducing a dialogic relationship between the past and the present self, or in different words, he introduced a constant dialogic interplay between two characters of the self: the 'I' and the 'Me'.

When one determines what one's position is in society and feels oneself as having a certain function and privilege, these are all defined with reference to an 'I'. However, the 'I' cannot be grasped directly by the subject. The 'I' for Mead is the active self, or the immediate response of an individual to others. We do not know how the 'I' will respond and therefore we know the 'I' only after the act has been carried out. For Mead, each individual's values and principles derive from the 'I' and it is through the 'I' that personality is formed. However, we are not conscious of the 'I'. The 'I' is on the stage, in the moment, talking to other people. Mead (1932) states that society gives form and content to the 'I', without which the individual would have no say, nor indeed any control over her/his conduct as an 'I'. For Mead, the form as well as the content of consciousness has social origins, and therefore it could be argued that speech/language/conversation is a social gift. Mead (1934: 175) defined the 'Me' as the organized set of attitudes towards the self, based on the views of significant others, such as friends and family. People are conscious of the 'Me'. The 'Me' involves conscious responsibility, and it is through the 'Me' that society dominates the individual. For Archer (2003), Mead's 'Me' is actually 'We' (Chalari, 2009).

The 'generalized other' for Mead is defined as the organized community or social group, which gives the individual her very unity of self. The attitude of the generalized other is the attitude of the whole community. It is in the form of the generalized other that the social process influences the behaviour of the individuals involved in it and carries it on, that is, the community exercises control over the conduct of its individual members. It is in this form that the social process or community enters as a determining factor in the individual's thinking and articulated speech. Therefore, it is only by adopting the attitude of the generalized other towards oneself that can one think at all, for only in this mode can thinking, or the internalized conversation of gestures which constitutes thinking, occur (Mead, 1956/1964: 218–20). The generalized other represents all forms that society takes in order to influence, form and shape the individual; it is the skeleton of each person's thought and speech.

Arguably, Mead's discussions on the 'I' the 'Me' and the 'generalized other' is not explicitly clear (Kuhn, 1964; Stryker, 1980; Chalari, 2009; Charon, 2011). His main contribution remains the realization that individuals are actors and that we all have a self. For Mead, we are both 'subjects' (actors) and 'objects' (selves). However, Mead is very clear in his views on social dominance over the individual, and these views remain stable and consistent throughout his work. For Mead, each self might be different, but all selves are formed in different ways from the social environment.

Goffman's concept of self: dramaturgy, performance and roles

Goffman remains one of the most influential theorists who applied through his empirical work, many of the concepts of symbolic interactionism, although he never identified himself through this term. Goffman's understanding of the self is deeply influenced by Simmel's view of the individual and Mead's perception of the connection between the 'I' and the 'Me'. As Charon (2011) explains, Goffman viewed the self as something that is completely built up on every occasion of social interaction. The self for Goffman is essentially social and it is not something an individual owns but something that others temporarily lend her/him. One of the most important books by Goffman on symbolic interaction is *Presentation of Self in Everyday Life* (1959) where he introduces the basic distinction between: what people expect us to do and what we want to do. Goffman explains that in order for people to maintain a stable self-image they perform for their audience. This idea is explained through his concept of '*dramaturgy*', which is defined as a series of dramatic performances analogous to those performed on the stage. Through dramaturgy Goffman attempts to define the self, not as a possession of an actor but the product of the dramatic interaction between the actor and the audience. The self 'is a dramatic effect arising [...] from a scene that is presented' (Goffman, 1959: 252–3).

Although Goffman himself does not provide an explicit definition of what the self is, Williams (1998) proposed an explanation of Goffman's self as consisting of three different aspects: a) the two 'selves' version, consisting of character and performer. The individual organizes the role/character of the performer; b) self as the product of social circumstances (or organization of interactions); and c) self as being able to change and manage oneself during events. Clearly, Goffman's understanding of the self is rooted in social, or in his terms, dramaturgical interaction. Individuals, or actors, want to present a certain sense of self that will be accepted by others and for that reason certain techniques are used. This is called, according to Goffman, '*impression management*' which is primarily oriented to prevent the possibility of unexpected actions (Manning, 2005). This is the reason why people act in polite ways, use kind expressions, follow appropriate manners and conform to society's/community's expectations.

Goffman's (1961a) understanding of the concept of self is related to the individual's ability to perform a wide number of roles in everyday life. However, as Goffman explains, only few people get completely involved in any given role. Goffman uses the term '*Role Distance*' to describe the degree to which individuals separate themselves from the roles they are in (a married man acting as getting married is not a good idea, or a professor acting as an ordinary teacher). The term '*Attachment or Commitment to a Role*', describes the repeated performance of the same role by an individual. Individuals have committed their self-feelings to it as demonstrated by their behaviour (some professionals take their job very seriously, for example, doctors who want to be perceived as 'Gods') (Ritzer and Stepnisky, 2014). Goffman very characteristically states that 'to embrace a role is to be embraced by it' (1961a: 106). Socialization for Goffman takes place through dramaturgical interactions, as actors perform their roles in front of their audience. He, therefore, believes that role is the basic unit of socialization. Following Simmel's thought, Goffman makes explicit that people are shaped through socialization and the individual learns to adopt social roles and rules.

Indeed, individuals are called to learn and consequently to perform successfully a wide variety of roles as they move on in life. Such roles and performances include people's 'basic social characteristics' namely to act as men or women, as white or non-white people, perform the role of religious or non-religious agents, perform the role of professionals, parents, partners, friends, sons, daughters and many more different roles, which have to be combined, synthesized and ideally performed in equally convincing ways. Inevitably, some of these roles might be in conflict (being enthusiastic professional and devoted parent) or some may be related in comple- mentary manners (being a popular student and disciplined daughter). In any event, Goffman's views on the self have contributed applicable ways of perceiving and understanding our everyday actions and interactions with others through role performance and dramaturgical settings.

Sociology of Emotions

Since the 1970s, the study of the sociology of emotions has attracted the interest of an increasing number of sociologists derived from various sociological disci- plines. However, the influence of symbolic interactionism remains predominant and profound. Hochschild (1983/2003) explains that there are two major models in the sociology of emotions: The first is termed 'the Organismic Model' deriving from the work of Darwin, James and Freud, which treats emotions as biological and some of them are universally shared (fear, anger, happiness and sadness). Emotions are not shaped by social actors; happiness, for example, remains inde- pendent of the culture in which it is expressed. Therefore, emotion is treated as passive as it cannot be managed or controlled by the person who experiences it. The second model is termed 'the Interactional Model' and derives from the works of Dewey, Mills and Goffman. Many interactionists agree that although there are some components of emotions which are indeed biological, social factors are inter- actively involved in the experience of emotions. Therefore, people are not passively receivers of emotions but they actively engage with emotions as they are expressed (Turner and Stets, 2005). Many of the above-mentioned interactionists emphasized the significance of emotions in their work: Cooley, through his looking-glass self explains that people develop self-feelings in response to their imagined perceptions of how others perceive us. These self-feelings are primarily based on the emotions of shame and pride. Mead mentioned the significance of connection between symbols, feelings and meaning whereas Goffman explained that self-presentation involved feelings such as those of embarrassment, stigmatization and alienation. Hochschild (1983/2003) and Turner and Stets (2005) perceive emotions as central components to social interaction and organization.

On the opposite side of the spectrum (coming from Critical Realism), emotions can be perceived as personal and private properties, experienced only by the individuals concerned. Archer (2000) maintains that emotions are the main aspects of our inner lives (an argument that originates from Simmel's (1950) understanding of the concept of inner life). Archer further explains that emotions are important because they are the fuel of our internal conversations (the conversations people have with themselves, in their head, silently, further discussed in Chapter 7) and she states that there are no people without emotions. The idea of emotions, according to Archer (2000: 195) is defined as 'commentaries upon our concerns' and she quotes Taylor (1985: 48) who explains that emotions are related to specific situations and our awareness of those specific situations. Therefore, emotions are seen as personal properties, occurring while people talk to themselves about what they feel, in a specific situation.

Methods and Methodology of Symbolic Interactionism

The school of thought of symbolic interactionism shaped unique model(s) of research techniques in order to study social interaction. These techniques originate from American pragmatists' perception of radical empiricism. Following James (1909) who believed that theory is a tool that allows the investigation of the social world, symbolic interactionism prioritized empirical research, which was based on specific theoretical foundations (discussed above). Symbolic interactionism rejects variable analysis and focuses on comparative analysis of formal features of social organization and activity. The purpose here is for researchers to reveal formal similarities and differences between social activities. Goffman (1961b), for example, in his study on *Asylums*, explains how specific forms of action in total institutions are shaped. These could be further compared with hospitals, the military and so on. Symbolic interactionism prefers qualitative data collection and analysis (although a variety of techniques may be employed) by proposing the investigation of real-world settings to be undertaken in 'fieldwork'. Fieldwork, is also described as 'participant observation' or 'ethnography'. This particular technique requires researchers to blend with the subjects of their investigation in order to better understand and appreciate the ways and forms social interaction and meaning-making is established and developed. Ethnography has offered fruitful and valuable findings and contributions to sociological, social anthropological and psychological knowledge; at the same time, it has also received extensive criticism primarily due to the inevitable subjective interpretations offered by the researcher that derive from her/his personal involvement and meaning-making processes (Dennis et al., 2013). In response to such criticism, symbolic interactionists through what is called the 'Iowa School', have attempted to develop what they consider a more scientific version of interactionism (Miller, 2011).

Ethnomethodology

Ethnography concerns the investigation of verbal (and non-verbal) forms of social interaction; symbolic exchange of meaning is primarily shaped through interactions that involve talk. The main way through which symbolic interactionists studied the social world is language, as a formal form of symbolic interaction, while it occurs in the field. In late-1960, a distinct approach was devised concerned with the ways individuals use language in everyday contexts. The term 'ethnomethodology' was coined by Harold Garfinkel in 1967 and refers to the folk, or lay methods people use to make sense of what others do and particularly of what they say. Heritage (1984: 4) defines ethnomethodology as the study of common sense knowledge and the various ways people use to make sense of, find their way in and act on the circumstances in which they find themselves. Garfinkel (1986) very characteristically explains that ethnomethodology is concerned with the organization of everyday life and Pollner (1987: xvii) adds that this is the 'extraordinary organization of the ordinary'. It is crucial at this point to clarify that ethnomethodologists do not believe that people are constantly reflexive, self conscious and calculative; they rather believe that most often individuals' action is routine and relatively unreflective. Perhaps this is why ethnomethodologists do not focus on agents but rather on 'members' of a specific interaction. Ethnomethodologists are preoccupied in analysing conversations as they are interested in analysing people's accounts, as well as the ways in which accounts are offered and accepted/rejected by others (Orbuch, 1997). Some of Garfinkel's students at UCLA (Harvey Sacks, Emmanuel Schegloff and Gail Jefferson) developed the latest and most important variety of ethnomethodology, called '*conversation analysis*'. Sacks in 1992, followed a distinct way of investigating language by focusing on the micro-analysis of the sequential display of common understandings within conversation, using recordings and transcripts of naturally occurring conversations as research tools. Conversation analysis studies social phenomena as they occur in naturally occurring conversations, as for example: turn-taking organization (Sacks et al., 1978), interaction and grammar (Schegloff, 1996), interaction and syntax (Chalari, 2012).

Summary

This chapter defined symbolic interactionism, by concentrating on the origins of this school of thought and by discussing the various aspects of this sociological and social psychological tradition. The fundamental concepts of interaction, thinking, socialization, meaning and symbols have been discussed, whereas interactionists' view on intra-action has also been considered. The social-psychological components of symbolic interactionism have been separately discussed whereas core sociological and psychological concepts associated with symbolic interactionism have been analysed: the concept of self has been further discussed by incorporating psychological and sociological aspects. Mead's and Goffman's contributions on the concept of self have been discussed separately. The separate discipline of the sociology of emotions has been briefly introduced as well as the methodological perspective of ethnography and the method of ethnomethodology.

• •

Concepts in Context

A heavily pregnant woman (who has arrived in the USA from Europe) needs to use the restroom in a restaurant. When she gets there she joins a very long queue. Although she is obviously pregnant nobody is offering to let her go through first. The woman thinks that perhaps being pregnant in American culture does not signify any special treatment and she therefore waits in the queue as all the other women. A few minutes after, another (American) pregnant woman enters the restroom. She looks at the queue, walks towards the beginning of the queue, stops in front of the woman who stands first, looks directly into her eyes and touches her tummy in a tender way. The woman who has been waiting for a quite long time, responds immediately by offering her turn in a very polite way. However, no other woman offered her turn to the first pregnant woman who still waited in the queue until her turn came, while struggling to make sense of what has happened.

This example outlines a case of a sequence of mainly non-verbal symbolic interactions that took place in a specific cultural context. Symbolic interactionism may offer a symbolic analysis of these sequences, by offering a convincing explanation to the pregnant European woman, who has been trying to make sense of the incident she has experienced. First, a symbolic interactionist would look for the meaning of the main symbols involved on this occasion. The main symbol here is the fact of the two women being pregnant. The one who comes from Europe is not familiar with the series of shared meanings American women in this restroom may share. Being a pregnant woman in North America signifies a woman who carries a baby in her, but does not necessarily require any special assistance or attention (unless she asks for it). In most European countries, being a pregnant woman signifies that a woman carries two lives, which is perceived as a very hard and extremely important thing to do; it is therefore considered polite, if not given, for others to offer any sort of assistance they can to a pregnant woman (without her having to ask for it).

• •

──── **SELF-REFLECTIVE QUESTIONS** ────────────────────

1. Why did the two pregnant women act so differently and receive such different responses?
2. How could a certain symbolic meaning (being pregnant) be interpreted in different cultures?
3. How important is other people's understanding of the ways these two women reacted?
4. How could similar roles (being pregnant) be performed in different ways?

Possible ways of exploring the questions offered in this chapter and Further Readings:

1. As Blummer might explain, the meaning of the symbolized feminine body, while carrying a baby may vary between different cultures/understandings. The fact that the first woman thought of possible cultural variations, reveals that the process of thinking is indeed shaped according to symbolized meanings and the definitions of these meanings. In terms of the non-verbal interaction that the second woman had with the woman who, in the end, offered to give up her turn: Reveals an act of socialization based on a different set of shared understandings: in Northern American culture, it is considered acceptable to demand what one needs or wants, especially if a woman is pregnant (this is what the second woman did).

Further Reading:

Blumer, H. (1969) *Symbolic Interaction*. Englewood Cliffs, NJ: Prentice-Hall.

2. But this interaction was not only about shared understandings. Cooley and Mead would emphasize the importance of the way others perceive us (it made no difference that both women were pregnant), and what we do about it (only the second woman demanded attention and assistance): The first woman was unable to define the meaning(s) of the series of social interactions she was involved with; however, the second woman was perfectly able to imagine correctly how others would perceive her and to respond to the potential unconcern expressed by others through this specific non-verbal interaction (it only took a direct look and a touch on her tummy).

Further Reading:

Charon, J.M. (2011) *Symbolic Interactionism: An Introduction, an Interpretation, an Integration* (10th ed.). New Delhi: PHI Learning Private Limited.

3.   Mead would also underline the shared understandings of the generalized other (the meaning of being pregnant and the way people use it to get what they want) in this context. Furthermore, Goffman would probably explain that: The first woman is taking some distance from her role as pregnant woman as she does nothing to indicate through performative means that she is actually pregnant and needs attention; the second is attached to her role as she is employing successfully performative means (touching her tummy in a tender way) to accomplish the successful completion of her performance.

Further Reading:

Dennis, A., Philburn, R. and Smith, G. (2013) *Sociologies of Interaction*. Cambridge: Polity.

4.   Perhaps, Goffman would have noted that the first pregnant woman did not even realize that she was involved in a dramaturgical interaction; she therefore failed to take her turn when she had the chance. In consequence, she remained 'invisible' by the audience.

Further Reading:

Goffman, E. (1959) *Presentation of Self in Everyday Life*. Garden City, NY: Anchor.

Goffman, E. (1961a) *Encounters: Two Studies in the Sociology of Interaction*. Indianapolis: Bobbs-Merrill.

In this example, the concept of self (or parts of the self) revealed by both women (actors/performers) of this series of interactions, entails passive characteristics for the first woman and active characteristics for the second. In both cases, it is the rest of the audience that enabled these specific characteristics to emerge.

3

Socialization

At birth, the individual human being is virtually helpless. Ahead lies a long and complicated process of learning to live in society. This process is Socialization. (White, 1977: 1)

Why is Socialization Important?

Socialization is one of the most central concepts in sociology. It is through socialization that an infant gets in contact with the social world and this process will continue throughout the life course. Socialization is probably the first and certainly the most important systematic link between the individual and society. The reason is that each individual enables her/him self to get in contact or interact with anything other than her/him self primarily through socialization. Therefore, socialization is based on inter-action (as well as symbolic interaction) and would naturally be about the exchange of action between the individual and something/somebody else. But is this the case? Is this exchange of action exclusively between individuals? Or is it within individuals as well? So is socialization only about interaction or could it also be about intra-action?

This chapter uses both sociological and psychological approaches to answer key questions in understanding the concept of socialization. The first question this chapter will try to explain regards: what do we mean by socialization? Specific schools of thought will be discussed and a variety of definitions will be involved. The second question tries to explore: what are the origins of socialization? The process of socialization throughout childhood will then be analysed. The last question this chapter explores has to do with: how does socialization take place? Certain aspects of socialization will then be explained, starting from childhood and moving on to life course.

EXAMPLE

A two-year-old boy points outside the window by saying 'ffff' and then he puts both his hands on his mouth. The boy cannot talk yet. However, he can interact.

The mother is trying to interpret the symbols. She is following the boy's instructions and she looks outside the window where the boy is pointing. She tries to understand what 'ffff' might mean. The boy and the mother share a common understanding of some symbols and meanings but they don't speak the same language. However, this boy knows very well what he means through his own language. And he is trying very hard to explain to his mother that he is pointing at something that he wants to put into his mouth. After a few days, the mother decides to observe her son while looking outside the window and repeating the same sounds and the same gestures. The toddler is neither stupid nor crazy. He knows what he wants but he doesn't know how to communicate it. The mother finally realizes that there is a deflated balloon outside the window that the boy wants to put it into his mouth and inflate. Was this realization the outcome of a typical form of interaction? Or was it the outcome of two separate (and interrelated) series of intra-actions? The boy knows what he wants and he uses his personal vocabulary and gestures to describe it and the mother is trying to imagine what these symbols mean by observing her son and using her imagination. The exchange of this symbolic interaction and therefore the accomplishment of some sort of communication is only achieved after the mother picks up the balloon and shows to her son that actually, this balloon is damaged but they can play with a new one. Why do we only recognize as 'interaction' and therefore 'socialization' the accomplished exchange of (sometimes meaningful) action? In this example, the mother and the boy exchanged meaningful action and they joined the process of socialization even before fully constructing shared meanings or understandings.

What Do We Mean by Socialization?

Sociological perspectives on socialization

The term socialization has been defined in a wide variety of ways. However, following the approach taken in the first chapter, it seems appropriate to begin the exploration of this term by using one of the most influential definitions offered by one of the four founding fathers of sociology (Marx, Weber, Durkheim and Simmel), that of Georg Simmel. Simmel was the first to analyse the interrelated concepts of interaction and socialization in such a detailed level that he promoted them into the core concepts of sociology. He believes that socialization forms the basis of society; this concept is perceived as the outcome of the endless combinations of interactions/relationships between individuals, which are constantly re-created and re-defined. Simmel used the term '*sociation*' to refer to the means through which social phenomena are produced and he explained that through sociation we try to understand the actions of others as well as our own. Craib (1997: 160) explains that for Simmel, sociation refers to the way in which we come into contact with each other in the pursuit of everyday lives and sociability is the play form of this activity. Therefore, sociation (or socialization) is based on interaction, or differently, on the endless combinations of ways that people exchange action. In fact, Simmel explains that sociology asks what happens to individuals and by what rules they behave, as they form groups which are determined through interaction (Simmel, 1950). In short, socialization for Simmel, can only be understood in terms of interaction. Following Simmel, Speier (1970: 189) synopsizes that socialization is the acquisition of interactional competencies. Today, sociologists regularly argue that socialization describes the ways each individual becomes fully human or a 'person' (Wentworth, 1980).

Relevant literature identifies three main explanations regarding socialization: a) the first approach deriving from *functionalism* (related to Durkheim), perceives socialization as something that 'happens' to individuals and concerns the ways individuals internalize values, attitudes and norms and how they interact within specific socio-cultural settings. Functionalists like Talcott Parsons (1937), believed that if individuals failed to play their expected roles or behaved strangely, then this means that the socialization process that they have experienced is probably incomplete or inadequate. Such views do not recognize individuals' uniqueness. b) The second approach derives from the *interactionist* tradition and specifically the work of Mead (1934) and Cooley (1902/1964) and perceives socialization as the 'development of linguistically mediated reflexive self-concept' (Turner, 2006: 591). Socialization is therefore seen as an interactive process during which individuals negotiate their definitions of the situation with others. Symbolic interactionists believed that socialization is a more dynamic process that enables each individual separately to develop her/his unique ability to think. Socialization is a two-way dynamic process as individuals influence and are getting influenced by the social environment. This school of thought does not distinguish self from society. However, c) the third, *critical* perspective, on socialization (deriving from Marxism and feminist theory) perceives socialization in terms of social control and prioritizes the significance of power imbalances in society and the reproduction of structures of inequality. Bourdieu, for example, explained socialization through the concept of 'habitus' and he suggests that individuals become gradually habituated to the customary ways of behaving, thinking and feeling common to others. Therefore, the element of adjustment to social conditions is prominent in this approach (Bourdieu and Passeron, 1977).

A different understanding of socialization has been offered by Wentworth (1980); he explained that socialization entails personal autonomy and freedom as well as structural formation and group influence. By sharing some similarities with Goffman's (1959, 1961a) concept of 'dramaturgy' (discussed in Chapter 2), Wentworth proposes three aspects of socialization related to: a) context; b) content and process; and c) potential results. a) 'Context' (or 'front' in Goffman's terms) is the stage in which socialization takes place and includes various social forms as culture, language, structures, norms, etc. b) 'Content and process' (or 'role' in Goffman's terms) is like the play or the scenario and determines the structure of socialization which includes certain forms of talk, behaviour and ultimately specific forms of interaction. c) 'Potential results' (or 'performance' in Goffman's terms) refers to the outcomes of the socialization, or of what happens next. It is thus understood that socialization may be perceived through different approaches and may contain separate aspects. Goffman, for example, associated socialization with different roles individuals perform during interaction: 'a role implies a social determinism and a doctrine about socialization' (Goffman, 1961a: 76–7) and he therefore suggests that the role is the basic unit of socialization as the individual is shaped through socialization and the individual learns to adopt social roles and rules. Wunder (2007) explains that socialization ensures that an individual will develop a social identity (or self) and have the motivation and knowledge to perform the roles she may need throughout the course of her life.

Socialization and internalization

Wunder (2007) further explains that socialization is the process through which individuals learn and internalize the attitudes, values and behaviours appropriate to people living in any given society (further discussion on internalization follows in Chapter 7). A number of authors have used the concept of 'internalization', in their attempt to further explain the concept of socialization. Durkheim (1912/1995) for example, believed that socialization results in the internalization of collective representations (shared thinking) and this is how ultimately 'society is represented inside us' (1912/1995: 16). For Durkheim, socialization is thus understood as the authority of society inside us. Parsons (1951) further elaborates this view by stating that internalization is the process of learning and therefore this is the way that important elements of culture are incorporated into personality. This is how culture gets into our heads. A similar and equally influential perspective on the internalization of socialization derives from the works of Freud (1961/2004), who believed that the purpose of socialization was to enable (or even force) individuals to internalize social restrictions and prohibitions which are in complete contradistinction with the individual's instinctive desires and sexual drives (further discussion follows in Chapter 6). This is how social inhibitions are internalized and therefore followed. According to White (1977), such deterministic views perceive internalization as a static process as they ignore the possibility of the agent developing her/his own free will.

As already discussed (Chapter 2), in contrast with this view, symbolic interactionism prioritizes interaction over internalization. Although this school of thought is also concerned with the ways individuals fit into society, the emphasis is placed on the individual's learning experience and the process of meaning-making through interaction. Socialization is seen as a life-long process. Mead (1934) for example, perceives socialization during childhood in terms of symbolic communication. Mead explains that children internalize symbols primarily through language. Once these symbols are internalized then the child is able to imagine situations or even possible responses from others. Mead explains that as the child talks to oneself, then s/he is able to imagine that s/he is someone else and therefore to objectify oneself (take different roles). According to Wentworth (1980), sociologists have generally come to believe that through internalization of socialization, social and cultural processes permeate, even constitute, the minds and bodies of individuals.

Perhaps one of the first founders of developmental psychology, Vygotsky (1978), has been one of the first to use this term (internalization) as he was explaining that children, through acquisition and use of language, eventually internalize and reproduce culture (further discussed in Chapter 7). However, his view did not agree with functionalism in terms of how society dominates our minds. For Vygotsky (1978: 57): 'every function in the child's development appears twice: first on the social level, and later on the individual level; first between people (inter-psychological) and then inside the child (intrapsychological)'. Interaction is indeed what comes first for Vygotsky. Children are able to internalize these interactions and then respond accordingly (if needed). The main difference between Durkheim's, Parsons' and Vygotsky's views has to do with the fact that although all three agree that socialization takes place through internalization of interaction, this does not necessarily mean that society dominates individuals through social-ization (as functionalism would have it). Vygotsky explains that it is common for children to produce self-directed speech (or egocentric speech according to the second founder of developmental psychology Jean Piaget) without being inter-ested if others would understand them. For Piaget (1926) this is a kind of 'antisocial' form of behaviour which eventually disappears as self-awareness increases. But Vygotsky explains that this speech eventually becomes internalized and the child stops producing this kind of speech out-loud. It is therefore trans-formed to 'inner speech' or as Vygotksy (1978) would describe it, a form of thought. As Chalari (2009) explains, although all individuals use certain forms of internalized language this does not mean that all individuals are affected by society in common ways. To the contrary, each individual internalizes aspects of the social world in unique ways and the ways this internalization is further processed pri-marily relies on each individual separately.

Archer (2003, 2007) would term this process as the ability of the individual to become reflexive towards her/himself and towards society. (More detailed analysis on how internalization of the social world takes place, will be discussed in Chapter 7.) According to Cosaro (2011: 20) socialization 'is not only a matter of adaptation and internalization but also a process of appropriation, reinvention and reproduction'. What might be important to realize at this point is that socialization takes place through internalization of the social world (or aspects of it). However, although certain schools of thought (like functionalism and symbolic interactionism) would conclude that this is how society controls our minds, different views (like Vygotsky's and Archer's) would suggest that socialization is a process that all individuals go through (from a very early age), but it is unique for each one of us. Therefore soci-ety (or else social structure) is indeed a determined parameter in the way individuals produce interaction and therefore get socialized, but as will be further supported in this book, it is not necessarily or exclusively the most decisive factor.

Psychological perspectives on socialization

Psychological perspectives on socialization try to emphasize the psychological contexts of this process. Such perspectives concentrate on the psychological state of the person being socialized and psychology primarily concentrates on the analysis of learning. Generally, psychological studies are primarily concentrated on the ways the child socializes, and therefore develops, through her/his interactions with parents, and certain agents of socialization (further discussion follows) (Slaughter-DeFoe, 1994). However, specific schools of thought perceive socialization in different ways.

Freud emphasized the importance of the unconscious (deriving from child-hood experiences) in the shaping of the individual's personality, behaviour and ultimately, socialization. He proposes that socialization is the process through which, individuals learn to suppress their sexual instincts and conform with social and cultural rules and expectations (Freud, 1961/2004). However, different perspectives on psychology would approach socialization differently. For example, cognitive psychologists would concentrate on cognitive (intellectual) development in order to explain how socialization occurs (Piaget's developmental stages). For behaviourism though, socialization is perceived according to the learning of patterns of behaviour through conditioning or through regular participation in recurring interactional activities such as observing and imitating. *Learning Theory* for example, introduced by Watson (1928), is based on the principle of rewarding or punishing behaviour. Skinner (1989) extended this approach by emphasizing the importance of reward as a more effective conditioning of behaviour. Following these views, *Social Learning Theory* (Bandura, 1969, 1977) is concentrated on the ways children imitate behaviours and supports the view that children learn through observation rather than reward. Socialization is therefore seen as a process conditioned by others. Personality psychology views socialization as the process of forming personality during early life through behavioural reinforcements and punishments (Zigler et al., 1982). White (1977) further explains that research in developmental psychology regarding socialization is related to the forms of interaction between the parent(s) and the child. Socialization is therefore studied in laboratory settings while social situations are recreated. Erikson (1950/1963) on the other hand is primarily interested in exploring socialization throughout the life course. He proposed eight stages of socialization beginning at birth and finishing at death. Cultural psychologists link culture with cognition as they explain that individuals internalize the cultural environment through socialization (Vygotsky, 1978; Bruner, 1990). In recent times many psychoanalysts and psychotherapists have tried to analyse the process of socialization by focusing on the relations individuals built with others as well as with themselves (further discussed in Chapter 6). The ways individuals form their relationship with themselves and with others, guide the way people live their lives (DeSuza, 2011; Luborsky, 1984).

Connections between sociology and psychology

Connections between sociological and psychological approaches to socialization can be seen in various approaches, for example, in the works of the symbolic inter-actionists (Mead and Cooley) as these views explore socialization in relation to the individual and the concept of self. To do that, Mead tried to explore the connection between the 'I' and the 'Me' (discussed in Chapter 2). Additionally, psychology and sociology could complement each other in terms of how socialization is studied, as many scholars coming from both disciplines would agree that in order to change society, we first need to change the way people bring up their children. Both sociology and psychology have contributed enormously in the study of childhood socialization, which, as will be further explained, constitutes the foundation of adult socialization. Therefore, for psychology and sociology, socialization consti-tuted the first unit of analysis, no matter if the subject of analysis is the individual, the society or both.

Socialization and intra-action

So far, the concept of socialization has been discussed by following a wide variety of theories, approaches and definitions. It could be summarized that socialization is generally understood as a lifelong process, which comprises of all possible com-binations of interactions an individual could have with others that enables us to learn how to live our lives within specific social settings. Following the approaches taken in the first two chapters on interaction and symbolic interactionism, intra-action is inevitably involved. Since interaction derives from intra-action (the way a mother scolds her child [interaction] derives from her own evaluation of what is right and what is wrong [intra-action]), then, socialization, which is based on inter-action, also derives from intra-action. Indeed, the mother who scolds her child, tries to teach her/him a lesson through this particular interaction. This lesson (for exam-ple to respect others), which will be repeated many times, will hopefully accompany this person throughout her/his life. This form of interaction then, becomes a spe-cific form of socialization through which this particular child is raised. Notably, this form of socialization is shaped according to the mother's principles and evaluations of what is right and what is wrong and what her child should or should not do. Therefore, this example of socialization derived from the mother's ongoing process of intra-action regarding what one should learn in life. But even when we refer to lifelong socialization processes like the continuous and repeated interactions indi-viduals form and shape (for example) in their workplace. These everyday contacts with others derive from our everyday contact with our self. Therefore, the aspect that should be added into the discussion on socialization, has to do with the endless intra-actions the individual experiences within oneself and allows us to learn how to live our lives within ourselves as we move on the life course. This missing part will be further explored and discussed in the following chapters and especially in Chaper 7.

The context of socialization

While discussing and analysing the significance in understanding the content of socialization, the aspects of interaction as well as intra-action should be employed. Equally importantly, the context of socialization should be considered. Admittedly, the literature used in this (and perhaps all) chapter(s) refers to studies, theories, views and approaches deriving from certain cultural, structural and moral settings. Socialization, has been (and will be further) discussed through the ways that Western culture has formed and perceived this social phenomenon. Non-Western societies and cultures, probably perceive the process of socialization through different means and ways, and therefore, certain aspects of the present discussion might seem disconnected to particular contexts of social reality (the socialization process is not as relevant with parenting, family, school and peers if we refer to war zones, refugee camps or certain forms of collective systems of children's upbringing). Even childhood socialization may be experienced as a completely different process than the one discussed in the following sections, if we refer to different cultural contexts. It is therefore crucial to clarify that the ideas discussed in this book's framework refer primarily to Western cultures, and the context of socialization may be perceived in completely different terms by readers coming from distinct social and cultural backgrounds.

Origins of Socialization: Childhood Socialization

In order to better understand what we mean by socialization (in Western cultures), it might be helpful to explore how individuals begin the process of socialization. Socialization begins very early in the infant's life. As Stern (1977) explains, infants aged three months old are already able to engage or disengage their caregivers (through smiling, crying, eye contact, touching). Upbringing can be seen as the most crucial time of socialization. Infants, and later on children, learn the language of their own group and come to understand the norms and values important to their family and society (Wunder, 2007). Developmental psychology is based on the work of the two most influential developmental psychologists (Jean Piaget and Lev Vygotsky) who have established different approaches regarding childhood socialization. Piaget (1926) for example explains that even at the age of four months, infants cannot differentiate themselves from their environment; he explains that the most important need of the infant is to be close to her/his mother and he describes distinct developmental stages in terms of the child's ability to socialize and ultimately learn. Vygotsky (1934) on the other hand, suggests that actually, even for infants, socialization is related to social structures and interactions. Vygotsky believes that interaction (and therefore socialization), even from a very early age, depend on structural constrains (class, status, etc.) as well as cognitive development.

Models of childhood socialization

Following the main approaches discussed in the previous sections, in order to define socialization as a concept, Corsaro (2011) explains that accordingly, childhood socialization is explained through two main models: a) *Deterministic Model* in which the child is seen as having a passive role; and b) *Constructivist Model* in which the child is seen as an active agent and learner.

a) The Deterministic Model derives from two separate approaches: i) *functionalism* (e.g. Inkeles, 1968) which prioritizes order and balance within society and consequently the child should be trained through socialization in order to fit and reproduce the structure of society. This model could also be supported by Durkheim (1995) who explained that through socialization the individual is taught how to follow collective representations (shared ways of thinking). He explained that the job of the parent and teachers is to produce a child who can take up a place in society. For example, children are taught to sleep at specific hours, respect others, do what they are told, etc. ii) *Reproductive approaches* (e.g. Bernstein, 1981) which emphasize the importance of social control through the maintenance and reproduction of, for example, class inequalities. Most upper class parents will try to provide expensive education for their children, even from an early age, by choosing prestigious institutions. Corsaro (2011: 9) characteristically says that according to this model 'society appropriates the child'.

b) The *Constructivist Model* on the other hand perceives the child as an active agent able to construct her/his own interpretations about the world (Corsaro, 2011). Piaget (1926), for example, explains that even infants are able to use and interpret information from the environment and then construct conceptions. This is probably why infants are able to develop a specific kind of bonding with their primary carer even if this person is not their biological parent. Piaget proposes certain stages of child development each of which entail certain forms of socialization. Furthermore, according to Vygotsky (1978), children's social development (and therefore socialization) is based on their collective actions, which are located in society. Children try to respond to societal demands in a collective manner through interaction. Think of how hard a child tries to mimic her/his parents from a very early age, or to learn what s/he needs to do to keep her/his parents pleased or to get them annoyed. The child develops socially and psychologically through her/his contact with others. First, through the contact with parents/care takers, then the extensive family, following that, the nursery/day care, the school and so on. Therefore, both Vygotsky and Piaget agree that children co-construct their perception of the social and physical world, through their first steps into childhood socialization. Mackay (1974) further promotes this approach by explaining that children are not passive, incomplete receptacles, rather they are active participants in the socialization process. Socialization is a two-sided process as children interact with adults while acquiring knowledge and the ability to reason. Corsaro (2011: 12) explains that according to the *Constructivist Model*, the 'child appropriates society'.

Corsaro (2011: 20–1), though, proposes a different approach to children socialization which he terms '*Interpretive Reproduction*' and explains that the main characteristics of this approach have to do with the fact that children are able to 'create and participate in their unique peer cultures by creatively talking or appropriating information from the adult world to address their own peer concerns'. Therefore, the child is not only involved in certain cognitive developmental stages that enable her/him to get prepared for the adults' world; nor is he/she only involved in interactions with adults that enable her/him to construct her/his own understandings and skills. Children also interact with other children and they create their own peer cultures (defined as a stable set of activities of routines, values or concerns). Therefore, children's socialization is about children interacting with adults, interacting with the social world and interacting with other children while following a specific cognitive development.

Effective childhood socialization?

Most (if not all) parents want the best for their children and naturally they try to follow the most effective (in their view) socialization process. Unsurprisingly, there are not any manuals offering instructions on how parents should socialize their children, but relevant (primarily Western) literature has been able to identify more or less helpful tendencies. However, the inevitable question one might ask is: what consists effective socialization? Notably, sociology cannot offer a specific answer to this question, as different cultures, in different chronological periods and dissimilar individuals in distinct social circumstances have followed an extensive variety of socialization practices regarding the ways children should be raised. In this context, relevant literature, and perhaps primarily psychological studies, offer specific views and interpretations of what might represent effective socialization practices. Such views, however, are products of certain cultures, beliefs and principles which may seem completely incomprehensible to readers coming from distinct cultural backgrounds.

For example, in Western societies, there is a common belief that caring and loving care takers are more likely to reinforce trust and respect in children. Similar views advocate that parents who can show that they are in charge of their own lives and they know what they are doing have better chances to be heard and followed by their children. The combination of discipline and love seems to be one of the most effective practices (Goode, 1977). Consistency in parents' behaviour is also considered vital in this context, along with the examples parents set through their own behaviour. However, occasional inconsistency in application of rewards regarding certain behaviours of the child is perceived as an effective way to reinforce desired behaviour. Psychologists call this approach 'intermittent reinforcement' (Kendall, 1974). According to relevant studies, participation in rule-making rather than direct enforcement of rules along with explanation of possible outcomes, may result in better ways of collaboration between the child and the parent. Furthermore, punishment, and especially physical punishment has been proven to be particularly unhelpful if not damaging in children's upbringing (Phelps et al., 1998; Dobbs-Oates et al., 2011). Such views derive from specific epistemological backgrounds, which have been produced within certain cultural, structural and moral contexts.

How Does Socialization Take Place?

Socialization occurs throughout the individual's lifetime but it has been researched primarily in two parts: a) *primary or childhood socialization*. This aspect of socialization is associated with family settings and the school period, it generally concerns learning skills of attitudes and behaviours. This first part of socialization can also be understood as the foundation of socialization. b) *Secondary or adult socialization* is related to a wide variety of settings deriving from primary socialization which are further developed, for example, higher education, working place or self exploration and it is mainly related to social influences. This part of socialization can also be perceived as the socialization through the life course. The process of socialization enables the individual to shape oneself in relation to other individuals, in relation to society and in relation to oneself. It is therefore vital to understand how the process of socialization takes place and what parts are involved in this process.

The wider part of (Western) sociological literature that explores these two parts of socialization, focuses on the 'agents of socialization', referring to those who do the socializing (Wunder, 2007; Giddens, 2009; Ritzer, 2015) or, the social contexts of socialization (already discussed as the first out of three main aspects of socialization according to Wentworth, 1980). Agents of socialization may include significant individuals (parents, partners), groups (family, peer group) or institutions (school, media) that provide structured situations in which interaction and learning takes place. In the same sense, social contexts of socialization refer to certain social settings that may influence the way people live their lives (parents may determine their attitudes towards their children through specific cultural customs or children who have been raised during the war years may be socialized in distinct forms and ways).[1] Therefore, as we discuss socialization we need to be conscious of the agents as well as the context of socialization.

The foundations of socialization

For many sociologists as well as psychologists, the foundations of socialization coincide with primary socialization and refer to the first contact of new borns, infants and young children with initial caregivers, social environment and culture. This stage, according to most psychologists, psychoanalysts and psychotherapists, constitutes the foundation of the individual's personality development (Rohlinger, 2007a). Primary socialization constitutes the initial process through which the individual (of an early age) abandons the physical limits of oneself and explores ways of co-existence with others. At that stage the future person begins to shape oneself in relation to others as well as oneself. This process is based on the acquisition of language(s) and introduces younger generations to the ways society(ies),[2] social structures and social institutions form. This procedure (also termed '*anticipatory socialization*') is primarily introduced by parents and siblings, and in some cultures by the wider family.

This section will discuss how specific agents and (primarily Western) contexts of socialization contribute to the future adult's understanding of the social world. Early social contact with family prepares future adults for later stages in life. It is within the family that initial social ideas are formed, like gender roles, cultural customs and practices, racial differentiations, class and status orientation, nationality characteristics and more broadly, social expectations and prohibitions. Perhaps, the most important influence deriving from family concerns the individual's fundamental principles, values and beliefs that form the basis of her/his future life. However, the traditional model of the 'nuclear family' is not as common any more, particularly in Western societies. New family models are now becoming more accepted (same-sex families, families spread in different countries, single-parent families, multicultural/racial/religious families). Naturally, forms of socialization vary tremendously between families even within common cultures. Nurseries and day care centres are now used more commonly from the age of even three months. This means that additional forms of interactions and therefore socialization occur in such early stages, undoubtedly contributing significantly to the formation of the future adult. Furthermore, as socialization is seen as a form of interaction, caregivers and parents are more often seen as being influenced by the child as much as they influence the child. School and peer groups' socialization routes contribute significantly to the child's understanding of the word. Additionally, gender formation is one of the first forms of socialization a child is called to learn. Media and the Internet are the most recent forms of socialization young adults are exposed to from a very early age.

Parenting and family

It is agreed between sociological and psychological literature that parents offer the first social training. Certain upbringing characteristics are considered favourable or unfavourable in terms of the child's opportunities to reach her/his developmental potential (White, 1977). Different cultural expectations are usually associated with children's upbringing practices and initial forms of socialization; such practices could vary enormously. A characteristic example is that of domestic violence; this violent act is treated as a criminal offence in some cultures whereas it is treated as common practice in others. Although children's socialization training and upbringing (in any culture) may include various deviant practices, today it is agreed (by primarily Western scholars and relevant practitioners) that emotional stability and security is vital in a child's life (further discussed in Chapter 6). Several studies (conducted primarily within Western cultural settings) suggest that consistent interaction patterns within family, constant demonstration of affection and play with parents along with repeated encouragement and stimulus of conversation and symbolic communication are as important for the child's complete development, as the basic requirements of adequate food, clothing and shelter (Naouri, 2008, 2005; Maccoby, 1992; Bowie et al., 2013). Indeed, the child's patterns in behaviour, habits and beliefs primarily derive from the models of interaction the child experiences and learns. Therefore, parents' and siblings' models of behaviour are the ones the child is more likely to imitate. The repeated expression of (cultural and personal) values by adults are learned and internalized by the child. Arguably, in cases when parental values are in contradiction with social norms or expectations, conflict is inevitably involved. For example, if a child is raised in a violent family s/he will possibly repeat violent patterns in out-of-family interactions (bullying). In cases like the above, the child might not be sure about which set of values to follow.

In the same vein, there is a tendency to agree with the premise that the most valuable socialization in the (Western) family setting is the one that causes the least stress for the child when s/he encounters a social situation in the wider society. Such children usually receive consistent parental love, encouragement and discipline whereas erratic handling causes anxiety and insecurity (White, 1977; Rogers, 1951, 1959, 1974, 1986). Furthermore, as Naouri (2005, 2008) has repeatedly demonstrated, the role of the father in the child's upbringing (and therefore primary socialization) is equally important with the role of the mother, especially if both parents work. However, as the mother usually spends most time with the child, she is considered the most significant socializing model for the child. Psychological research (perhaps primarily following Freud's core ideas) consistently promotes the significance of the establishment of a meaningful connection between the mother and the young child. Even in cases that the mother cannot fulfil this expectation, the presence of a stable adult model is essential. Mother or father's withdrawal of affection often creates difficulties in socialization. Furthermore, the child is more likely to receive a consistent and systematic form of socialization if parents are the only adult models in the family (Naouri, 2005, 2008).

Parenting and family practices constitute the first contact of the child with the (developed) social world. However, the cultural, social and political circumstances where such socialization might take place determine the values, principles and beliefs associated not only with the upbringing practices, but also the dominant social norms regarding what might be more or less desirable or effective socialization practices. Therefore, we need to keep in mind that we primarily refer to Western psychological and sociological literature being in agreement when proposing that the way primary socialization takes place, determines in many respects the way the future individual will live her/his life. Although there are various occasions where children who are raised in deprived environments thrive and others raised in privileged settings fail to fulfil their potential, the principles of: security, stability, acceptance, understanding, caring, affection, encouragement and discipline constitute the essential characteristics of a supportive primary socializing experience. It is therefore becoming understood, that the centre of attention regarding primary socialization is the young child and her/his contact with her/his parents, siblings and family, although in reality this might not be necessarily the case in different cultural settings.

School

By the time young children (again in Western societies) begin school, they spend most of their days interacting and socializing with peers and teachers, trying to learn, and making sense of the world by combining their life experience at home and school. Socialization that takes place in school is considered the second most important agent of Western socialization. The role of education relates to the completion of the fundamental process of learning to take one's place in society. This process is also called '*anticipatory socialization*' and refers to the teaching and learning of what will be expected of one in the future (Ritzer, 2015). Educators are called to instruct the learners systematically into the ways of the whole (although usually very specific) culture. The school offers the first formal and structured socialization to young individuals (White, 1977). Schools teach values and attitudes as well as family, but the process of education includes more systematic forms of learning and teaching which include for example: the importance for working for rewards, the significance of neatness and punctuality, orderliness and respect for authority. Students are expected to remain quiet in class and follow the rules of school discipline. Teachers evaluate students' performance in multiple levels whereas the reactions of teachers may affect the expectations children have about themselves (Persell, 1990; Giddens, 2009).

The process of education in Western cultures has been studied extensively and various approaches have been established. In terms of socialization though, the main approaches followed in this chapter perceive socialization in education in different terms: a) functionalism emphasizes the importance of education in terms of teaching the child how to be fully integrated into society (the child learns core social expectation that s/he is asked to meet, like study in university, get a decent job and create a family); b) symbolic interactionism prioritizes the interactional element of the educational process (between the student and the teacher as well as between the students) while also allowing self-expression of individuality (exploring and cultivating a specific talent); then c) Marxism reveals the function of education as a system of social selection as it is through education that future individuals are selected to follow specific occupations related to status, authority, power and income (the kind and level of education offered in state schools is considered to be different in relation to public schools). Therefore, education (and hence school) offers a structured socialization process that takes place at multiple levels. The ways each child experiences these forms of school socialization vary tremendously and all individuals have different memories of their school years. Therefore although this specific form of socialization is offered in similar ways to certain groups of children (organized primarily according to age), and even though younger children and later on adolescents are exposed to this specific kind of socialization on an everyday basis, it is undeniable that each young individual internalizes this process in unique and even unpredictable ways.

Peers

An additional and equally significant aspect of school socialization relates to the forms of interactions between students. This part of primary socialization is called peer socialization and becomes increasingly important especially in developed societies during the high school years (Fine, 1987; Bennett and Fraser, 2000; Steinberg and Monahan, 2007). Peer group is defined as a group of friends of about the same age and usually the same status. Up until the age of two, children seem to play together but in fact they do their own particular thing. After this stage the child is more able to respond to orders, and to requests or needs of other children. Children need the supervision of adults as well as the comfort they offer. As they develop this need is abridged. Actual peer groups are formed as early as the first or second grade and children over the age of four or five usually spend a great deal of time with friends of the same age. The kinds of socialization formed between children in nurseries and day care centres mainly relate to playing with toys, imitating one another, following teacher's instruction but children also learn to share, care, respect and be patient. Peers may also reinforce behaviours that are reproduced both by parents and school, for example prevent aggressive attitudes, encourage appropriate behaviours for boys and girls, support good manners. These basic but fundamental forms of interaction constitute an increasingly important part of primary socialization

(Corsaro, 2011). The significance of family socialization is given and most of the time it can be relevantly easy to see similarities between young children's and parents' behaviours, habits, attitudes and values. However, in the case of peer groups, such observations are not as clear (Harris, 1998).

As the young child moves through school, peer influence becomes more significant. Peer concerns may involve music, movies, sports, sex, relationships or in some cases illegal activities. Peer groups may provide social rewards like praise, prestige, attention, acceptance and understanding (Persell, 1990). It has been supported that such rewards are more important for young individuals who have not experienced, to a satisfactory degree, such feelings through family socialization (Rogers, 1986). A number of studies reveal that the influence of a supportive family remains strong with regard to the young individual's future life (Krosnick and Judd, 1982; Fairlie et al., 2012; Pugliese and Okun, 2014). Girls form different kinds of peer groups in comparison to boys. The stereotypical 'girly' concerns might be at odds with what boys care about. It is not until the later stages of adolescence that peer groups consist of both boys and girls. Gender, therefore, constitutes an additional aspect of socialization that one needs to consider.

Gender

Gender (further discussed in Chapter 4) socialization refers to the transmission of norms regarding what girls or boys can and should do (McHale et al., 2003; Rohlinger, 2007). Parents are the first who teach their children how to behave in a gendered manner. Parents dress infants in certain colours according to their gender, buy specific toys, teach specific manners, talk in certain ways. Additionally, certain social expectations are learned from an early age; boys for example are expected to be more active and aggressive whereas girls are expected to be more sensitive and caring (Beasley, 2005). These 'automatic' behaviours are generally perceived as natural expressions of masculinity and femininity. By the age of two, children have some sort of understanding of what gender is. By the age of five or six they start understanding the sexual anatomical differences between boys and girls and the purpose of these differences. Once gender is 'assigned', society expects individuals to act accordingly. However, these stereotypical perceptions have been heavily challenged for example by Feminism (Lorber, 2000) that questioned the privileged social treatment males have been receiving from birth. Gender socialization and reinforcement of gender role behaviours is typically encouraged in family and school settings, sports groups and the media. The media and the Internet are another agent of socialization that becomes increasingly significant in the ways individuals interact and socialize.

Mass media and the new technologies

Media socialization concerns a variety of communication forms that do not require personal contact, such as books, magazines, newspapers, radio, films, television and the Internet. Media plays a large role in shaping our understanding of the world and therefore in the ways socialization takes place. Over the last decades, children have been extensively socialized through television but more recently especially through the Internet. The numbers of hours a child spends in front of a screen (laptop/ tablet/smartphone) or TV is endless (Comstock and Scharrer, 2007). Parents begin using media as a form of socialization from a very early age. For many years television has been considered the 'children's closest friend'. Today, various forms of new technologies are offered for the entertainment of young (and older) individuals such as smartphones, video games and tablets (Rideout et al., 2010). Increased precautions have been introduced regarding the limited time a child should watch any kind of media programme. The NHS, for example, instructs parents to prohibit their children to watch any kind of programme for more than thirty minutes per day before the age of three and several forms of parenting control in terms of programme content (for TV, Smartphones, tablets, relevant applications) are now available. Social networking sites become ever more popular whereas Facebook and Twitter are already considered old-fashioned by younger generations (Buckingham, 2008; Watkins, 2009). As the forms of mass and social media alter so rapidly, along with technology, it becomes extremely difficult to be certain of the exact ways and degrees of influencing socialization. What remains certain, however, is that such influence is becoming increasingly powerful.

Socialization through the life course

Individuals will never stop the process of socialization, for as long as they are in contact (even limited) with others. As Erikson (1950) proposed (by developing eight stages), socialization continues through the life course for as long as the individual gets in contact with the social world. As we move on in life, individuals need to work in particular settings, perhaps continuing in higher education or trying different jobs. In all cases, people need to follow institutional rules and regulations, reprioritize their expectations, needs and wants and reconsider their plans, ambitions and anticipations. This is an ongoing process, which has been termed by some as '*resocialization*'. Primary socialization refers to socialize something new whereas resocialization regards the readjustment of a specific socializing process (work in a different job). Certain kinds of socialization may be considered in this context such as in the cases of total institutions (Gambino, 2013; Goffman, 1961b), in these cases, like in the army or prison, rules and regulations should be followed blindly and completely. The effect of 'institutionalization' is prominent in these cases as individuals find it hard to operate outside given barriers. Still, for most individuals, socialization remains a life project, which involves endless encounters with and between people, groups, institutions, cultures, structures, norms, attitudes and habits.

In all cases we refer to the connections individuals have with anyone or anything outside their selves. However, and as it has already been suggested, it might also be helpful to consider whether the process of socialization also involves the ways the individual gets in contact with oneself (this idea will be further developed in later chapters). These ongoing processes can only be explored if we begin to study the actual ways the individual (as an agent) gets in contact with society (as a structure). Simmel very correctly stated that socialization is indeed the basis of society, however, it may well also constitute the core foundation of the human being. It is therefore vital to further explore some of the endless fascinating ways that the individual is connected to society.

Summary

This chapter explored the concept of socialization by using both sociological and psychological approaches. Socialization has been defined initially through the work of Simmel, whereas additional and more recent views have been involved. Psychological and sociological perspectives regarding socialization have been discussed separately and a synthesized overview followed. The connection between socialization and intra-action has been discussed and the importance of the context of socialization has been recognized. The origins of socialization have also been included in the discussion by concentrating on childhood socialization. Specific forms of socialization have been explained including parenting, family, school, peers, gender, mass media and new technologies whereas the ongoing process of socialization through the life course has been briefly discussed.

• •

Concepts in Context

A German professor in a UK university falls in love with a Canadian colleague. They decide to live together and have a family. They have a child in Canada and spend the first year of their boy's life with the Canadian part of their family. The couple decide to move back to the UK as that is where both parents work, although they occasionally visit the German side of the family. The boy spends the second year of his life in the UK, enjoying long hours in a British nursery. Both parents work and they spend the rest of their time with their son. The boy learns both German and English whereas by the time he begins school his British accent is obvious. This is just one of the characteristics that distinguish him from his parents.

This could be a case of a multicultural family that tries to find the most appropriate way to enable the younger part of the family to socialize with others, with different cultures and with oneself. In this case, each member of this family comes from different cultures and all three cultures contribute significantly in the boy's upbringing (German, Canadian, British). As the boy learns the different languages, he acquires better (although never full) access to his German and Canadian roots. However, as he grows up in Britain, he will probably be perceived as being British with German and Canadian roots. Socialization for this boy has been quite complex, as various different aspects should be considered. Still, his parents raise the boy by allowing him to be exposed to different cultural settings, different languages and different family heritages.

• •

──── SELF-REFLECTIVE QUESTIONS ────

1. How could we study this case of socialization?
2. How could we identify the aspects of intra-action related to socialization?
3. What is distinct about this case of childhood socialization?
4. How important is the contribution of family in this example of socialization?

Possible ways of exploring the questions offered in this chapter and Further Readings:

1. One way to study this case of socialization would be through functionalism. However, relevant approaches might fail in explaining how this child could/should go through the socialization process, as it is not clear in which culture he needs to fit. Should he be exclusively integrated into the British culture? What kind of contact should the parents maintain with their own cultures? Which cultures should be learned at home? Symbolic interactionism might be more helpful in explaining that the acquisition of different languages may allow this boy to get a better understanding of the different cultures and his own heritage. But, how much should parents try to teach their son of these different cultures and languages? What level of understanding of these differences is considered acceptable? Marxist/critical views would probably emphasize the unequal treatment this child might receive, as he is different compared to other children. But is this difference necessarily disadvantageous? Is there any chance that this child might use his unequal position to his own benefit?

Further Reading:

Ritzer, G. (2015) *Essentials of Sociology*. Thousand Oaks, CA: Sage.

2. In cases like the example discussed, the complexity of the socialization process might become more obvious. However, at the same time, what remains important

relates to the fact that this boy, just like any child, will eventually find a way to lead his life and bridge the different components of his upbringing. The plurality of ways this boy can use to communicate with others (and thus go through the process of socialization) may also relate to the ways he will use to relate to himself. This boy might feel more strange between his Canadian or German family and perhaps less strange between his British friends. The ways he will find to balance the different parts of his socialization process are more related to the ways he might produce intra-action rather than interaction.

Further Reading:

Chalari, A. (2009) *Approaches to the Individual: The Relationship between Internal and External Conversation*. London: Palgrave Macmillan.

3. The uniqueness of this boy's upbringing has to do with the ongoing exposure to different cultures throughout the different stages of his cognitive, social and emotional development. As both parents are getting equally involved in his childhood years, the boy is involved in a number of different kinds of interactions and exchanges of symbolic meanings (different languages, traditions, norms) that could potentially enable him to have easier access to more ways of thinking and better understanding of different kinds of behaviour. But at the same time, this might mean that this boy's upbringing might be more difficult as this boy needs to figure out how different ideas and values can co-exist within his mind and his everyday life in a meaningful way.

Further Reading:

Corsaro, E.A. (2011) *The Sociology of Childhood*. Newbury Park, CA: Pine Forge Press.

4. Perhaps, the parental contribution in this case of socialization might be more complex in relation to other cases. As both parents anticipate that their son will be involved with three different cultural heritages, they have to work harder in order to find a balanced way to raise their son. It might be even more difficult for these parents to pass on to their son the values and principles that they were raised with and feel that their child should also learn. At the same time, through their son, these parents expand their own process of life course socialization as they learn more about the British culture, values, principles and norms. Therefore, this case might be a rather extreme, but not rare case of a multicultural family, that tries to combine different forms of socialization through meaningful ways.

Further Reading:

Bowie, B.H., Carrère, S., Cooke, C., Valdivia, G., McAllister, B. and Doohan, E.A. (2013) 'The role of culture in parents' socialization of children's emotional development'. *Western Journal of Nursing Research*, 35(4): 514–33.

Maccody, E.E. (1992) 'The role of parents in the socialization of children: an historical overview'. *Developmental Psychology*, 28(6): 1006–17.

This example discusses the foundations of this individual's socialization experience (including childhood socialization) which will be followed by the experience of socialization through the life course and all different components of this complicated process will allow this person to move on in life. As each individual's case is unique, so is the socialization process s/he experiences. What might be helpful though would be to explore how individuals (like this young boy) manage to get in contact with their own self and eventually construct their identity, especially in cases like the one discussed, where a wide variety of different elements are involved. The next chapter will explore the identity formation process.

Notes

1   For further discussion see: Sagi–Schwartz (2012).
2   Plural refers to increasing cases of infants/younger children who are raised in multicultural families or even between different cultures and acquire from an early age more than one language.

4

Identity

What I am as a self, my identity, is essentially defined by the way things have significance to me. And [...] these things have significance for me, and the issue of my identity is worked out, only through a language of interpretation which I have come to accept as a valid articulation of these issues. (Taylor, 1990: 34)

Why is Identity Important?

This chapter will explore the meaning of identity. Identity is one of the core concepts in sociological and psychological literature and both sciences have contributed enormously to the understanding of this term. However, this concept – along with the concept of self, which will be discussed separately – is highly problematic. The reason is exactly the fact that this concept has been searched and explored in such enormous detail, by such a wide variety of approaches, that it has been impossible to produce a single definition of what identity is. Still, it is unmanageable to explore the relationship between the individual and society without providing an explanation of what identity means. The solution to the problematic definition of the complex meaning of identity might instead be to use more specific terms to refer to exact social and psychological properties (e.g. intra-action). This is the attempt by the following chapters of this book which concentrate on more specialized terminology and walk away from generalized conceptions. However, before we move on to the detailed analysis of more technical terms, the definition of identity remains an epistemological challenge. In my attempt to provide as much inclusive definition(s) as possible, both sociological and psychological (social-psychological) approaches will be followed. Inevitably some perspectives will not be included due to lack of infinite space. Still, this overview aims to cover the most prominent perspectives of identity.

This chapter begins by providing initial and general explanations of what we mean by identity. The specific areas of personal, social/relational and collective identity will be discussed by incorporating sociological and psychological perspectives.

Then certain identity theories will be analysed, including role identity theory, identity theory, affect (and identity) control theory and queer theory. Specific categorized identities will be also explained, like those of stigmatized, gender, sexual, race and ethnic identities. As explained, the concept of identity covers a wide variety of approaches but this chapter focuses on those views that can better explain how the individual may be related to society.

EXAMPLE

A young academic had been struggling for years in her continuous attempt to form her identity. She believes that this life process or life 'project' as she calls it, is the most difficult ongoing experience she has ever had. She was born and raised in Cyprus by a traditional Greek-Cypriot family and she realized at a very early age that she was different compared to other children. She felt more comfortable being around girls rather than boys. She also realized quite early that this is not acceptable, actually she thought that being gay was not normal. She kept this part of her identity secret for many years. In the meantime, she decided that she needed to move away from her family and the place she grew up although she valued her family and homeland tremendously. She also wanted to be respectable and successful. She studied in London and started a very promising academic career. After long years of struggling with herself about who she is, she decided to come out, to tell her friends, her family, her colleagues. It wasn't an easy thing to do but perhaps not as hard as she was worried it would be. She moved on in her career by becoming a professor before she turned 40, she received British citizenship, she managed to keep a very good relationship with her family and she visits Cyprus very often. She thought that this was when she would feel fulfilled. But she always felt she was mistreated because she was too feminine to be gay or because she was unmarried and single or because she was too young to be respected as a professor or because her English is not as native as her colleagues'. She is still trying to make peace with herself about who she is but probably she is far more worried about who others believe she is.

What Do We Mean by Identity?

Jenkins (2008: 5) quite successfully states that identity is 'the human capacity [...] to know who is who (and hence what is what). This involves knowledge of who we are, knowing who others are, them knowing who we are, us knowing who they think we are, and so on.' Identities are made not given. Following the previous chapters, identity derives from social and symbolic interactions between people and groups of people, socialization throughout the course of people's lives and through

intra-action. If an individual belongs to a particular group of people then the characteristics of this group also characterize this person. As Vryan (2007) explains,
identity affects self-conceptions and other intra-psychic structures and processes
and perhaps this is the reason why identity is defined by various scholars in relation
to the concept of the self. Although these two terms do not coincide, it may
become particularly complicated to differentiate the one from the other. As the
following chapter is dedicated to the definition of self, this chapter will concentrate
on the essence of identity. Still, it might be helpful to provide an initial distinction
by clarifying that the 'self refers to the process and organization born of self-
reflection whereas identity is a tool [...] by which individuals or groups categorize
themselves to the world' (Owens, 2013: 206). Identity can also be defined as the
'self- and hetero-valuative determination of the self or/and social groups'
Emmanouil (2014).

A slightly different approach is offered by Edwards (2009: 19), who explains that
the essence of identity is similarity. Similarity refers to the 'sameness' of the
individual's personality 'at all times or in all circumstances' which means that this
person is the same and no one else. Identity constitutes a continuity, which in many
instances constitutes an uninterrupted passage through life which maintains its main
characteristics even when major changes occur. Therefore, identity on a personal
level has to do with the ongoing integrity of a person. *Personal identity* makes one
feel unique and different from other people and others perceive her/him as such.
Personal identity is also understood as *'personality'* and includes, according to
Edwards (2009), our individual traits, characteristics and dispositions. Personal identities for Owens (2013) are both attached to individuals (their traits, personality
characteristics) and are internalized by them. The naming of a person is a characteristic indication of people's attempt to become differentiated. Quite correctly,
Edwards (2009) explains that the uniqueness of each individual is not defined by
the unrepeated psychological components that no other individual possesses. This
cannot be possible. All individuals share some common characteristics but the combination of those characteristics is unique for each one. In fact, each individual
blends his/her personal characteristics with certain social contexts and the constantly recreated outcome may produce what this chapter defines as the 'essence' of
identity. Inevitably, it becomes understandable that personal identity is intrinsically
connected with what is called 'social identity'.

Naturally, identity refers to the continuity of the individual itself but also there
are important connections between the individual identity and 'groupness'. In this
case we refer to *'social identity'* which is about 'a connectivity born in history and
carried forward through tradition' (Edwards, 2009: 19). Social identities tend to
attach to groups. For many sociologists, people's personal characteristics derive from
the socialization (discussed in the previous chapter) of each individual within specific groups to which they belong (family, peer group, school, close friends).
Personality characteristics are influenced by the particular social context within
which each individual comes in contact with others. For example, if a child is raised

in a religious, conservative family, there is a good chance that her/his personality will be influenced by this particular social environment, although admittedly, in an unpredictable manner. Therefore, individual identities will be both components and reflections of particular social (or cultural) identities. The social identities individuals share may include stereotypical characteristics (Edwards, 2009). Typically, boys are raised as being more aggressive and active, girls are raised as being more caring and passive. Social identities should be differentiated from '*collective identities*' that may attach to demographic categories (Northern Americans, Bostonians, immigrants) but are primarily used in social movements discourse (relevant discussion follows). Burkitt (1999) explains that collective identities are also based on similarities and therefore, to be identified as environmentalist, activists, academic or student can be the source of group solidarity.

A more 'compressed' definition of identity is offered by Vignoles et al. (2011: 4) who explains that identity comprises of four separate but interconnected components: the personal, the relational (social), the collective and the material components of identity. The authors explain that taken together these four components of identity may provide an integrated operational definition of identity. Therefore, viewed by an individual person, identity consists of the combination of the person's self-chosen or ascribed commitments, personal characteristics and beliefs about oneself; roles and positions in relation to other individuals; the person's membership in certain social groups and categories; and the individual's identification with treasured material possessions and the individual's sense of where she belongs in geographical space. Therefore people are characterized by complex combinations of identity components, which may complement each other (a hard working man and conservative Christian); may contradict one another (a laid back surgeon). Moreover, people may not be fully conscious of some of their identity components (a devoted, caring but manipulative mother). More importantly perhaps, people are not necessarily aware of the processes by which identity categories are formed (such as gender or race identities) which are generally regarded as 'natural' and 'given'. These approaches refer to identity formation as social constructions (Segal, 2010). Vignoles et al. (2011) quite correctly explain that people have a number of means at their disposal to reconcile apparent inconsistencies in their sense of identity and to preserve a sense of self-continuity. Indeed, different people develop their personal ways to go through life. As will be further discussed in later chapters, current social theory offers new concepts to explore the fundamental question of how the individual is connected to society and therefore how people manage to preserve a sense of self-continuity.

The following section will provide more analytical accounts on three main aspects of identity: personal identity, social/relational identity and collective identity.

Personal identity

For McCall and Simmons (1966) personal identity refers to the uniqueness of individuals in relation to various categories and Thoits and Virshup (1997) add that personal identities are unique identifiers and therefore may be associated with a personal name, a body and appearance (a stylish clothing style), a biography and personal history (within a particular family network, e.g. 'the Kennedys'), a unique gathering of social identities (member of the local rowing club and graduate of Cambridge University) and a set of specific personal characteristics and traits (being generous, kind, polite with good manners) (Vryan, 2007). Statements like the following might clarify this point: 'I am John Smith. I am married to Susan Smith and I have two sons, George and Paul. My parents are Mary and Jason Smith and I have a sister, Ann. I am a medical doctor and I graduated from Trinity College, Cambridge University.' Symbolic interactionism has influenced extensively the ways personal (and social) identity has been defined; the core explanations of this term define personal identity as a set of meanings and expectations specific to a given individual. Stryker (1968, 1980) proposed that identities are perceived as parts of selves formed during and through structured role relations. Personal identities carry expectations related to present and future interaction associated to other individuals. This view, is derived from Stryker's identity theory (discussed later) and is based on fundamental concepts of symbolic interactionism like the unbreakable connection between Goffman's concept of self and the idea of role performances (Burke and Tully, 1977; Ervin and Stryker, 2000) discussed in Chapter 2. Notably, personal identity is considered the most enduring and essential representation of an individual, although its content may be presented differently to different audiences and may be redefined over time. Still, personal identity determines the individual as unique as it is impossible (even in the case of identical twins) for two individuals to share the exact same set of social identities or the same personal history or even personality (Vryan, 2007). Following symbolic interactionism, Stryker (1991: 22–4) outlines four main principles: a) individuals are actors and reactors; b) action and interaction is shaped through sharing of meanings and common understandings and definitions; c) people's understanding of themselves and others define interaction; and d) self-conception is the outcome of others' responses to the person. Following symbolic interactionism's emphasis on language, Edwards (2009) explains that language and identity are ultimately inseparable as language is central to the human condition.

Psychological perspectives

Owens (2013: 215) explains that the early psychological definition of personal identity is offered by James (1890) as the 'reflective process' that is, involved in 'our abandoning the outward-looking point of view and of our having become able to think of subjectivity as such, to think of ourselves as thinkers'. Personal identity here is also defined as the coherent picture that is composed of myriad 'facets' of oneself (Schwartz, 2001) that one shares with oneself and others. Psychological definitions of personal identity are primarily influenced by the work of Erikson (1950). Erikson's psychoanalytic views were concerned with the passage from childhood to adulthood and conceived identity as a process that is internal but also includes the relationships that individuals form with others during the life course. Weigert (1983) explains that Erikson distinguishes routine 'personal identity' as the normal way we are seen and interpreted by others from the technical use of his *'ego identity'*. For Erikson, 'ego identity' relates to the awareness of self-sameness and continuity not only on an individual level but also at the level of the immediate community (Erikson, 1946). In contrast to Freud's antagonistic relationship of the individual with society (further discussed in Chapter 6), Erikson proposed a constructive relationship; he believed that the individual and society form a unity within which mutual regulation takes place (Rapaport, 1958: 105). Erikson was also concerned with the concepts of inner identity, identity diffusion, wholeness and identity, racial group identities, psycho-social identity and developmental identity over the life course (Weigert, 1983).

'*Identity synthesis*', derives from Erikson's main principles and refers to the individual's anticipated future, however, '*Identity confusion*' refers to the inability to develop a workable set of ideals on which to base an adult identity (Schwartz, 2001). Davis (2009) defines personal identity as the way in which individuals 'manage' their multiple social identities. This approach is further developed by Boulu-Reshef (2015) who defines personal identity as the process which individuals undertake when trying to maintain multiple social identities in a way that is consistent with their conception of themselves. This view is inspired by the philosophy of personal identity approach which defines personal identity as the aspect of the self that is specific to the individual. Generally speaking, psychological perspectives are more concerned with the agentic role of the individual in creating and discovering her/his own identity (Côté and Levine, 2002). In this vein, endless studies have been conducted related to goals, values and beliefs (Marcia, 1966, 1993), standards for behaviour and decision making (Atkins et al., 2005) and self-esteem and self-evaluation (Sedikides and Gregg, 2008).

Social/relational identity

According to Owens (2013), social identity derives from the group, statuses and categories to which individuals are socially recognized as belonging. Vignoles, et al. (2011) use the term '*relational identity*' which refers to the role(s) attributed to any individual in relation to other people. Similarly, Vryan (2007) points out that social identities define a person or a group of people according to the meanings and expectations constructed by a specific group or category of people about this person in relation to the group (being a sister, mother, partner, colleague). These roles are defined by the individuals who experience the roles and the people related to these roles. Relative or social identities cannot be established by the individuals on their own, rather they are established and recognized through the interaction with the people to whom they are related. Individuals are therefore defined as members of particular groups and hence no others (being British, therefore different from being French); any membership is associated with particular expectations of the group towards each member (being proud of being British) and act accordingly (defend the pride of Britain in any instance). Owens (2013) clarifies that these views on social identity are related to dramaturgy theory introduced by Goffman (discussed in the previous chapters). In fact, social identity has been studied mainly through specific social categories related to sex/gender, family, race and ethnicity, nationality, religion, occupation, sexuality, age and voluntary subcultural memberships. As Vryan (2007) clarifies, social identities may be based on any distinction socially constructed or interactionally defined as significant (being a member of a peer group that enthusiastically explores a rare kind of butterflies). As Goffman would maintain, an individual may possess (or perform) a variety of social identities (and therefore roles) but the significance of each one may vary according to the social setting, circumstance and indeed the individual concerned. For example, a professor delivering a lecture in class is defined (and perceived) through his role and the social identity related to the fact that he is the professor who teaches during the lecture. Most probably the additional social identities he may possess as being for instance an Asian, middle aged single man, may not be significant. However, if the same man attends a traditional wedding ceremony in his hometown, the additional social identities he possesses may become notably significant, as he would probably be considered as an excellent potential husband. Therefore, social identities also represent how a person may fit within socio-cultural structures and social networks.

Psychological perspectives

According to Owens (2013) psychological perspectives employ 'Social Identity Theory' as they perceive social identity as a cognitive tool individuals use to categorize and explain their social environment and their own place within it (Tajfel, 1981; Tajfel and Turner, 1986). Social identity theory is particularly concerned with the examination of the effect of specific group memberships on how people define themselves. In particular, inter-group relations and conflicts, self-esteem motives as well as in-group and out-group categorizations (particularly related to prejudice and bias). Social identity theory assumes the superiority of the mind; therefore, social identity is perceived as 'the part of the individual's self-concept which derives from his knowledge of his membership in a social group[s] together with the value and emotional significance attached to that membership' (Tajfel, 1981: 255). Being a priest, for many individuals may seem merely a profession, but for some others as a mission or even a way of life. Psychological perspectives, emphasize not only the 'role' of the priest and what the relevant performance may entail, but also how significant this profession might be to the person who possesses the 'role'. The emotional fulfilment that a priest may experience while offering help, support and comfort constitutes the personal elements associated to this profession or social identity. Therefore, social identities are also perceived in relation to their significance for the individual who possesses them. Naturally, certain social roles may be perceived as a burden for some people (becoming a father of an unwanted child) whereas for some others the same social identity may be perceived as a blessing (becoming a father after trying for years to have a child).

Collective identity

According to Whooley (2007) collective identities are formed according to the common interests, experiences and solidarities of a group of people. Collective identities are primarily used by social movements' approaches which are concerned with people's identifications with the groups and social categories to which they belong and the meaning they give to these social groups (Vignoles et al., 2011). Melucci (1989: 34–5) defines collective identity as a conceptual tool for understanding the micro-development of socio-political collective action and social movements. At the same time it concerns a shared and interactive definition produced by a group of people aiming at defining the orientations of actions, opportunities and constraints in which the action is to take place. Polletta and Jasper (2001: 285) define collective identity as the 'individual's cognitive, moral and emotional connection with the broader community or category or even institution' and they emphasize that collective identity is a perception of a shared status or relation. Collective identity for Whooley (2007), is the outcome of ongoing struggles involved in the interactions of political actors. More specifically, collective identity can refer to membership in any form of social group or category including: ethnicity, nationality, religion and gender as well as smaller face-to-face groups such as families and work groups (Vignoles et al., 2011).

Elliot (2009: 14) emphasizes that collective identity gains its power through the establishment and recognition of common interests, built upon forms of solidarity involving battles over, for example, social exclusion and inequalities. A different view is offered by Dennis et al. (2013) who explain that collective identities may also be formed through leisure activities, for example, through children's play or merely through clothing styles. Such collective identity has also been termed as 'leisure ethnicity' (Kelly, 1983). A characteristic example would be through athletic activities as athletes could be profoundly characterized through a specific 'athletic identity' (Allen-Collinson and Hockey, 2007). A wider term used by Dennis et al. (2013) to describe such collective identities is *'affiliated identities'*.

Which level of identity analysis?

As has been discussed, identity can be approached through various levels of analysis, the most dominant being that of personal, social and collective. Psychological perspectives tend to focus more on studies related to personal or individual identity formation; for example, neo-Eriksonian perspectives are related to the exploration of identity status and the area of self-psychology (Schwartz, 2001). Relational/social and collective identities are primarily explored though sociological, social-psychological and discursive perspectives, by focusing on certain social processes (Wetherell, 2010). Notably, sociological and social-psychological perspectives perceive personal and social identities as being interconnected and interdependent as they are both shaped by the social context (Turner and Onorato, 1999). On the contrary, Elliot (2009: 14) characterizes the above-mentioned identity categories as 'traditional', which have dramatically loosened in our age of light mobility, liquid experiences and dispersed commitments. In fact, Elliot believes that identity categories might not be as much related to personal and private troubles, which cannot be resolved collectively. For this reason, he explains that there is a shift from identity to the self as a new marker in our times as there is increased interest in the individual's experiences and the new forms of domination and exploitation. Indeed, this book shall further investigate this shift on the self in later chapters.

Identity and intra-action

As was indicated at the beginning of this chapter and in the previous section, the concept of identity might not be as insightful in explaining the ways society and the individual are connected. As has been understood, identity is primarily related to interaction in a multi-level of analysis no matter if we refer to personal, social or collective identity. The idea of identity is almost inseparable from the concept of interaction. At the same time, the understanding that each individual may have about her/his identity(ies) can be fully defined only by the individual concerned. No matter which social categories are involved or which theorizations are followed, each individual may hold: (a) specific (or even multiple and constantly changing) perception(s) of her/his identity(ies) which might be in agreement or at odds with (b) other people's perception about this particular individual. Inevitably, intra-action is definitely involved in this process, as it is the process through which each individual is able to create, maintain or change any perception created by oneself and/or others regarding her/his own identity. Intra-action enables individuals to exchange views, understandings, perceptions, beliefs or values with oneself and therefore form, re-form or alter any aspect of identity formation they may be involved with. Consequently, intra-action plays a central role regarding identity formation processes and ultimately, might be a more helpful term to be used in the exploration of the ways individuals are related to society. Further discussion follows in Chapter 7.

Identity Theories

As discussed above, the concept of identity has been approached through various ways and a number of separate explanations have been offered. Although it remains practically impossible to include every single aspect on this over-researched area of exploration, it is vital to mention the most related theories as they seem to be used repeatedly in the relevant literature.

Role identity theory

McCall and Simmons (1966) explain that role identity theory is concerned with the character and the role the individuals devise for themselves when occupying specific social positions. Deriving from symbolic interactionists' thought, role identity theory refers to the imaginative view that a person has about her/him self in relation to a specific position or, in different words, role. Influenced primarily by Mead's thought, role here is seen as the main plan of action. Role identity theory views individuals as capable of becoming creative and spontaneous regarding the performance of any given role, but at the same time individuals are guided by the requirement of their social position. There is a variety of roles that any individual possesses with oneself. But role identity theory is about the hierarchical ordering of these roles. This means that following Goffman's views on dramaturgy, there is an emphasis on the degree of the commitment to a particular role identity and the successful performance of this role (the self-esteem of a committed surgeon who successfully completes a complex surgery). There is also an emphasis on the view of the significant others regarding the performance of the role (the evaluation of the patient's family regarding the specific surgery) (Owens, 2013). In 1963, Berger started expanding role identity theory by emphasizing the biographical meaning of role identity formation.

Identity theory

According to Owens (2013), identity theory has been primarily developed by Stryker (1968, 1987). This theory's main ideas derive again from symbolic interactionism and assume that individuals have the possibility of choice, even though choices are constrained by social structure and social interaction. Stryker's identity theory is based on two main concepts: that of salience and commitment to role relations and the hierarchical ordering of identities. Identity salience is defined by the probability of a particular identity being revealed in a particular situation (a father being unwilling to play with his son when they are alone, therefore being distant as a father; however, the same father may become fully engaged with his son's activities if his colleagues are around). Relational commitment refers to the intensity of the interactions involved during the performance of the role identity and it also involves the significance others place on the role identity the given person performs. In the example above, relational commitment would refer to the intensity of the father's engagement to his son's activities (intensively engaged in the presence of his colleagues or poorly engaged in the absence of their company), and also how significant his colleagues believe his role as a father to be. Thus, this father might not be particularly engaged with his son's activities on an everyday basis, but if his colleagues view of him as an engaged father is important for his work-life and work-development, this father will gladly perform the identity role of the good father in front of his colleagues. Therefore, this person can choose to perform the role identity of the good/engaged father in given circumstances and can deny to do so if the circumstances alter.

Following a similar, although not identical theoretical vein, Stone (1981) defined identity as a coincidence of 'announcements' and 'placements'. An identity announcement consists of anything that a person can interpret as an identification of the role that the actor intends or wants to enact in a situation. For example, the entrance of the judge in a courtroom announces that s/he is in charge. Identity announcement may be intentional or unintentional; a well known singer who shops in a department store hoping that he will not get recognized but some people who recognized him started cheering. In this case, the singer announced his identity unintentionally and the relevant response by others followed. Stone (1981) explains that in the case that an identity is announced, others certify our announcement of that identity by 'placing' us in terms of it. In the case of the judge walking into the courtroom, everyone has to stand up, as a signal of recognizing and accepting this person's authority. However, if any of the people attending the trial refuse to stand up then possible consequences may be involved. In this case, announcement and placement do not coincide and therefore potential for disrupted or paralysed social interaction is considerable. In the example discussed, if the defendant of a trial refuses to stand up and therefore fails to recognize the authority of the judge, then the entire interactional process of the trial might be disrupted or may even collapse.

Affect control theory

Affect control theory was introduced in 1970s by Heise (1977) and it concerns another theory based on symbolic interactionism processes that emphasize the role of language in relation to social categorizations. Affect control theory consists of quantitative models that simulate social interaction, emotional response to events and labelling/attribution processes. The main themes of this theory relate to '*affective reaction*': people respond affectively to interactional events; and '*affect control*': actors interpret events in order to confirm '*social sentiments*' (shared affective meanings within a culture). An example would be the case of a married man meeting an ex-girlfriend. This man could produce a warm and kind greeting when he would first meet his ex-girlfriend (affective reaction) but would probably avoid any expression of physical intimacy (hugging, kissing), as this response might not be considered appropriate due to an intimate past (affect control). According to this theory, people behave in order to experience sentiments consistent with the identities they are trying to confirm in a situation; the term here used is '*situated identities*' (accidentally meeting an ex-girlfriend) and the emotions they experience signal the extent to which they have been successful (or not) in doing so (feeling vulnerable or emotionally exposed). A group of researchers further advanced this theory by recalling it 'Identity Control Theory' (Burke, 1991; Stets and Tsushima, 2001); this approach has been focusing on predicting negative emotion from an interactional discrepancy (Owens, 2013).

Queer theory

Queer theory derives from postmodern and post-structuralist thinking and its main principle regards the challenging of any perception of real identity and of the truth of personal narratives. For example, according to post-structuralist Foucault (1978) any form of categorizations, such as identities, are not pre-given, unified or fixed. Identities (including self-identity) are constantly reconstructed and reinvented. In similar terms, queer theory defends the view that the concept of identity mistakenly assumes that all people have essential, in-built character traits and essential sexual desires. Queer theory is concerned (although not exclusively) with marginalized identities, and also emphasizes the uncategorized and unmarked desires and forms of social relationships. Queer theory 'queers' social life by emphasizing the in-betweens, the hidden spaces and the invisible zones that contribute to the formation of any identity perception and understanding. To many scholars, queer theory is concerned with a wide variety of identity categories and subcategories such as gay, lesbian, bisexual, transgendered, transsexual, curious, intersexed, questioning and allied identities. Alternatively, this is also perceived as non-identity or anti-identity theorization (Ritzer and Stepnisky, 2014).

Categorized Identities

After discussing the main identity kinds or levels of analysis and the main theories associated to identity, we can now turn to certain categories of identity that have been used repeatedly in relevant literature. Such categories are also used in our everyday lives and most of the time we do not even think that we use them. Still, these identity categories have been analysed in a systematic way that reveals a common characteristic: all identity categories are social constructions. This section will deliberately concentrate on some of the most commonly used identity categories (stigmatized, gender, sexuality, race and ethnicity identities) without intending to include all possible identity categories identified in sociological and psychological literature.

Stigmatized identity

Goffman (1963) was particularly interested in the theme of appearances, identity and meanings of self-in-situations. He investigated the gap between what a person ought to be ('*virtual social identity*') and what a person actually is ('*actual social identity*'). Many scholars emphasize Goffman's contribution to the concept of embodiment, although his initial concern was to study 'stigmatized' identities. Stigma describes the dramaturgical interactions between stigmatized people and 'normal' people. Goffman explains that some disabled people can be stigmatized on the basis of observable physical impairments defined as '*discredited stigma*'. The main character-istic of this identity is the loss of control over the presentation of self and the management of individual identities. In the case though that the impairment is not directly observable (chronic depression) then the individual concerned can hide it more easily; this may allow the individual to control and manage their identity. This is defined as '*discrediting stigma*'. Goffman has not been explicitly clear in his definitions on identity *per se*, but as Weigert (1983) explains, Goffman's concep-tualizations of identity allowed him to interpret the individual in relation to cultural stereotypes associated with social identity (like stigmatization); Goffman has also been concerned with the processes of information control and the man-agement of discrediting information in the interactional maintenance of a creditable personal identity in situations. Rohall et al. (2007) explain that the significance of Goffman's approach on stigmatized identity is fundamental as he reveals on the one hand the ways people use as they try to make themselves look like 'normal' people, and on the other, the ways people use to 'cover' their prob-lems from others. Any kind of variation in relation to what is perceived as 'normal' is defined as '*deviant*'. Stigmatized identities are also termed deviant identities and relevant studies concentrate on the management of those identities (Heckert and Best, 1997; Schur, 1971). Notably, and rather accurately, Goffman believes that all individuals at some point in their lives have been stigmatized in one way or another.

Gender identity

Gender (and sexual) identity formation are processes that have been approached by various theoretical perspectives (feminism, postmodernism, functionalism, symbolic interactionism, queer theory). Gender is defined through sex (based on biological difference). However, gender is not restricted to sex differences as gender is expressed through behavioural, interactional and personality characteristics. The most prominent approach regarding gender and gender identity formation is deeply influenced by symbolic interactionism. Following this approach, possessing a gender identity, means that individuals learn gender (and sex) difference from a very early age; we learn to act accordingly just as we learn our native language. For Goffman (1979), gender identity relates to gender performances in everyday life, which are shaped through ritualized performances within various social situations. Butler (2004) explains that individuals are compelled to perform as male or female accord-ing to specific social/gender structures and expectations from a very early stage in life. Following Goffman's view, Butler agrees that male and female performances are perceived as given, natural and fixed facts. However, such perceptions are based on patriarchal, hierarchical systems shaped by power (Foucault, 1978). Butler explains that by performing as men or women we just reproduce the standard social norms. These repeated performances shape our gender identifications (who we really are, a man or a woman?), our sexual desires and sexuality. She also emphasizes that the distinction between the two separate identity categories, that of being a woman or a man is fundamentally unstable as being a woman means not being a man (and therefore not to act in any kind of a masculine way), and *vice versa*. Such distinction also refers to sexuality as being straight (or having a straight identity) means not being gay (and therefore not to act as such). Burkitt (2008) explains that there is a degree of self-making in gender as there is in all identity as we try to adjust ourselves with images and voices within us as well as around us. Therefore, gender identity may be perceived as an ongoing project in all individuals' lives, which is not fixed or static. Following the symbolic interactionist tradition, gender identity (like any identity category) is recreated or reinvented by individuals as social circumstances change and personal perceptions alter. For example, a young woman living in a liberal Western society might not be particularly concerned about how she presents or maintains her gender identity as she probably perceives it as given. However, if this woman has to move and live in a county in the Middle East she needs to follow very strict social regulations regarding the ways she is expected to act, behave and present her female identity.

Sexual identity

Sexual identity though is defined by our sexual orientations namely, who we desire, with whom we are connected (Scott and Schwartz, 2008). Sexual orientation forms four basic categories: a) heterosexuality (sexual desire of the opposite sex); b) homosexuality (sexual desire of the same sex); c) bisexuality (sexual desire for both sexes); and d) asexuality (lack of sexual desire) (Kim, 2011). Certainly, additional categories can be added and discussed although such attempt would expand beyond the purposes of this section. Indeed, extensive variations exist regarding how people express their sexuality and the ways sexuality may by related to gender. Notably, gay and lesbian studies explore systematically the concept of identity as it studies and theorizes the lives and experiences of gay and lesbian people. Such experiences have been historically marginalized (Giffney, 2004). Following the explanation of gender identities, sexual identities are not a given either. Just like women were perceived as lower human beings for hundreds of years, gay people were stigmatized until recent years. Unfortunately for both cases, in certain societies, this is still the case. Sexual identities and the wider acceptance of the concept of 'being different' especially through media, allow the formation of various sexual subcultures, for example, related to certain dressing styles ('drag'), specific locations (Manchester's Gay Village, The Super Paradise Beach at Myconos) and so on. Some environments are more accepting than others and different people are more or less willing (or open) to any expression of sexual identity. Both gender and sexuality are powerful determinants of our interactions with others. Stereotypically, even in the most developed Western cultures, a prestigious job would be more easily offered to a middle-aged, white, straight, family man rather a black, lesbian, single mother. Therefore, although a wider range of gender and sexual identities have become more accepted, certain stereotypical perceptions are still applicable.

Race and ethnic identity

Race and ethnic identity are terms that have not been systematically defined within sociological or psychological literature, even though both race and ethnicity have been extensively studied and explored by both disciplines. Although the terms race identity and ethnic identity are used quite often, relevant literature does not provide explicit definitions, rather these terms are based on 'common sense'. Some of the few systematic definitions offered about these terms derive from the work of Chávez and Guido-DiBrito (1999). They explain that initially, race identity has been perceived as a biological category, which derives from the physical and gene characteristics of individuals accompanied by specific character qualities. However, today, the authors explain that racial identity is primarily described as social construction, which 'refers to a sense of group or collective identity based on one's perception that he or she shares a common heritage with a particular racial group' (Helms, 1993: 3, quoted by Chávez and Guido-DiBrito, 1999). Still, race identity is often used by people to characterize others according to skin colour in order to differentiate and distance themselves from others. Racial identity is a surface-level manifestation based on what we look like yet has deep implications in how we are treated. In similar terms, Chávez and Guido-DiBrito (1999) explain that ethnic identity is also considered as a social construct as well and it is viewed as an individual's identification with 'a segment of a larger society whose members are thought, by themselves or others, to have a common origin and share segments of a common culture and who, in addition, participate in shared activities in which the common origin and culture are significant ingredients' (Yinger, 1976: 200, quoted by Chávez and Guido-DiBrito, 1999). Individuals with common ethnic identity may share common beliefs, traditions and values and quite often feel proud of sharing these characteristics (for example, feeling proud of being Irish). Analogously, an individual may feel uncomfortable if s/he does not wish to share the values and principles that may describe her/his ethnic identity. In more general terms, ethnicity is defined as a 'personal identity collectively ratified and publicly expressed' (Geertz, 1973: 268). Chávez and Guido-DiBrito further explain that identity development concerns the individual's awareness and identification with certain cultural values, behaviours, beliefs and traditions and they emphasize that ethnic and racial identity models provide a theoretical structure for understanding individuals' interpretations of their own and other cultures. Jenkins (2007) suggests that the broader concept of ethnicity entails communal, local, regional, national and racial identities which are locally and historically specific, but at the same time notably fluid. Jenkins argues that racial and ethnic identities may make a considerable personal difference to individuals, both in their sense of self and in their judgement and treatment of others.

Summary

This chapter provided a rather general overview of definitions and sociological and psychological perspectives related to identity. An initial definition of identity was defined followed by the specific areas of personal, social/relational and collective identity which were to be discussed by incorporating sociological and psychological perspectives. Certain identities have been analysed, including role identity theory, identity theory, affect (and identity) control theory and queer theory. Specific categorized identities have also been explained, like those of stigmatized, gender, sexual, race and ethnic identities. As explained, the concept of identity covers a wide variety of approaches but this chapter focuses on those views that can better explain how the individual may be related to society. The aspect of intra-action will be further discussed in the following chapters as it may be more related to definitions of self rather than identity.

• •

Concepts in Context

John Phillips is a senior manager who has spent his life travelling around the world, working for big event organizations and changing residence every two years. He was raised in the Netherlands but he has been travelling for the last twenty years. His brother lives in Los Angeles and he visits him as often as he can. The rest of his family lives in Amsterdam and he visits them once a year. He speaks three languages, he has double citizenship (Dutch and American), he is currently a permanent resident of Rio de Janeiro, as he has been living there for the last two years. He has friends in most of the cities in which he has lived. He doesn't own a house, he is not married and he doesn't want to have a family. He enjoys changing partners and learning new cultures through multiple intimate relationships with both genders. He lives a comfortable life and he plans to keep on travelling and working in different continents for as long as he is able to.

This is an example of a person who might be called 'cosmopolitan' as he is living his life while travelling around the world. However, this particular person doesn't really care how he might be characterized as all these different people he has to work with constantly characterize him in various ways depending on the given social context on each occasion. Every time he changes country of residence he is the 'stranger' until he finds a way to blend and become as accepted as he can. He mainly works with upper class executives, visits the wealthier parts of each city, drives the most expensive cars and flies business class. He enjoys his life, he enjoys making and spending lot of money and he doesn't feel that he needs to fulfil any particular stereotypical identity role to become accepted, as he does not remain in a specific social or cultural context long enough to care if he will become accepted by locals. The people he works with and most of his friends share certain common characteristics with him, namely being international nomads making good money and living comfortable lives. Perhaps an epigrammatical characterization for this person's identity would be something like, 'a joyful lack of any kind of stability'. Apparently this person cannot be easily identified, categorized or characterized.

●●●

——SELF-REFLECTIVE QUESTIONS——

1. How can we study the identity of John Phillips?
2. Which theories of identity could we use?
3. Which combination of identity categories would describe this person best?
4. How is identity formed?

Possible ways of exploring the questions offered in this chapter and Further Readings:

1. In terms of his personal identity, like any person, he combines various characteristics that differentiate him from any other individual. He is John Phillips, who does not have a permanent job, permanent residence, permanent relationship, permanent friends or family. He is a person who performs successfully the professional roles he is ascribed and he is able to adjust quickly and in a relatively painless way to new environments. His social identity is the outcome of the combination of his sense of belonging to certain social groups. Furthermore, he performs the role ascribed to various social identities, like that of the successful manager, tireless traveller, wealthy lover, joyful friend, charming stranger. He doesn't enjoy collective identifications, as he prefers not to bond permanently with others in any level or way.

Further Reading:

Burkitt, I. (2008) *Social Selves: Theories of Self and Society*. London: Sage.

2.   Role identity theory could help us explore the significance of the commitment
      John Phillips places to particular role identity(ies) by considering the successful
      performance of this role. John Phillips is a very committed professional who works
      endlessly and others can rely on him. He is very convincing in offering consulta-
      tion in his area of expertise and he is thus considered a valuable executive in the
      company he works for. Identity theory would help us explore further the concept
      of 'identity salience' (the probability of a particular identity to be revealed in a
      particular situation) as John Phillips might be very reluctant in revealing, for
      example, his sexual identity within a professional context, but he would explicitly
      display his sexual desires while spending some of his nights in elite clubs and privi-
      leged 'adult entertainment' environments. Affect control theory would probably
      explain why this man never shares any information regarding his personal life with
      his colleagues. He wants to avoid any sort of emotional connection and therefore
      potential emotional exposure. He feels safer if he is able to control potentially
      unpleasant emotional engagement by avoiding any form of sentimental connec-
      tions. Finally, queer identity could probably explain the balanced way that John
      Phillips has succeeded in combining all aspects if his identity as he doesn't really
      care how he will be characterized. The time he spends in each place is not enough
      to allow others to produce stereotypical views of him. So, he has found a way to
      'escape' the potential of becoming stigmatized or even marginalized.

Further Reading:

Burke, P.J. and Tully, J.T. (1977) 'The measurement of role/identity'. *Social Forces*,
    55: 880–97.

Weigert, A.J. (1983) 'Identity: its emergence within sociological social psychology'.
    Symbolic Interaction, 6(2): 183–206.

3.   John Phillips is a single bisexual (sexuality), white (race), European (ethnicity),
      middle-aged (age), wealthy (class) man (gender), who has spent the most part of
      his life travelling and working at different places, meeting a wide range of different
      people, finding ways of relating to them and maintaining some connection with
      his family. But, would such a description help him (or any other person) to ascribe
      an even generic identity for this person?

Further Reading:

Jenkins, R. (2008) *Social Identity* (3rd ed.). London: Routledge.

4.   Could we follow a specific theory of structure to explain the way(s) this individual
      identifies himself, or is identified by others? Certainly, any identity(ies) that could

characterize this person are formed through and during endless and continuous interactions, forms and means of socialization and ways of connecting to others and himself. Any role(s) this person enacts derive and are shaped by such a wide variety of cultural and social characteristics that it probably becomes impossible to track down its origin.

Further Reading:

McCall, G.J. and Simmons, J.L. (1966) *Identities and Interaction.* New York: Free Press.

Could any stereotypical identity categorization describe this individual? Probably not. And probably the reason is that the concept of 'identity' might not be the most helpful scientific tool to allow social scientists to understand who this person is, or who other people believe this person is. Several aspects of identity exploration will certainly help us understand some of the ways each separate and unique individual is connected to society, to groups of people, to specific ideas, beliefs and values. But as this book will reveal in later chapters, different sociological and psychological terms and concepts (e.g. intra-action) can become more helpful in allowing us to understand how the individual is connected to society and ultimately with oneself.

5

The Self

(Sociological and Psychological Definitions)

The individual [has] 'the capacity to decompose himself into parts and to feel any one of these as his proper self'. (Simmel, 1950: 58–9)

Why is the Self Important?

The definition and understanding of the meaning of the self is crucial and fundamentally important when we try to explore the connection between the individual and society. Such exploration is as problematic (if not more so) as the examination of the concept of identity. Following the complexity of the definition of identity, self is another term that has been extensively studied, explored and outlined by a variety of social sciences such as psychology, sociology, social anthropology, political science, economics, to name just a few. However, the roots of all these explorations derive from the 'mother of all sciences', namely philosophy, and particularly the Ancient Greek philosophy. Ever since, the question 'Who am I?' has been one of the fundamental existential problems each individual experiences at some point in life, and a plethora of relevant researchers have tried to give an answer. Unsurprisingly, there is no such thing as a universal understanding of what the self is. As this chapter will show, the plurality of approaches, definitions and associated terms end up creating a rather 'complex' area of sociological and psychological investigation. However, following the rationale of the previous chapter, the plurality of approaches and the inconsistency of definitions, indicate the increasing need to choose different conceptual tools in order to explore what the self might mean. The following chapters will introduce more specific (and on certain occasions more helpful) terminology (e.g. intra-action), but the exploration of the meaning of self through sociological and psychological literature is considered imperative in our attempt to understand the ways that society is connected to the individual.

This chapter begins by introducing central sociological approaches to the self, departing from the works of the four founding fathers of sociology (Simmel, Marx, Durkheim and Weber). Although American Pragmatism is primarily a philosophical school of thought, the views of the four main pragmatists (James, Mead, Dewey and Peirce) will be discussed as they have influenced core sociological and psychological understandings regarding the notion of the self. Symbolic interactionism and the views of Goffman in relation to the idea of the self will be further explained. Furthermore, certain recent sociological approaches will be introduced by focusing on the concept of reflexive self. Psychological approaches to the exploration of self will follow by providing an additional attempt to define the idea of self. Further links with core psychological terms will follow, such as those of self-concept, self-awareness and self-consciousness and selfhood. The last section of this chapter discusses synthesized approaches to the self by analysing the connection between the ideas of self and identity and briefly introducing the perspective of social cognition as a distinct discipline aiming at defining the notion of the self.

EXAMPLE

A woman aged 70, lost her husband two years ago. They were married for over 40 years. They had their ups and downs but she never accepted that she might lose him. She has two children and three grandchildren and she is in good health. She finds it very difficult to be on her own. She always wants to be around others and especially her close family. There are times that she admits that she has to learn to live her life on her own but it is too hard for her to actually do it. Her sadness is profound but her difficulty to be on her own is perhaps more intense. She has quite a few interests, as she enjoys travelling, reading, having long walks, cooking but she experiences great joy when she is taking care of others. Now, she admits that she has none to take care of and she doesn't know how to take care of herself. She feels uncomfortable doing things for herself as she never had the chance to live a life like that. So now she needs to reinvent herself and understand what she really wants; she needs to explore what she likes and what brings joy to her life. She needs to explore and perhaps even re-introduce herself. But where does she need to look in order to find her self?

Sociological Approaches to the Self

Sociological approaches to the self have included a commendable plurality of perspectives. Unsurprisingly, sociology and social psychology share common ground but each discipline follows separate theoretical foundations. This section focuses on the most influential sociological perspectives regarding the exploration of self; although some theories have already been mentioned in the previous chapters, this section will try to reveal how separate sociological perspectives perceive the notion of self.

Classic social theory and the self

The exploration of the sociological origins of self will depart from the thought of the very first sociologists, in our attempt to understand how the idea of self has been sociologically shaped. Classic social theory treats the self as part or component of what is called society. The first three founders of sociology (Durkheim, Marx and Weber) do not perceive the self in their works, as individual self, and therefore limited discussion is offered in this section regarding their contribution. In particular, Durkheim, Marx and Weber, refer to the self, exclusively in relation to their study of industrial Capitalism. On the contrary, and as already discussed (in Chapters 1 and 3), Simmel, the fourth founder of sociology, was the first to distinguish the individual self from the social world by introducing terms and ideas associated to the inner life and private self. Simmel did not prefer to use the term 'self' directly, rather he used the concept of the 'individual'. Still, his discussions are much closer to the realization of what the notion of self might refer to. Nevertheless, the views of Marx, Durkheim and Weber on the idea of self, remain fundamentally significant in the sociological thought.

Georg Simmel

As discussed in previous chapters (1 and 3), Simmel's contribution to the exploration of socialization and interaction is of high significance in sociology, as Simmel was one of the first to introduce the idea of human interaction through the process of socialization ('sociation') and formation of people's relations. But Simmel was also one of the first to point towards the direction of intra-action as a way to explore the connection between the individual and society. Although his work was organized around the concept of the individual, the idea of self also becomes understood and perhaps more explicitly studied.

For Simmel (1950), there is a clear distinction between the idea of individual and the concept of society although these two concepts are constantly interconnected. As discussed in previous chapters, Simmel uses specific terms as he refers to the distinction between the individual and society; the term 'content' is related to the individual's instincts, interests and tendencies and the term 'form' is related to inter-action, influence and relationships between individuals. Such a clear distinction reveals the acceptance and awareness of psychological properties (e.g. feelings, thoughts, needs) (Spykman, 1965). The recognition of such properties is not included in the sociological explorations of the other three fathers of sociology (discussed below). However, Simmel is the only classic sociologist to be concerned with the study of society as well as the idea of the individual; characteristically he claims that 'the really practical problem of society is the relation between its forces and forms, and the individual's own life' (Simmel, 1950: 58). Therefore, for Simmel, the individual (or self in this sense) and society constitute two separate albeit inter-connected concepts.

More specifically, Simmel (1950) suggests that purely personal qualities, such as strength, beauty, depth of thought, kindness, courage, purity of heart, have their own autonomous significance. These qualities, are independent from social qualities. They are values deriving from human existence, thus they are different from social values, which rest upon individual's effects (Levine, 1971). Therefore, for Simmel, the individual (or self) consists of certain and specific qualities, of which we (as social scientists) need to be aware and be able to distinguish from social qualities and influences. Therefore, although individuals identify themselves through other individuals (during and through interaction) at the same time, the differences between individuals are more important than similarities, in terms of the individual's identification. Such differences related with the Simmelian concept of 'content' or in other words the purely personal qualities each individual possesses (related to intra-action). Furthermore, for Simmel (1950), the individual experiences inner freedom which allows each individual to find the space to develop a unique personality. While Simmel considers the individual and the individual's interactions to be the basis of society, and although he cannot separate the individual from the society, he insists at the same time that the individual needs to develop a unique personality separately from the social environment.

Simmel does not use the term 'self' often. In one of the few quotes that he actually refers to this notion, he suggests that the individual has 'the capacity to decompose himself into parts and to feel any one of these as his proper self. Yet, each part may collide with any other and may struggle for the dominion over the individual's action' (Simmel, 1950: 58–9). Therefore, an individual consists of different (often conflicting) parts. Perhaps these different parts could also be seen as different 'performances' or 'roles'. In fact, and as already discussed, symbolic interactionism (a school of thought deeply influenced by the social theory of Simmel) perceived the self in exactly this way. The self (especially according to Goffman) is seen as an actor able to perform separate roles according to specific social circumstances (further discussion follows). Simmel (1950) explains that through such performances each individual presents a specific aspect of her/himself which enables her/him to connect to certain social circles (e.g. family, friendships, intimate relationships, professional relations), although the adaptation of different 'selves' may result in conflicting contradictions (e.g. a caring mother and wife to act as passionate 'divorce lawyer'). In contradiction to symbolic interactionism, and the classic sociologists, Simmel was very careful to recognize both the significance of social influence and structure as well as the private life of the individual (or the self) which is equally legitimate and significant in terms of sociological analysis.

Notably, Simmel, was the only classic theorist who acknowledged the significance of the analysis of personal qualities in his attempt to study the social word, and he clearly tried to separate the concept of the individual from the notion of society. However, his work has been repeatedly criticized as he does not explain explicitly what the individual (or the self) consists of (or derives from), although he analytically discusses the concepts of 'inner freedom' and 'inner needs' (already discussed in previous chapters). Although Simmel's views influenced symbolic interactionism, his attempt to place equal attention on the exploration of the social and the personal level as two distinct aspects of social reality, was not further evolved. Still, he remains one of the very few sociologists to recognize and promote the personal and private qualities of the human beings and to incorporate them in his (admittedly) incomplete attempt to define the notion of self.

Unlike Simmel, the following (and more recognized) three founders of sociology, prioritized the detailed exploration of social structure rather than focusing on the definition of the self. The following section offers brief overviews of the aspects of each theorist's work that is related to their understanding of what the self might mean.

Karl Marx, Emile Durkheim and Max Weber

Marx, like Weber and Durkheim did not distinguish the idea of self from the concept of society. Marx's work was not related to the direct exploration of the individual self and he perceived the self primarily as part of a social group (class, culture, religion). As explained by Burkitt (2008), for Marx each individual is defined according to the social group(s) s/he belongs to, and more importantly, according to the division of labour occurring in Capitalism (Marx and Engels, 1970). In case an individual wanted to change her/his personal situation (change social group), then, collective/massive acts and political reactions should take place. 'Alienation' is one of the few individual characteristics or feelings discussed by Marx, which refers to the 'distance' that the individual experiences from oneself, fellow workers and the product s/he produces. Therefore, Marx perceives the meaning of self in relation to society or through society. Collective identity was an approach Marx repeatedly used, especially regarding class consciousness and class conflict; still, collective identity denotes a shared form of self reference.

In accordance to Marx's rationale, Durkheim also perceived the self in relation to the division of labour. Durkheim (1984) explained that in simple/traditional societies, people were connected through 'mechanical solidarity' as each individual belonged to and represented a specific group of people (community), sharing common beliefs, values, principles. In modern Western Capitalism, people are connected through 'organic solidarity' in which individuals depend on one another and each one has a specific task(s) and place within society. In this case advanced specialization in terms of division of labour allows people to adopt various self-identities. Durkheim used the term '*collective consciousness*' to describe the shared beliefs, views, values and ideas formed within society according to which, each individual forms her/his own thinking and feelings. However, he recognizes that collective consciousness is not as significant in modern societies, as people are too individualized and isolated without social values and therefore they have lost the meaning of their lives. This experience is described as '*anomie*' by Durkheim and it is defined in relation to division of labour (organic solidarity) and the ways people connect. Anomie (among other reasons) could lead to suicide according to Durkheim (1952). Individualism (people prioritizing their own interest rather than the social) is clearly problematic for Durkheim (1969) as he believed in a moral collective regulation of social order (Burkitt, 2008). Durkheim approached the self through the specific ways (division of labour) people are connected with one another.

Weber (1930), was the third founding father of sociology who approached the idea of self in relation to industrial Capitalism. He perceived the self through the ascetic principles of Calvinism, that allowed Capitalism to flourish in the Western World. Weber focused on the eternal agony of Calvinists' salvation, through living an ascetic life and hoping to become the God's chosen one for salvation. Therefore, people were living a life highly regulated by the church. This way of life is defined by Weber as the '*Protestant ethic*'. Furthermore, Weber praised the importance of the rationalization of the Western world by explaining the tendency of individuals to follow bureaucratic principles and values. However, Weber uses the concept of the '*iron cage*' to describe the limitation of people's lives into bureaucratic systems (Burkitt, 2008). Perhaps Weber, in relation to Marx and Durkheim, was the only one to recognize that individuals have the ability to freely choose their own values and actions. Still, in accordance to Mark and Durkheim, the self is again approached in relation and through society (particularly Capitalism) or aspects of it.

American Pragmatism and the self

American Pragmatism is known as a philosophical school of thought (primarily deriving from William James, Georg Herbert Mead, John Dewey and Charles Sanders Peirce), which inspired the analysis of various sociological approaches. Although it is not considered to be a central sociological source of theoretical thinking, American Pragmatism has shaped the views of symbolic interactionism and influenced the thought of social psychology scholars who tried to explore the notion of self. Particularly, the works of James and Mead constitute the 'roots' of psychological and sociological understandings regarding the notion of self. As a philosophical school of thought, American Pragmatism proposes that the individual's knowledge is not like a mental copy of things that exist in reality, but is, rather, an attempt to understand the social world in order to make practical sense of it and to act effectively. The pragmatistic theory of truth consists simply of those ideas that happen to work. Therefore, knowledge is true only if it helps us to achieve our practical aims and objectives (Chalari, 2009).

Pragmatists thought that ideas are produced through dialogue within groups of interacting individuals and therefore ideas belong to culture and are 'tools [...] that people devise to cope with the world in which they find themselves' (Menand, 2002: xi). In other words, ideas are tools that allow humans to be active in the world, and human consciousness is not simply a mirror image of the environment, but a creative and imaginative part of the activity that shapes it. Therefore, what we make to be truth is not the knowledge that best reflects or represents a given word but what works for us. For example, (any) religion is helpful and meaningful and therefore followed by its believers if the returns offered could work beneficially for them (eternal happy life in Heaven).

An innovative explanation of the contribution of American Pragmatism regarding the ways that the notion of self is perceived, is offered by Wiley (1994) who defined how, according to pragmatism, the self interacts with herself (further discussion on Wiley's views follow in Chapter 7). Although Wiley's views consist of an interpretation and a creative synthesis of separate theoretical approaches deriving from American Pragmatism, it seems particularly helpful to use his interpretations, before discussing each pragmatist's views separately. Wiley (1994) explains that two conversational poles were proposed by Mead (I and Me) and by Peirce (I and You), each thus incorporating one pole overlooked by the other. By combining the two theories, Wiley developed the trialogue I-You-Me or, as he calls them semiotically, I-present-sign, You-future-interpretant, Me-past-object. Human existence thus consists of the elements of present, future, past (the triad I-You-Me), all of which overlap, displaying connectedness and are capable of achieving solidarity (Wiley, 1994). Notably, none of the pragmatists offered a complete definition of the notion of self (or the individual). Instead they all offered their own descriptions about various aspects or properties or elements of the self. The following sections provide brief summaries of each pragmatist's point of view related to the idea of self.

William James (1842–1910)

According to James (1890), the individual is defined as the total sum of the interactions that s/he has with the social environment, including her private property (material possessions). More specifically, James proposed that the 'self' consists of three separate aspects: a) the '*social self*' that represents the recognition the individual receives from others; b) the '*material self*' which is related to the body and its functions; and c) the '*spiritual self*' that concerns the individual's inner subjective being and psychic faculties (James, 1890: 292). These sub-divisions, together with the pure ego, constitute the empirical self, the 'Me'. James, defines the 'Me' as the 'self as known', or the 'empirical ego'. He defines the 'I' as the 'self as knower', or the 'pure ego'. At any given moment, the 'I' is conscious, whereas the 'Me' is only one of the things of which the individual is conscious. For James, the 'I' is a wider concept, which includes the 'Me' within it. James, like Mead, use the terms 'I' and 'Me' albeit in different ways.

Both the 'I' and the 'Me' are used by James (1890) to define the notion of self: the 'I' or the 'self as subject' is described as the self-as-knower. In turn, the 'Me' of the 'self as object' is described as the self-as-known. The 'I' is characterized by clarity and will, and metaphorically reports on the actions of the 'Me'. Furthermore, the 'I' interprets the movements of the 'Me' within a particular storyline. James explains that the fundamental function of the 'I' is thought. Therefore, whatever we think about relates to each individual's 'I'. However, the 'Me' constitutes each aspect of the individual, each social property of the self, every distinct element of which the self consists. Control among those elements derives from the 'I' which functions as thought and is therefore able to process every aspect of the 'Me' (Chalari, 2009).

Georg Herbert Mead (1863–1931)

Mead (also discussed in Chapter 2), following James, used the same terms (the 'I' and the 'Me') to define the notion of self, which he perceived as an object which arises in social interaction. As discussed in Chapter 2, Mead (1934) was particularly interested in the ways individuals react and respond to other people's views about them. These views and attitudes are termed 'the generalized other'. Mead's definition of the self, is based on the concept of the 'generalized other' as he perceives the self through human and particularly symbolic interaction (e.g. language) with others. Through language the individual can interact verbally with (the generalized) other(s) as well as with oneself. Furthermore, through language the individual internalizes the 'generalized other' and shapes her/his behaviour according to possible reactions of the 'generalized other'. Therefore, one of the reasons why people are able to become, for example, polite is that they know that this kind of behaviour is likable and acceptable to others.

Regarding the self in particular, Mead used the terms 'Me' and the 'I'. He emphasized that the self is related to reflexivity and the ability of the person to become the object of her/his own attention. Every time we consider what we have done, what we have said, why we have acted the way we did, then we become the object of our own attention, examination, monitoring and evaluation. Mead perceived the term 'Me' to be more related to the individual's interactions and associations with others (e.g. joining the gay rights movement) whereas the 'I' is related to the cases that the individual is trying to distinguish herself from others and preserving the self (e.g. defending one's personal right to be gay). Therefore, for Mead (1934), every behaviour derives from the 'I' but is communicated through 'Me' within the social limitation of each occasion. The self is therefore primarily associated with the 'Me' as according to Mead (and symbolic interactionism) the self is shaped and formed through and during human interaction (rather than intra-action). Mead (and later on Goffman) explained that the self consists of numerous 'selves' that represent aspects of certain social structures. The totality of self reflects the entire social structure (Burns, 1979). For example, a person can be an adventurous global explorer, a cultivated scholar, an enthusiastic activist and a recognized professional. All these components of this person's self reflect specific aspects of certain social structures that characterize this person, who is able to: take advantage of globalized mobility, to further develop his upper class prestige, to participate actively in social movement(s) and remain successfully employed. All these (and perhaps many more) characteristics probably define a white, upper class, middle-aged man coming from the Western world. Unlike James, Mead believes that the self should fit into the social order and he clearly states that self and society are inseparable.

John Dewey (1859–1952)

Dewey's work is perhaps the one out of the four founding fathers of American Pragmatism who has received the least recognition. Dewey began his exploration regarding the connection between the concept of the individual (or self) and culture from the recognition of the individual's superiority over the social structure. However, he continued by realizing culture's determinant influence and concluded by demonstrating social dominance over the individual. Therefore, although he is more interested in exploring aspects of the idea of self at the beginning of his work, he gradually becomes more engaged with cultural influence and dominance. Perhaps, this radical change in his thought, eliminated the originality of his work. Still, his contribution to the study of self remains pivotal.

Dewey (1971) initially defines the 'ego' as the source of volition, the cause of any choice. The 'ego' is perceived as an internal representation of the self, which is always free and acts according to its freedom. Dewey also uses the term 'inner life' (also used by Simmel) which represents a feeling, a state of mind or an interesting event (the birth of a child) which has its own significant career. Inner life thus consists of imagination and emotion, inner reveries and enjoyment, whereas, outside the individual, everything (study, science, family, industry, government) is socially constrained. Thus, for this pragmatist, the individual is free to think, feel, experience any aspect of life, at a private, personal level. However, while this individual comes in contact with the rest of the world, then s/he needs to adjust accordingly. Dewey explains that an individual's road to freedom by escape into the inner life is no modern discovery, but used many times by 'savages', by the oppressed and by children. However, Dewey (1940) radically changes his views about the individual as his ideas develop. Dewey very characteristically concludes that: 'The idea of culture [...] points to the conclusion that whatever are the native constituents of human nature, the culture of a period and group is the determining influence in their arrangement' (Dewey, 1940: 18–19). His later works gradually move away from the idea of the individual having a private part, inner freedom, inner life and independence of consciousness. Eventually, he comes to perceive these as cultural conceptions and the individual as a cultural construction. The cultural beliefs, ideas, values and principles are internalized by the individual and inevitably replace any element of inner freedom. There is a shift from an individual-centred perspective to a cultural/social-centred one (Chalari, 2009). Therefore, Dewey ends up perceiving the self as a cultural product.

Charles Sanders Peirce (1839–1919)

Peirce (1940) was probably the only American pragmatist who clearly distinguished between the internal world (or the world of thought) and the external world (of fact). He states (1958) that phenomena individuals experience may be internal or external. Internal phenomena require an internal explanation by necessary internal properties. This recognition is critical as none of the previous scholars promoted such an approach. Peirce (1958) posits that there are internal mechanisms used by humans to understand their existence, primarily associated with the process of thinking. For example, through thinking we can realize that we may be critical towards our selves or demanding or perhaps too strict.

According to Wiley (1994) Peirce believed that the 'ego' consists of: the past ('Me', the 'object'), the present ('I', the 'sign') and the future ('You', the 'interpretant'). Although Wiley also explains that Peirce does not use these exact terms he defines the above-mentioned term as follows: a) the past 'Me' termed 'critical self', refers to a summation of the past, providing us with an orientation to the future/individual's consciousness; b) the 'present self' termed 'I' describes a source of creativity and innovation; and c) the 'potential future self', termed 'You', moves up the time-line and assumes the position of the acting 'I'. All people are able to experience the different 'chronological' aspects of their self. We often look back at what we once did or said and we may become disapproving of our actions. And then, we might consider that if we had the chance to experience the same situation today, we would have acted differently. And we may even keep on dreaming about how things would have been if we had acted in specific ways. In other words, Peirce identified the interaction between the three phases of ego (and thus intra-action), the interrelation between the past, the present and the future. This realization remains at the core of various psychological and sociological interpretations about the self and the individuals which will be further discussed in Chapter 7. Additionally, for Peirce (1935), there is a definite distinction between the inner and the outer cosmos of the individual, which means that the individual is clearly distinguished from society.

Symbolic Interactionism, Erving Goffman and the Self

Symbolic interactionism is a school of thought deriving from American Pragmatism, and is particularly concerned with the exploration of the idea of self. The approaches offered by symbolic interactionism are based on the central role of human interaction and therefore, the definition offered in relation to the notion of self constitutes the outcome of interaction. As has been extensively discussed in Chapter 2, symbolic interactionism emphasizes the ways and forms that interaction is produced and more importantly explained. Interaction is shaped according to the meaning people give to shared symbols used while producing interaction. Language remains the most characteristic example to describe this theorization: individuals interact verbally by exchanging words, phrases, utterances, while following a specific kind of turn-taking while they talk. Each language is organized according to a meaningful structure of symbolic elements (letters, words, grammar, syntax). Although each word has a specific meaning, during a discussion the meaning might change according to the context of what is said. This (and any) meaning is shaped during verbal interaction. Symbolic interactionism explains that although each individual may interpret certain forms of interaction differently, social/cultural meanings become prominent through shared interaction. The self is the product of the endless symbolic interactions taking place between different people. As the main form of symbolic interaction is language, the self can be studied and explained primarily through language formation and exchange of verbal interaction. Therefore, the notion of self and the concept of society become inseparable and inevitably interdependent (Charon, 2011).

Erving Goffman (1956, 1961) offers an extension of symbolic interactionism by offering a dramaturgical definition of the self (also discussed in Chapter 2). For Goffman, each individual puts on a 'show', a performance by trying to manage the impressions he gives to others about her/him (being a loving grandmother, a considerate mother, a committed wife). These performances represent short-term selves focusing on the role that has to be performed during different occasions. These short-term episodes are organized according to endless different 'scripts' which are followed to the end (at Christmas grandmother may offer a generous family dinner, where all members of the family will be delighted and full of joy). Therefore, the self consists of short-term selves adjusting to certain roles according to specific circumstances. This approach is better understood in terms of social identity, as short-term selves actually constitute separate social identities. Blumstein (2001: 184) explains that 'identity (...) refers to the face that is publicly displayed [during] interaction (...). Identity is Goffman's "presented self" and as such it requires no private commitment on the part of the actor or audience to its being a valid reflection of the "true" self.' Therefore, in the example of this particular grandmother, her family may be convinced that she is a cheerful, lovable and caring senior woman, whereas they might never realize that this person is in desperate need of care, attention and acceptance. Still, as original as Goffman's dramaturgical approach may be, it remains incomplete in terms of a specific definition of what the notion of the self may be. In Goffman's work, ideas of self and society are in a constant and recurring interplay.

Recent approaches to the self

In sociology, the exploration of self is deeply influenced by the thought of symbolic interactionism and the work of Goffman. For example, Rosenberg (1979: 593) explained that self 'arises out of social experience and interaction; it both incorporates and is influenced by the individual's location in the social structure; it is formed within institutional systems; it is constructed from the materials of the culture; and it is affected by immediate social and environmental contexts'. Blumstein (2001) further supports that even if the self can be part of the mechanics that motivate the actors' behaviour, the self finds expression in behaviour during interaction. The self shapes and it is shaped by interactional behaviour. People project identities (defined as enacted behaviours) through interaction, sometimes not at all related to the actual self. Various scholars have offered a wide variety of similar approaches, like Burkitt (2008) who very characteristically explains that there is no individual self, but rather, it is more accurate to refer to social selves. The reason is that people are born into social relations that were not chosen by them. Therefore, the selves we become are formed according to the family, neighbourhood, social class, gender, ethnicity, beliefs and values in which we are educated. Burkitt further explains that the search of self is related to 'what we do'. Consequently, the self is constantly reconstructed as people consider the question 'who do I want to be/become'? The author supports that to try to become what one wants or anticipates becoming, involves some kind of political struggle especially in relation to race, gender and sexuality identity formation (as discussed in the previous chapter). Adams (2007: 12), fully supports this view as he explains that self is 'inseparable from the social, cultural, relational, discursive fabric in which it is constructed'. In turn, social control becomes an additional way through which the self is perceived; this view derives from the work of the post-structuralist Michel Foucault who maintained that power constitutes our subjectivity (in a kind of 'subjectification') from the moment in our childhood when we enter the language system (Wetherell and Maybin, 1996). Language if further linked to discourse and more specifically narratives of self (further discussed in Chapter 7); 'our sensitivity to narrative provides the major link between our own sense of self and our sense of others in the social world around us' (Bruner, 1986, cited in Wetherell and Maybin, 1996: 258).

On the other hand there are various scholars who use the principles of American Pragmatism in a different way, by perceiving the notion of self through the idea of reflexivity. Reflexivity, or on some occasions 'reflexive self', has been used as an approach that allows the examination of the relationship between the ideas of individual and society. This relationship could be perceived as a 'dualism' or as a 'duality' between structure and agency (the concepts of individual and society), depending on the recognition attached to the autonomy that characterizes each concept without diminishing the interdependent connection between them. Various views relating to reflexivity perceive the individual as able to produce intra-action namely to find ways of interacting with oneself, to explore, understand and evaluate her or himself. Chapter 7 discusses reflexivity in further detail, and the work of the most prominent scholars associated with this perception will be discussed. For now, it is crucial to consider the meaning of self through the individual's ability to become reflexive. As will be further explained, the definition of 'reflexive self' might provide one of the most complete, wide and at the same time specific explanations regarding the connection between the ideas of self or individual with society. For now, a short summary of various sociological (and some psychological) approaches will be discussed.

Reflexive self

Owens (2013: 207) defines reflexivity as 'the ability to view oneself as an object capable of being not just apprehended but also labelled, categorized, evaluated and manipulated; reflexivity hinges on language'. In other words, for Owens, 'reflexive self allows people to view themselves from an external point of view, just as other people might view them through varying degrees of detachment' (p. 207). Elliott (2009) explains that self is reflexive to the degree that people constantly monitor, or watch their own activities, behaviours, thoughts or emotions. Owens (2013) clarifies that an individual can reflect back on oneself and this ability allows people to plan ahead, worry about personal concerns, ruminate about past actions or even experience feelings and emotions. Benson (2003: 61) associates the self with its reflexive ability to function adaptively.

Owens (2013: 206) further explains that the self can be understood as 'an organized and interactive system of thoughts, feelings, identities and motives that: (1) is born of self-reflexivity and language; (2) people attribute to themselves; and (3) characterize specific human beings'. Such views reveal the intra-active aspects of self as it describes ways that interaction within oneself can be experienced. Owens' conceptualization of the self derives from American Pragmatism's distinction between the 'I' and the 'Me' attempted by both James (1890) and Mead (1934), as well as Cooley's 'looking-glass-self' (1902) (already discussed in previous chapters). Rosenberg (1979) explains that the self-concept (further analysis follows) is tied to the 'I-Me' dualism found in the self and describes the ability of the individual to be both the knower ('I') and the known ('Me'). The self is the outcome of the individual's own objectification and can stand outside her/himself and react to her/himself as detached objects of observation. Therefore, the self is both the subject and object of investigation. As will be further discussed in Chapter 7, the concept of reflexivity will be analysed as the main way through which the individual is connected to society. For now however, it is important to realize, that 'reflexive self' has been used repeatedly in sociological and psychological literature as a distinct attempt to define the notion of self.

Social psychological perspectives define 'reflexiveness' as people's capacity to turn back on ourselves, to take ourselves as objects and guide our actions accordingly through evaluative processes. As already discussed, this is a central concern of Meadian symbolic interactionist theory: our perceptions, concepts and theories about ourselves as persons become at least partly constitutive of who we are as a person. How we construe ourselves is an essential component of who we are (Epstein, 1973). Smith adds that selfhood has to do with guiding what one does and appraising what one has done at least partly through reflection on one's performance; feeling responsible, at least sometimes, for one's actions and holding others responsible for theirs (Smith, 1991: 20). The self cannot be conceived outside of the social and relational context. Glăveanu (2010) explains that the essence of the self lays in the space of intersubjectivity of the relations between the 'Me' and the 'Other' and emphasizes that representations, attributions and culture constitute both the environment and the fabric of self. Such approach is termed 'synergetic', which reveals the value of creative syntheses, of exploring potential selves and incorporating various postmodern cultural possibilities (Gergen, 1991).

Gekas and Burke (1995) further support the association of self and reflexivity by explaining that the concept of self refers to the process of reflexivity that originates from the interplay between the 'I' and the 'Me'. The authors perceive reflexivity as 'self-awareness' and they define it as the individual's ability to be both subject and object of oneself; they clarify that reflexivity is the consciousness of oneself, which is also understood as the most fundamental feature of the human condition. Therefore, the self is seen through the process of reflexivity whereas the products or consequences of the reflexive activity is called the '*self-concept*' (discussed in the following sections). Leary and Tangney (2003: 8) conclude that the underlying capacity of the individual that all approaches to the self reveal is that of reflexive thinking, which is defined as the object of one's attention and thought. More complete discussion on reflexivity can be found in Chapter 7.

Psychological Approaches to the Self

Psychology has been perceived as the most suitable discipline within social sciences to provide a complete definition about what the notion of self might be. However, following sociology's incapability to produce a specific and universal definition of this term, psychology has been another discipline to produce and suggest an equally (if not more) impressive plurality of approaches, definitions and explanations regarding the notion of the self.

Defining the self

Leary and Tangney (2003: 6–7) quite correctly explain that the concept of 'self' has been used in such a wide variety of ways from both sociology and psychology, that it remains impossible to provide a universal definition about this term. However, they have identified five ways through which psychology in particular, has used this term: a) 'Self as Total Person'; the term self is used instead of the term person. Self refers to the person of her/him self. However, the usage of self as a person does not necessarily entail psychological meaning. b) 'Self as Personality'; the term self coincides with the whole or part of an individual's personality. c) 'Self as Experiencing Subject'; self refers to an inner psychological entity that is the core or the subject of the individual's experience. Self is experienced as 'something' inside our heads. d) 'Self as Beliefs' about oneself; self is understood as the perceptions, thoughts and feelings about oneself. Self-concept is usually associated with this definition of self. e) 'Self as Executive Agent'; self is seen as the decision maker and doer as the one that regulates the person's behaviour. This perspective is also understood as the executive feature of the self, or self-control and self-regulation. The authors explain that none of these categories are complete and therefore a more specific definition of the general term of the self is needed (always depending upon the specific context within which it is used).

McConnel and Strain (2007: 52) further explain that there are different psychological perspectives on the definition of self as there are also different ways of investigation (lab-based experiments versus longitudinal studies). Furthermore, there are different ways of assessing constructs (private *vs* public measures). The authors explain the personality psychologists' view that the self is more stable and invariant. For example, the notion of self-concept has been researched by personality psychologists in relation to well-being and mental health (John, 1990; John and Srivastava, 1999; McCrae and Costa, 1999; McCrae and John, 1992). Following the results of the above-mentioned studies, the self-concept is comprised of the following personality attributes: extraversion *vs* introversion, agreeableness *vs* antagonism, conscientiousness *vs* lack of direction, neuroticism *vs* emotional stability and openness *vs* closedness to experience. On the other hand, those who oppose personality psychologists, particularly those with behaviouristic and psychoanalytic orientations such Epstein and O'Brien (1985), argue that such positions exaggerate the collectivization of the self and underestimate the extent to which the self is individualized and invariant across situations.

Social psychologists perceive the self as a fluid response to changing social situations. Linville and Carlston (1994) explain that social psychology defines the self as a collection of multiple, context-dependent selves. This perspective assumes that people possess many and different self-aspects (daughter, mother, friend, lover, activist, professional) and that social contexts (in certain cultures women may be socially excluded) may activate one of these self-aspects, which in turn guides behaviour (e.g. activist woman) (Markus and Wurf, 1987). Cognitive psychology suggests that the self is comprised of a relatively large amount of information within a substantial cognitive structure. Self in this context is generally conceptualized as a set of cognitive representations reflecting a person's personality traits, organized by linkages, across representations created by personal experience and biography. Self is sometimes extended to include things besides trait attributes, such as social roles and even identities; self is thus seen as a cognitive structure incorporating elements such as intelligence, perseverance, honesty, etc. (Greenwald and Banaji, 1989). The exploration of the notion of self through the area of social cognition will be separately discussed in the following sections.

Social psychology has been deeply influenced by symbolic interactionism which has provided a distinct approach on self (already discussed in Chapter 2). What might be important to consider, is that self is viewed by this school of thought as an ongoing and continuously changing process, through which we construct a sense of who we are through interaction with others. As already discussed, self is formed through interaction and therefore it is examined in relation to how people present themselves during interaction; the self comprises of different and complex parts and adopts different forms and shapes according to the social circumstances. As self is perceived as an ongoing process, this concept cannot be defined through consistent terms; however, according to symbolic interactionism the outcome (or snapshots) of the self as process is the self-concept which is defined as the sum total of thoughts and feelings we have about ourselves as an object (Rohal et al., 2007). Following the principles of the symbolic interactionists' school of thought, Hewitt (2003) further explains that the acquisition of self is closely tied to the acquisition of language. The author emphasizes the developmental implications of how a child learns the social world since when the infant is born it is unable to distinguish itself from the social world. As the child matures s/he becomes able to be the object to itself. Maturation is achieved through developmental stages and the ongoing process of socialization.

The self-concept

The self-concept is a term mainly used in social psychological literature. Rosenberg (1979) defines the self-concept at the totality of an individual's thoughts and feelings about her/him self. Burns (1979) explains that for psychologists the self-concept plays a key role in the integration of personality as it motivates behaviour and achieves mental health. In physical and mental illness the self-concept is often disrupted, distorted and damaged. The main question psychologists are trying to answer remains: 'who am I?'. Shavelson et al. (1976) described the self-concept as the perceptions of a person about him/herself, which are formed in relation to this person's social environment. These perceptions are especially influenced by the evaluations of the significant others, by reinforcements and the attributions of this person's behaviour. According to Rosenberg's (1979) 'self-concept theory' the self-concept development is characterized through four general principles: reflected appraisals, social comparison, self-attributions and psychological centrality. Rosenberg also adds that individuals are motivated by the principles of: a) self-esteem (provoke individuals to think well of themselves); and b) self-consistency (people struggle to validate their self-concepts) while they are trying to maintain and protect their personal self-concept. According to the self-concept theory, the individual observes, evaluates and eventually concludes about her/him self. It is beyond the scope of this section to further explain each of these principles and concepts; it should be mentioned however, that certain theorists have elaborated on different aspects of self-concept, like Shavelson et al. (1976) who propose the following major features of self-concept (Diagram 5.1) as explained by Marsh et al. (1992: 50).

Byrne et al. (1992) explain that up until the 1980s, self-concept research has been noted for lack of rigour in its theoretical models and measurement instruments. Notably, the majority of self-concept research focused on the relation between self-concept and other constructs. The authors further explain that the elaboration of multidimensional approaches has enabled a more comprehensive description of the 'self-concept'. They distinguish between two kinds of studies that explore the 'self-concept': a) within network studies that explore the internal structure of self-concept (outlining different dimensions like the physical, social or academic self-concept); and b) between–network studies that attempt to establish the relation between measures of self-concept and other constructs.

However, a wide variety of studies on the self-concept use a plurality of sub-categories to explore this concept. For example (Diagram 5.2), Shavelson et al. in a study conducted in 1976, tried to divide the general self-concept (called *General Self-Concept*) into more specific self-concepts (e.g. academic self-concept and non-academic self-concept). Then they divided the non–academic self-concept into even more specific self-concepts (such as social self-concept, emotional self-concept and physical self-concept) and then, they divided each of these into even more specific self-concepts (e.g. the social self-concept is further divided into the categories of

Diagram 5.1

1	It is organized or structured, according to people's categorizations of the extended amount of information they have about themselves in relation to one another.
2	It is multifaceted, that the particular facets reflect a self-referent category system adopted by a particular individual and/or shared by a group.
3	It is hierarchical as it is based on perceptions of personal behaviour at the base moving to inferences about the self in sub-areas rather than to inferences about self in general.
4	The hierarchical general self-concept is stable but as one descends the hierarchy, self-concept becomes less stable as it increasingly situation specific.
5	Self-concept becomes increasingly multifaceted as the individual moves from infancy to adulthood.
6	Self-concept has both a descriptive and an evaluative aspect such that individuals may describe themselves.
7	Self-concept can be differentiated from other constructs such as academic achievement.

Marsh et al. (1992: 50)

peers and significant others). And each sub-division could be further divided into even more specific categories. This is just one example of a multidimensional hierarchical self-concept study.

It is important to emphasize that as Marsh et al. (1988) explain, there is not a universal definition of the 'general self-concept' and in different psychological studies this term is perceived in a number of different ways. In fact, in psychological literature, the self-concept is not usually studied *per se*. Rather different aspects related to self-concept receive much more detailed attention. For instance, studies have focused on the self-concept in relation to: self-esteem (Rogers, 1951), self-worth (Taylor and Brown, 1988, 1994; Crocker and Park, 2004), self-enhancement (Taylor et al., 2003; Colvin et al., 1995), self-control (Langer, 1975) and self-verification (Swann, 1997). It is therefore important to note that in terms of psychological literature the theoretical definition of the 'self' or any other relevant term used for similar purposes, remains incomplete and for that reason it is extremely difficult to even categorize the endless definitions used in a huge variety of studies that explore the self or aspects of this concept.

In accordance with this realization, McConnel and Strain (2007) propose the perspective of self-complexity through which the self can be explored and combines all possible self-aspects and attributes (traits) related to oneself. Self-complexity derives from the idea that each person can have many different selves which are combined in complex combinations. The authors add that self-complexity theory 'predicts that life events will have greater impact when people have: a) relatively few self-aspects; and b) have greater structural overlap in their self-concept attributes' (p. 59). An additional way of investigating the self has been proposed by Brinthaupt and Erwin (1992), which is through self-report. There are certain ways

Diagram 5.2

Example of a multidimensional hierarchical self-concept study:

General Self-Concept

⇓   ⇓

Non-academic self-concept   Academic self-concept

⇓   ⇓

social self-concept, emotional self-concept, physical self-concept   (....)

⇓   ⇓   ⇓   ⇓

peers   (....)   (...)   (...)
and significant
other(s)

Adapted from Shavelson et al. (1976)

that one can use self-report: a) accessibility and organization of self-relevant knowledge; b) contextual, situational and cultural factors; and c) individual and developmental differences. Still, it remains clear that psychology studies primarily focus on areas related to self and not self as such. It becomes evident that psychology is using different means and ways to define and investigate this concept but this discipline (and most sub-disciplines within it) are primarily interested in exploring the self in relation to another concept(s) through various means and ways.

Self-awareness and self-consciousness

Self-awareness and self-consciousness are two terms often used primarily in social psychological literature associated with the individual's realization or understanding of oneself. Researchers have used a wide variety of related terms in their attempt to study and explain the ways individuals use to become aware and conscious of themselves. Notably (and following the problematic nature of the notion of the self) although such specific terms are used repeatedly in relevant literature, the definition of those terms is not consistent. The following discussion offers a selective summary of representative studies, revealing the detailed exploration of the ideas of self-awareness and self-concept.

According to Morin and Everett (1990), 'self-awareness' is the unique capacity of the self to reflect upon itself, or rather, the condition according to which the individual becomes the object of its own attention. Self-awareness theory (Duval and Wicklund, 1972; Wicklund, 1975) views conscious attention as dichotomous: attention is directed either towards the self or the environment. Fenigstein et al. (1975) proposed a self-consciousness scale and they presented two different dimensions: private self-consciousness (the tendency individuals have to pay attention to their inner thoughts and feelings) and public self-consciousness (which is a measure of the consciousness of the fact that the individual is a social object that influences other individuals). Self-consciousness has been viewed by Rime and LeBon (1984) as being dependent upon past experiences, marked by more or less frequent exposure to self-focusing stimuli. According to Duval and Wicklund (1972: 2) in the self-aware state 'consciousness is focused exclusively upon the self and consequently that individual attends to her conscious state, her personal history, her body or any other aspect of herself'. Hull et al. (2002) mention that one could expect that self-aware individuals are especially likely not to be influenced by external primes, particularly if these primes are inconsistent with personal standards.

Duval and Wicklund (1972) associate the self-awareness state with a conscious, reflective process when they describe the nature of self-focused attention. Carver (1979) adopted Duval and Wicklund's term 'self-focused attention' to define the self-aware state, although in 1981 Carver and Scheier explicitly distinguished self-attention from consciousness, they described self-awareness as involving an awareness of various aspects of the self, and private self-consciousness as the tendency to be aware of one's thoughts, feelings, private motives and desires. Hull et al. (2002) mention that it is hard not to describe individual differences in self-consciousness (in the terms discussed above). Gibbons (1990) adopted Duval and Wicklund's definition of self-focused attention and linked this to a more general self-assessment process that includes awareness of internal states.

Carver and Scheier (1985) maintain that some aspects of the self are covert, hidden or private, and that other aspects of the self are overtly social or public. Sometimes, attention is focused selectively on the private self and sometimes it is directed to the public self. This private–public distinction was first highlighted in the development of the self-consciousness scale (already discussed) which measures private self-consciousness and public-consciousness with separate sub-scales. According to Carver and Scheier, the individual can somehow separate her private from her social being. Thus, although there is recognition of the social and private parts of the individual, the researchers see those two parts as being able to operate independently. Self-regulation means attempting to be who you think you should be; this is done by trying to live up to principles specified by your perception of who you should be. In turn these principles are realized in programmes of action. Scheier and Carver (1983) state that one of Freud's most influential assumptions is that people are largely motivated by internal, and implicitly private concerns (as will be further discussed in Chapter 6). The authors suggest that the multifaceted nature of the self should be acknowledged, and that more attention should be given to the possibility that different self-facets can each contribute to behaviour in different ways, at different times, and in different contexts. People differ in the degree to which they habitually attend to themselves. The disposition to be self-attentive has been labelled as self-consciousness, in order to distinguish it from the manipulated state of self-awareness.

In the same vein, Trapnell and Campbell (1999) proposed that self-consciousness is probably multidimensional and Joireman et al. (2002) suggested that self-consciousness may sometimes both impede, and at the same time facilitate empathy. More specifically, they believe that self-rumination is likely to impede whereas self-reflection is likely to facilitate adaptive forms of empathy. Furthermore, in 1995 Tan and Moghaddam argued that reflective positioning is a process by which one intentionally or unintentionally positions oneself in unfolding personal stories told to oneself. This process can take various forms, the most elaborate of which might be the writing of one's private diary or autobiography (further discussion related to inner speech follows in Chapter 7). Furthermore, Trapnell and Campbell (1999) suggest that the chronic state of attending to private thoughts and feelings *per se* stimulates greater differentiation, integration, accuracy and cognitive accessibility of self-information; that is, it enhances self-knowledge. They also propose that chronic, private self-attention appears to enhance self-knowledge at the expense of psychological adjustment. Buss (1980) suggested that in private self-consciousness, people regularly inspect their bodily processes and moods, reflect about their motives and goals and frequently fantasize about themselves.

As a result of repeated self-reflection they know themselves very well. Therefore, it could be understood that self-reflection is related with self-consciousness which leads to self-knowledge.

Morin (2002, 2005) analysed further self-reflection (enjoying analysing the self) and self-rumination (not being able to shut off thoughts about the self). Morin suggests that self-awareness represents a higher form of consciousness which makes it possible for humans to become the object of their own attention and acknowledge their own existence. As the author notes from past studies, people with a high degree of self-awareness know themselves better than those that are less self-aware. He recognizes that people must analyse themselves differently. According to Morin (2002) self-rumination is identified as the anxious attention paid to the self, where the person is afraid to fail and keeps wondering about her self worth. On the other hand, self-reflection refers to a genuine curiosity about the self, where the person is intrigued and interested in learning more about her emotions, values and thought processes. Morin concludes that all people analyse their inner thoughts and feelings (self-awareness), but some people feel anxious about what they might discover about themselves (self-rumination) while others feel intrigued and fascinated about themselves (self-reflection). According to Trapnell and Campbell (1999) self-consciousness does not represent a unitary construct (i.e. focusing on the self), but is instead made up of 'self-rumination' and 'self-reflection'. Trapnell and Campbell suggest that each type of introspection would lead to very different cognitive and behavioural consequences.

Once again it becomes understood that although various studies have been directly involved with the study of the self in relation to personal and social aspects, there is not a specific form of consistency regarding the terms of concepts used. A wide plurality of perspectives are indeed offered, which incorporates empirical evidence but somehow the definition of the idea of self remains incomplete or perhaps unclear.

Selfhood

Another term frequently used in psychological literature regarding self-exploration, is that of 'selfhood'. Jenkins (1996: 52) prefers to use this term as it allows the minimization of the tendency towards reification implicit in 'the self' and this term emphasizes the 'processual' character of selfhood. Elliott (2009: 15) states that 'selfhood is sameness' and he refers to the continuity of identity over time and for all time. Smith (1991) explains that for psychology, selfhood explains what it means to be human and involves being self-aware or reflective; selfhood is perceived as an evolutionary, historical and personal achievement, which is not given nor within limits. Elliott (2002) explains that selfhood refers to the person's sense of self and it usually incorporates the elements of personality and character which remain stable and durable. He further explains that the concept of selfhood may imply a 'core' self which remains fixed and permanent; however, Elliott (2009) states that actually selfhood is flexible, fractured, fragmented and fragile. For Mead (1934) selfhood is related to symbolic communication and selfhood includes both the 'Me' and the 'I' and it is not a passive social product. For Mead, the 'Me' is related to role taking and has social origins whereas the 'I' emerges through conversation with others and with the 'Me' and is able to transform the 'Me' in the process.

Smith (1991) follows three characteristic psychological perspectives (deriving from symbolic interactionism) in order to examine selfhood: the first is the perspective of *evolution* and he explains that selfhood as we now experience it emerged with language and he further supports Mead's (1934) view that humans can only be understood and explained through the reflexiveness of language which allows them to perceive their self as object, to view themselves through the eyes of others and become the audience of their own voice. The second perspective on selfhood is *cross-cultural and transhistorical* and he further supports Geertz's (1973) view that certain cultures minimize individualized selfhood. In this vein, Gekas and Burke (1995) explain that the nature of selfhood is not only contextual but it is also historically and culturally conditioned, since selfhood is a historical emergent in a changing world of cultural diversity. An alternative conception of selfhood is emerging, primarily from studies of Asian cultures as well as minority groups which is termed '*interdependent construct of self*'. The third perspective on selfhood relates to *developmental* perspectives. Piaget (1952) was the first to explain that infants achieve selfhood as they explore and learn the world through interaction. However, although at the beginning of the life course individuals interact with the environment, after, things get more complicated as symbolization (e.g. language) is also involved. For example, Rom Harre (1998: 68) clearly states that 'what people have called 'selves' are (...) produced discursively', namely through dialogue (and consequently language). However, although Harre states that 'selves are not entities' (1998: 68), Archer (2000: 3) clarifies that 'our sense of selfhood is independent of language' (these views will be further discussed in Chapter 7). Still, even if the idea of selfhood is perceived in different ways, it definitely constitutes an open-ended project entailing ongoing forms of interaction (as well as intra-action) and constant recreation of social and personal meaning.

Synthesized Approaches to the Self

Inevitably, sociological and psychological approaches on the notion of the individual and the self share indeed common ground. The following sections discuss characteristic approaches derived by both disciplines that have produced amalgamated explorations of the notion of the self.

Identity and self

As has been discussed in Chapter 4 on identity, self and identity are two inseparable concepts, occasionally treated by relevant sociological and psychological literature

as identical terms. Various attempts have been reported to characterize the relationship between identity and self (Blumstein, 1975; Gergen, 1968; McCall and
Simmons, 1966; Swann and Read, 1981; Wiley and Alexander, 1987). Although
these two terms are indeed complementary, they remain distinct. Perhaps the reason
for using self and identity as indistinguishable terms is that both concepts attempt
to answer the same question: who am I? Gekas and Burke (1995: 42) explain that
identity refers to who or what one is, to the various meanings attached to oneself
by self and others. Owens (2013: 206) clarifies that self is a process and organization
born of self-reflection (as already explained) whereas identity is a tool by which
individuals or groups categorize and present themselves to the world. A characteristic description of the connection between self and identity is offered by Blumstein
(2001: 186–7) who explains that the 'actor's desires/goals can best be served by the
identities they choose to enact' but repeated enacted identities eventually become
selves that grow out of motivational states. The term 'ossification' is relevant here as
it refers to the 'repeated enactment of identities that produce selves'; this is how we
become the person we have enacted (Blumstein, 2001: 184). In addition, according
to social psychologists (e.g. Huntington, 1957; Kadushin, 1969; Turner, 1978), roles,
or certain social identities shape selves like the marital role, provider role, the home-
maker, the parent and the lover role.

The closest connection between self and identity is included in the kind of
identity called 'individual or personal identity' (discussed in Chapter 4) as it refers
to aspects of self-definition at the level of the individual person. Following psychological explanations, these may include goals, values, beliefs, standards for behaviour
and decision-making, self-esteem and self-evaluation, desired, feared and expected
features of selves and one's overall 'life-story'. Theories of personal identity are
primarily interested in individual-level processes, by emphasizing the agentic role
of the individual in creating or discovering her/his own identity (Vignoles et al.,
2011: 3). Benson (2003) might add that the identity of a person concerns the ways
in which a person can be picked out as unique compared to all other individuals
in terms of her/his appearance, finger-prints, eyes, personal historical identifiers,
DNA and so on.

As discussed in the previous chapter, in sociology, the concept of identity is used
in order: a) for individuals to produce self-categorizations in relation to group
memberships and therefore produce various social roles and social categories; and
b) for an individual to display various character traits so that others will be able to
recognize the actor and her/his performance (Goffman, 1956, 1961). In this case
identity is seen as the most public aspect of the self. In fact, self subsumes identity,
just as self includes the self-concept (discussed in the following section). As symbolic
interactionism would suggest, the self contains various identities that a person may
possess, all the possible combinations of the connections between those identities
and therefore the self ends up taking the shape of any identity(ies) that the individual may experience at any given time. Elliott (2009) explains that identity is fluid,
not fixed. The self can be understood as a symbolic project as people constantly refer

to their sense of identity as a guiding orientation to their lives, to other people and to society. In that sense, for some women, being mothers is the most important and prominent component of their selves, although they may also simultaneously experience complex combinations of identities such as being efficient professionals, devoted wives, loving daughters and sisters. The self, in such cases is taking indeed the shape of the identity(ies) this particular person experiences at this given time. In the near future the same individual may experience completely different combination(s) of identity characteristics such as being divorced, unemployed and even a single mother. The identity of mother remains prominent but the self has to be reshaped due to the change of the peripheral identities. As Elliott (2009) would say, in such a case this woman is constantly working on producing and reproducing her defining sense of self.

Still, in this example, and probably in all cases, there are various forms of identities that are not based on the self, such as forms of collective identities. Therefore, this woman can choose to identify her self as wife, professional or even mother but she cannot choose to identify herself in any nationality, or race she may prefer. Therefore, Elliott suggests that self is rightly understood to consist of subjectivity, emotions and personal feelings which in turn influence the experience of social and collective elements of identity such as gender, sexuality, race, ethnicity, disability and so on. In that way, it becomes understood how self and identity become indistinguishable concepts as most attempts aiming at providing 'parallel' explanations for each term, end up producing a synthesized definition for both self and identity.

Social cognition and the self

An additional academic field (combining both sociological and psychological elements) concerned with the exploration of the notion of self is that of social cognition. According to Howard (2001) social cognition has been a highly individualist field although socio-political and cultural contexts shape everyday cognitive responses. Fiske and Taylor explain that the study of social cognition is guided by a basic assumption that behaviour is a function of people's perception of their world, rather than of objective descriptions. Thought intervenes between environmental stimuli and an individual's affective and behavioural responses to these stimuli (Fiske and Taylor, 1984). Howard (2001) supports that individual thought is influenced by social contexts and therefore the individual behaviour is not accounted for exclusively by personality traits. Cognitive processing of social information includes attention, encoding of information, the retrieval of information through memory and the formation of a variety of inferences.

Howard (2001) also explains that individuals structure their perceptions about themselves and others by means of abstract social categories (social identities or social roles). These categories are consequently internalized as aspects of their self-concepts, and that social cognitive processes relating to these self-conceptions produce self-behaviour. But they do not explain how they shape 'individual behaviour'. The author explains that perhaps the concept of '*attribution*' may be helpful here. Attribution is defined as 'the formation of a causal inference, a judgement of what factors may have produced a particular outcome, or a trait inference, the assignment of a trait to an actor on the basis of her or his behaviour' (Howard, 2001: 106–7). The main assumption of the main models of attribution (e.g. Heider, 1958; Kelley, 1967, 1973; Jones and Davis, 1965; Jones and McGillis, 1976) is that the cause of behaviour can be categorized into either internal factors, factors associated to the individual or external factors deriving from the environment. Therefore, there is an oppositional relationship between internal and external, or individual and social factors. This means that in the case of social cognition the individual and society are treated as two separate concepts that may entail conflicting aspects.

Self and intra-action

Following the concept of identity, the notion of self remains a key term used in sociological and psychological literature while exploring the connection of the individual with society. As this chapter reveals, this term, as prevalent and as essential as it might be, still lacks a complete, specific, concrete and universal definition. Probably the reason might be that the word 'self' is such an agentic property, which can only be fully experienced by each individual separately. Still, this term turns out to be rather vague and therefore not as advantageous in its use while investigating the ways that individuals relate to society. However, self, like identity, is primarily related with the principle of interaction and admittedly any understanding regarding this term would include the aspect of interaction. Therefore, inevitably, intra-action is profoundly related to the idea of self although it cannot and it should not coincide with it. Intra-action refers to everything that is happening inside ourselves that allows us to be in contact with everyone including ourselves. Intra-action (like reflexivity) is a part, or a process or a property of the self that allows the self to be related to oneself and others. Therefore, intra-action may be a term that could be used in more concrete ways while referring to the relationship between structure and agency (further discussion follows in Chapter 7).

Summary

This chapter has been concerned with the ways that the idea of self has been defined through sociological and psychological literature. Self has been discussed through the works of the founding fathers of sociology (Simmel, Marx, Durkheim and Weber). Although American Pragmatism is primarily a philosophical school of thought, the views of the four main pragmatists (James, Mead, Dewey and Peirce) have been briefly discussed as they have influenced core sociological and psychological understandings regarding the notion of the self. In this context, symbolic interactionism and the views of Goffman in relation to the idea of the self are particularly relevant. The sociological exploration of the idea of the self also includes certain recent approaches by focusing on the concept of reflexive self. The second part of this chapter provides an overview of psychological approaches regarding the exploration of self. Further links with core psychological terms will follow, such as those of the self-concept, self-awareness and self-consciousness, and selfhood. The last section of this chapter discusses synthesized approaches to the self by analysing the connection between the ideas of self and identity and briefly introduces the perspective of social cognition as a distinct discipline aiming at defining the notion of the self.

• •

Concepts in Context

A middle-aged man lives for the last ten years in an isolated monastery as a devoted monk. He lives with a small group of monks, which follows in a very disciplined manner, a rather ascetic way of life. For the biggest part of his day, this monk remains silent. He only talks when he has to, as he prefers to spend most of his time on his own. He prays very often, reads a lot and is taking part in all spiritual liturgies (like all group members) and to all sorts of religion-related functions organized by the monastery. When he was asked why he decided to live this kind of life, he explained that he wanted to be closer to himself and closer to God. He admits that he feels connected to his inner 'spirit' and spends long hours trying to understand who he is. He has realized that there is something 'deeper' inside him that he sometimes calls 'God' and he feels obliged to follow his 'inner' voice that calls him to remain devoted, isolated and quiet.

• •

──── SELF-REFLECTIVE QUESTIONS ────────────

1. How can we study this person's 'self' by incorporating classic sociological perspectives?
2. How are these perspectives related to more recent sociological explanations?
3. How can we study this person's 'self' by incorporating psychological perspectives?
4. How could the perspectives of self-concept, identity and social cognition be employed?

Possible ways of exploring the questions offered in this chapter and Further Readings:

1. Certain sociological approaches may become helpful in recognizing this man's ability to experience 'inner life' (as defined by Simmel) although at the same time he is following a strict structural routine imposed by the specific religion he wishes to follow. However, this kind of 'inner freedom' he experiences may be explained through American Pragmatism as his own ability to communicate with aspects of himself. Perhaps, this monk is discussing with God while praying, and on this occasion most of the pragmatists would agree that this man is experiencing an inner dialogue with himself between the 'I' and the 'Me'.

Further Reading:

Burkitt, I. (2008) *Social Selves: Theories of Self and Society* (2nd ed.). London: Sage.

2. Mead and the school of American Pragmatism would probably emphasize the fact that the monk's spiritual beliefs (shaped by this specific religion) actually control the ways he thinks and therefore, as Goffman would say, this monk constantly performs very specific roles in his attempt to come closer to what he calls God. Some others (perhaps more recent sociologists) might identify this man's ability to think and act in a reflexive way and they might emphasize the fact that he is able to monitor and even control his thoughts in his attempt to understand himself.

Further Reading:

Elliott, A. (2009) *Concepts of Self.* Cambridge: Polity.

3. Additionally, psychologists coming from different psychological sub-divisions might emphasize different aspects of this man's life and self: personality psychologists might emphasize his personal isolation, whereas cognitive psychologists might explore further specific psychological traits and even this person's intelligence. Social-psychologists would probably explore the different social roles the monk has to get involved with and the specific (albeit limited) interactions he forms with others.

Further Reading:

Gekas, V. and Burke, P.J. (1995) 'Self and identity', in K.S. Cook, G.A. Fine and J.S. House (eds), *Sociological Perspectives on Social Psychology.* Needham Heights, MA: Allyn and Bacon, 41–67.

4. Psychologists interested in the formation of the self-concept could concentrate on specific aspects of this man's self like this person's: self-esteem, self-worth, self-enhancement, self-control and self-verification. The assessment of this man's

self-awareness and self-consciousness would be one of the central social-psychological evaluations. However, some of those focusing on the understanding of selfhood might conclude that this person's identity is disrupted as he has not maintained a continuity of his identity over time and for all time, as he decided to radically change the way he lived his life. Additionally, psychologists trying to understand this person's individual or personal identity would concentrate on this man's personal self-definition which could include his own goals, values, beliefs, standards of behaviour and decision-making, self-esteem and self-evaluation, desired, feared and expected features of himself and his overall 'life-story'. Finally, social cognition might reveal and explain what factors (internal or external) may have produced a particular outcome, like this person's decision to change his life in a such a radical manner.

Further Reading:

McConnel, A.R. and Strain, L.M. (2007) 'Content and structure of the self concept', in C. Sedikides and S.J. Spencer (eds), *The Self.* New York: Psychology Press, Taylor and Francis Group, 51–73.

Even if many of the above-mentioned related social sciences 'join forces' in their attempt to decode this (or any) person's actual self, they will probably produce a sophisticated description of who this person is at this particular time, given the information they can use. This means that no matter the school of thought or the discipline followed, the notion of self remains an idea that is constantly reshaped and is still extremely difficult to define in a universal manner. This chapter offered a wide plurality of approaches, some of which will be further analysed as new terms and alternative approaches will be discussed.

6

The Unconscious and Conscious Self

(Psychoanalytic and Psychotherapeutic Approaches)

The notion of an unconscious mental state implies accessibility to consciousness. We have no notion of the unconscious except as that which is potentially conscious. (Searle, 1998: 152)

Why is Unconscious and Conscious Self Important?

The concepts of conscious and unconscious self derive from the thought of Sigmund Freud and the principles of psychoanalysis. These two terms have influenced enormously sociological, psychological and psychotherapeutic approaches on the exploration of the self as well as the formation of society. It is considered vital to explore the significance of these two powerful concepts associated to the understanding of the notion of the self and evaluate their contribution to the ways the individual is connected to society. The exploration of consciousness and unconsciousness belong to the wider sphere of psychology and more particularly to the theoretical as well as applied therapeutic techniques of psychoanalysis and person-centred approach and psychotherapy. Therefore, this chapter will be primarily focused on the principles of the above-mentioned approaches, whereas sociological interpretations will also be added.

This chapter begins by explaining the relevance of psychoanalysis regarding the exploration of the idea of self. The notion of the self is then defined through Freudian psychoanalysis, Neo-Freudian approaches, the Frankfurt School views, post-Freudian ideas and Lacanian-psychoanalytic perceptions. After completing this wide psychoanalytic review the chapter will focus on the contribution of person-centred approaches by defining the self through Rogers' theory. The last section of this chapter explores self-related therapeutic techniques by discussing first psycho-analytic and then person-centred applications of therapeutic approaches to the self. Comparisons and contradictions are discussed whereas limitations are also revealed through the Foucauldian criticism of therapeutic discourse.

EXAMPLE

A student from the Czech Republic arrived a few months ago in England to begin her studies in a British University Business School. She was very excited to be in a different country, studying what she always dreamed of, but she had also started feeling distressed and lonely. She misses her family and it is rather hard for her to make new friends. Although at the beginning she was very eager to attend all her classes, after a while she had second thoughts as to whether the degree offered by the business school is the right discipline for her. She felt that she can't settle into university life, that she is a stranger, that nobody understands what she is saying or the way that she feels. It became very difficult for her to explain why everything seemed so confusing and complicated. She used to be a sociable, extrovert girl back at school but as a university student, she preferred spending time in front of the TV hoping that another day would pass. Her mother became very concerned with her daughter's attitude, she thought that she has not been herself lately. She worries that her daughter's character is not strong enough to cope with such frustration. So she advised her to see a therapist and ask for help. The girl followed her mother's advice and had a few sessions with the university counsellor. After a while, the girl was feeling better, she started attending classes, seeing friends and moving on. When her mother asked her what had happened and how such change occurred, the girl said that therapy has helped her to know her self better. But when her mother asked her how exactly that happened, the girl could not find the words to explain.

Why Psychoanalysis?

As discussed in the previous chapter, a wide variety of sociological and psychologi-cal approaches have been employed in order to explore the ways through which the notion of self has been studied. Furthermore, an equally extensive selection of sociological and psychological explanations have already been discussed (in previous chapters) regarding the ultimate purpose of this book: to explain how the individual is connected to society. One distinct area of exploration and explanation, related to the idea of the self, is offered through psychoanalysis. While a number of philosophical, sociological and psychological theories have tried to explain the connection between the individual and society, Freudian psychoanalysis has offered provocative illuminations by revealing that the unconscious desires constitute the organizing principle of all human thought, action and social relations (Elliott, 1992). As will be discussed, psychoanalysis was introduced by Sigmund Freud (1856–1939) but subsequent (and usually extreme) developments have extended psychoanalytic thought in a rich, albeit vague, theory and practice of self exploration and therapeutic analysis. It is therefore vital to reveal the diverse and remarkably influential psychoanalytic contribution in terms of how the self is constructed and analysed. The psychoanalytic explanation of the sources of the self has shaped a large number of sociological and psychological (as well as psychotherapeutic) elucidations of the ways the individual is related to her/him self and society.

Defining the self through Freud's psychoanalysis

According to Elliott (2002), classic psychoanalysis, which is based on the thoughts of Freud (1900, 1901, 1905, 1915–17), perceives the self as the 'tip of the iceberg' of subjectivity. Self consists of two main forms of subjectivity. The one called 'conscious self' and the other called 'unconscious self'. In psychoanalytic terms, the self consists of three main areas (Burns, 1979):

a)   The '*ego*' represents the conscious self. Although different psychoanalytic approaches perceive Freud's concepts in distinct terms, the ego is generally described as the sane and rational mental life in contrast to irrational unconscious. The ego is thus perceived as a set of psychological processes (perceiving, thinking) that control consciousness, or in different words the purposive motivated behaviour. Sometimes the ego is depicted as meaning the totality of a person whereas on other occasions the ego is seen as the factor that secures the balance between the 'id' and the 'superego'. Furthermore, the ego is explained as the core that controls and drives personality and represents the conscious awareness and the subjective experience of the individual. The ego is rooted in the unconscious.

b)   The '*superego*' or '*preconscious*' mediates between the 'ego' and the 'id'. It is described as the organized part of the personality structure which is mainly but not entirely unconscious. The superego includes the individual's ideals, spiritual goals and conscience that criticizes and prohibits one's drive, fantasies, feelings, and actions. Furthermore, it aims for perfection and works in contradiction to the id whereas it directs the individual to act in a socially appropriate manner.

The superego, controls our sense of right, wrong and guilt. More importantly, it helps us fit into society by getting us to act in socially acceptable ways.

c) The '*id*', also termed the *unconscious* consists primarily of feelings and sensations that are repressed. For Freud, 'id is the dark, inaccessible part of our personality'. The unconscious consists of all those wishes which are repressed by the demands of everyday life and reality and in particular the repressed desires of infancy. The id, or the unconscious, is a sphere of a conflict between ideas, wishes and (mainly sexual) desires. The access to unconscious life is limited because of mental repression. However, it returns all the time to disrupt the consciousness in the form of dreams, slips of the tongue, jokes, neurotic symptoms or perverse behaviour. According to Freud (1953–74: 141) 'thoughts emerge suddenly without one's knowing where they come from, nor can one do anything to drive them away'. The id or unconscious represents the irrational part of the individual.

According to Freud (1953–74: 143) 'what is in your mind does not coincide with what you are conscious of'. Following the Freudian tradition, psychologists generally perceive the human mind as having two regions. One of these contains conscious experience (thoughts, feelings and behaviours we are aware of at the moment) and the other contains memories, currently outside awareness, but able to enter awareness easily (Carver and Scheier, 1996). As discussed, Freud added a third region, which he referred to as the unconscious. According to Freud, these three regions (introduced above) constitute the mind's topography or in other words, the self. Therefore, Freud used the term 'conscious self' to refer to the part of the mind that contains all of which we are currently aware. People can verbalize their conscious experience and can think about it in a logical way. The 'preconscious' or 'superego' is that part of the mind that represents ordinary memory. Although it remains outside awareness, it can be readily brought into awareness. In turn, the unconscious refers to that portion of the mind that is not directly accessible to awareness, and is in part a repository for the urges, feelings and ideas that are associated with anxiety, conflict or pain. Once they are in the unconscious they remain there and exert a continuing influence on later actions and conscious experience (Rhawn, 1980).

According to Elliott (2002) the self is perceived in psychoanalytic theory as entailing the (often conflicting) split between the conscious and unconscious sides of the self. The unconscious self is understood as a 'hidden self', which we have limited access to, whereas the conscious self, is perceived as the self we are aware of. Burns (1979) explains that the self is primarily understood as the ego, because the ego is the only part of the self (conscious side) that we have access to. Therefore, at the heart of psychoanalytic theory is the idea that human behaviour can be explained in terms of the relationship between the conscious and unconscious elements of the mind. People are seen as being motivated by unconscious drives.

These are emotions of which they are unaware, or that they experience only in a distorted form. Their conscious lives are dominated by the attempt to control the expression of these drives. Psychoanalysis, then, examines the relationship between the surface structure of consciousness and the deeper structure of the unconscious. Freud believed that the truly important operations of personality take place in the unconscious. He further states that the biology of the human body generates unconscious drives and desires, in particular the drive for pleasurable experiences aiming to satisfy bodily needs. Human action is shaped by the continuing struggle between the unconscious, instinctive drives and the conscious and rational control exercised by the ego (Freud, 1915–17).

However, James in 1890 stated that 'the unconscious is the sovereign means of believing whatever one likes in psychology and of turning what might become a science into a tumbling ground for whimsies' (p. 163). Through this statement James exposes the uncertainty which surrounds the unconscious. According to Carver and Scheier (1996), researchers have found that many aspects of people's experience are influenced by processes that occur outside their awareness. Such influences occur when we are forming perceptions and impressions of other people, and when we are making judgements as to how likely something is to happen. Such influences can also affect the individual's mood state and his or her actions. Recent psychologists might object to the exact nature of unconscious, but they would accept its existence and its relatively unclear content.

Elliott (2009) explains that according to psychoanalysis the relationship between the self and society is based on the repression of desires, feelings and pleasures which, of course, leads to conflict, tension and contradiction. Any experience of dissatisfaction, depression or unhappiness is therefore treated as inherent problems of the self, rather than forms of inevitable conflict between the individual's personal needs and social restrictions. Freud's originality relates to the idea that the repressed sexual drives and sensations initially experienced in childhood constitute the source of psyche and inner being. The Oedipal syndrome (Elliott, 2009: 62–76) constitutes an attempt to theorize the child's (and particularly the boy's) attachment to the mother through employing the child's sexual desire towards the mother. The way that each child ends up resolving (or not) this developmental phase determines the extent to which the unconscious, hidden and unconfused sexual desires of the adult will 'haunt' the conscious self and the ego. Freud's theory of the self remains radical and one of the most criticized as well as influential in sociological and psychological literature. It might be helpful to keep in mind that Freud's work was produced during the (particularly sexually) repressive period of the Victorian era, and therefore expression of sexuality was indeed limited and controlled.

Neo-Freudian approaches to the self

Primarily, Carl Jung and Alfred Adler, who have worked closely with Freud, formed the Neo-Freudian school of psychoanalytic thought. One of the main ideas shared among Neo-Freudians is that the self is learned through social contact and experience and through interpersonal relationships. In Jungian theory, the self signifies the coherent whole, unifying both the conscious and unconscious mind of a person. According to Jung (1960), there are two centres of the personality. The ego is the centre of conscious identity, whereas the self is the centre of the total personality – including consciousness, the unconscious, and the ego. Therefore, the self forms both the whole and the centre. The self is described as an equilibrium between the conscious (ego) and unconscious levels. For Adler (1927) the idea of self is associated to the personalized subjective means through which the individual interprets and gives meaning to her/his life. He believed that in order to understand the individual, we have to perceive it a unified whole instead of a collection of bits and pieces, and we have to understand each individual in the context of their environment, both physical and social. Following Jung and Adler's attempts to distinguish the idea of self from that defined by Freud, Sullivan (1953) and Horney (1945) saw the self as a system arising out of anxiety. Moreover, they further promoted the significance of interpersonal relations as a source of anxiety experienced by the self.

The main figure out of the Neo-Freudians who focused extensively on the idea of self-identity was Erikson (1965). Erikson provides an extension of Freud's view on the ego by explaining that the ego develops as it gradually resolves conflicts related to the social world that each individual interacts with. He supports that personality development (or in other words, maturation process) includes the entire lifespan although he was predominantly interested in how children (and later on, adolescents) socialize and how this affects their sense of self. He defines identity as the subjective sense of sameness and continuity, which is related with the direct experience of self. Identity is not static, rather it is a continuing process, which expands self-awareness and exploration of the self.

The Frankfurt School approaches to the self

The Frankfurt School is a social and political philosophical movement of thought initially located in Frankfurt, Germany and after 1933 moved to Columbia University, New York. The Frankfurt School is the original source of what is known as 'Critical Theory' and it was founded with the aim of developing Marxist studies. Two of the most prominent critical theorists were Marcuse and Adorno, who tried to explain the way the individual psyche is related to cultural forms. This was probably the first systematic attempt to incorporate Freudian analysis into sociological theory. To do so they introduced 'Drive Theory' which is based on the idea that the consciousness emerges gradually from a differentiation with the unconscious, as the external reality (society) intervenes and regulates the individual's life. Marcuse (1956) explains that the ego represents an 'outgrowth' of the id and it remains a secondary process. Therefore, the unconscious constitutes the core of consciousness. Social oppression is fundamental in Marcuse's and

Adorno's thought, although Marcuse clearly states that the personal core of self-hood and the principles of self-identity always remains in the unconscious. He further explains that civilization inevitably transforms the two principle instincts of life and death and represses the core instinct of pleasure and satisfaction through social and political control. In a similar vein, Adorno (1966/1973) believes that psychoanalysis explains the process of identity formation although he became critical towards Freud's definition of the ego; Adorno explains that there is a contradiction within ego as it consists both the conscious (an agency of self-reflection) and the unconscious (the repressive agency). Adorno explains that in order for the ego to operate in society, it should overcome the conflicting/contradictory co-existence between the conscious and unconscious and the repressive tendencies and prohibition of the modern social world. Adorno (along with Horkheimer) further promotes critical theory's main principle: the capitalist world led to nega-tivism (Adorno, 1966/1973). As the liberal phase of Capitalism prevails, Adorno felt that the struggle between the conscious and unconscious components of the ego along with the intensified social repression of the ego as such, undermines the autonomy of the ego and eliminates self-differentiation. Consequently, both Adorno and Marcuse perceived the self through the repressive force of the late capitalist world and the central (albeit increasingly repressed) drive of pleasure deriving from the unconscious world. This results in a form of self-control which eliminates the autonomy of the ego (Elliott, 1992).

Post-Freudian approaches to the self

According to Elliott (2002) post-Freudian approaches of the self, are not con-cerned as much with the conflicts of the inner world (between the conscious and the unconscious and the repression of sexual drives) but rather, an increasing interest is displayed towards the connection of the self with the other(s) by focus-ing on the emotional relations between individuals. There are two main post-Freudian schools of thought: the American and the British. American post-Freudian tradition entails two areas of focus: a) '*ego-psychology*' which is mainly concerned with the genesis, development and adaptive capacities of the ego. This approach promotes the capability of the powerful ego to produce rational action. According to Anna Freud (1937) such ability derives from the way the initial interaction between the infant and the mother has been formed, followed by specific forms of separation. b) The '*interpersonal/culturalist model*' of American psychoanalysis focuses on the rational capacities of selfhood in relation to social and cultural conditions. Broadly speaking, the emphasis of self-autonomy is seen as the basis of equal interpersonal relations.

The British post-Freudian tradition explores the complex links between the self and others and it is termed '*object-relation theory*'. This approach is more con-cerned with the self as being an emotional connection(s) with others. A central role, in the way the self is formed, is attributed to the mother-infant relationship and the emotional need for connection this relationship represents. Socially destructive, or in other words, problematic or dysfunctional relationships are seen as responsible for preventing the ability of the self to relate to others. Winnicott (1965), for example, further emphasized the crucial significance of the relationship between the infant and the mother, as through this connection, the infant will be introduced to individualized existence and consequently selfhood. Winnicott uses the term 'good enough mother' to describe the period that the mother offers her presence through affection and devotion while allowing the small infant to get a sense of independence through imagination and creativity. This is the way (liberating and supporting relationship with mother) that according to Winnicott (1974), a young child experiences aloneness in a meaningful way which results in an authentic selfhood and forms a stable form of selfhood. Winnicott used the concept 'true self' to describe a person capable of creative leaving whereas 'false self' describes a person unable to establish stable emotional relations with others (Elliott, 2002).

Lacanian psychoanalytic approaches to the self

Lacan (1949) was one of the first to employ symbolic language in his attempt to expand the psychoanalytic thought, perceiving the idea of self through the person's visual identification with her/his image in the mirror. Lacan explains that infants, between the ages of eighteen months and six years, acquire the ability to identify their own images in reflective surfaces (mirrors). At this time, infants are lacking in most physical and mental abilities possessed by older human beings (*Stanford Encyclopedia of Philosophy*, 2015). Lacan believes that the reflection of the infant in the mirror (like the reflection of a person in a mirror) is an illusion, as behind the mirror there is not a real person. For Lacan, this metaphor can explain the fact that the ego is an object rather than a subject. The ego, or self, which is reflected in the mirror is not part of the individual's subjectivity, but rather is something outside her/his own being, and therefore it becomes an object. In other words, the ego, or self, does not coincide with autonomous agency, or a free, true 'I' determining its own fate (*Stanford Encyclopedia of Philosophy*, 2015). The self constitutes an ideal imaginary projection, or it is formed through Freud's concept of 'narcissistic fantasies'. Later on in life, the adult will realize that her/his self is shaped through cultural and social meaning and this will enable her/him to overcome the perception of oneself as complete and unified (as experienced during the mirror stage and narcissistic fantasies). Lacan perceived the unconscious as a series of symbols, which, for a variety of reasons, remain below conscious awareness, making people unable to think certain thoughts (unable to remember specific incidents, explain certain reactions or feelings) and causing confusion. Lacan explains that the psychotherapist can read these series of symbols as they reveal themselves through slips of the tongue (or even through dreams). For Lacan, the true self consists both of the conscious ego and the unconscious id as both are the result of the symbolic use of language, which labels and processes each individual's raw desires (Fink, 1995). Lacan (1949) explains that to be a member of society, individuals inevitably use language as speakers or listeners. Therefore, physical life is closely related or even shaped through symbolic codes of language.

Limitations

In classic Freudian psychoanalytic thought the autonomy of the self is perceived as being limited due to unconscious desires. Freud believes the unconscious will eventually become conscious self and will reclaim individual control. Harre (1979) explains that human helplessness is profound because of the repressed, albeit powerful unconscious core of the notion of self. Action is controlled by hidden motivations and only the psychoanalyst is able to reveal and explain them. Therefore, it is up to the psychoanalyst to transform the unconscious into conscious. Consequently, according to Harre (1979), Freudian psychoanalytic theory perceives the self as unable to control the unconscious and therefore unable to control itself. Neo-Freudian explanations as well as approaches deriving from the Frankfurt School and Lacanian thought maintain the core significance of the powerful unconscious self while they remain unable to fully explain and define it. Post-Freudian psychoanalytic tradition moves away from the controlling influence of the unconscious and focuses on emotional relations by promoting the significance of the mother–infant relation. The self is thus formed according to the ways that mothering is offered and perceived. Once again the self is formed according to external powers and reorganized following learned forms or emotional connections.

Why Person-centred Approach?

Carl Rogers (1902–87) was an American psychologist known for his influential psychotherapeutic method known as client (or person)-centred approach (further discussed in following sections). Rogers' theory is considered one of the most influential in contemporary psychology and his unique therapeutic method influenced a wide variety of therapeutic approaches (particularly counselling). His theory provides thorough explanation of what the definition of the self might be, but his most analytic approach regards what he terms 'self-actualization'. According to Rogers the notions of self and self-concept are defined as the organized, consistent set of perceptions and beliefs about oneself and include all experiences available at a given moment, both conscious and unconscious (Rogers, 1959). Self (as a wider concept) develops through interactions with others and involves awareness of being and functioning; the self-concept is 'the organized set of characteristics that the individual perceives as peculiar to himself/herself' (Ryckman, 1993: 106). Rogers perceives the self as consisting the inner personality, and can be linked to the soul, or Freud's psyche. However, unlike Freud, Rogers is not so much concerned with the unconscious and he does not prioritize the component of the self as related to unconscious repressed aspects. However, Rogers is not explicit or clear when he mentions (even peripherally) the role of the unconscious. Instead, he is quite explicit when he explains that the self is shaped by the personal experiences each individual encounters, primarily related to childhood and other people's evaluations.

Defining the self through Rogers' theory

The (wider meaning of) self according to Rogers, is 'composed of characteristics of the "I" or "Me" and the perceptions of the relationship of the "I" or "Me" to others and to various aspects of life, together with the value attached to these perceptions' (Rogers, 1951: 200). Notably, Rogers uses terms closer to Mead and James but he does not distinguish between the 'I' and 'Me'. Rogers differentiates the notion of self from the self-concept, as the latter is one part of the former. Burns (1979) provides an overview of Rogers' theory of the self by focusing on the following aspects: Rogers' phenomenological account of the self is based on the principle that individuals live in a personal and subjective world. The self-concept is formed through the individual's perceptions about oneself and it governs the individual's perceptions and understandings about the social environment. 'Self-actualizing tendency' (to actualize, maintain and enhance the experiencing individual) forms the part of the self related to a learned or inherent need to receive positive evaluations from others. This need of positive self-regard or self-esteem is vital as the individual is trying to confirm her/his own positive evaluations about oneself through the positive evaluations of others. The self-concept is used in two ways by Rogers; it is initially described as the way the person sees and feels her/himself. Furthermore, it is a process of controlling and integrating behaviour (behaviour is defined as the goal-directed attempt by the individual to satisfy her/his needs). The individual is constantly seeking actualization; the self-concept is seen as part of the individual that influences the individual's actions but does not direct them. For Rogers, each individual can actualize her/his ideal self through psychotherapy. The notion of self consists both of the self-concept and the ideal self and it usually coincides with the usage of the word 'person' (Burns, 1979).

Rogers claims that '*the process of the good life involves the willingness of becoming and achieving one's potentialities. It also involves the courage to proceed and the determination of oneself to be fully engaged into the stream of life*' (Rogers, 1961: 184–5, my emphasis). In this vein, Rogers developed the client-centred therapy as a technique to modify self-conception while going through a psychological adjustment. As explained by Burns (1979), during the process of this psychological adjustment, the individual tries to maintain the self as known and therefore resists change. However, Rogers (1951) believes that man's nature is positive, moving towards maturity and self-actualization and that 'change' is the result of maturing and enables the individual to come closer to the 'true self' (what the person can truly become). As will be further discussed, during therapy the client learns about herself and the new aspects of herself and new ways to relate to others. The client explores her feelings and attitudes related to the problem areas 'followed by increased insight and self-understanding' (Rogers, 1951: 133). This kind of psychotherapy enables the individual to come closer to herself and know better herself. Often, Rogers explains, the client is initially interested in certain unsolved problems, however, during therapy the concern alters, and the client starts to explore herself. The self is thus understood as 'the core' of the individual which constantly alters and evolves.

According to Mearns and Thorne (2007) during psychotherapy the self becomes the centre of the client's and the therapist's attention. In that way the individual is supported by the therapist to explore her/him self, improve it or even change it. The therapist provides the individual the means through which s/he can come closer to her/his inner existence. Consequently, the way that psychotherapy enables the individual to 'look inwards' is the nature of the relationship between the client and the therapist. As Kahn (1997) maintains, the way this relationship is formed influences the 'paths' the individual will follow to explore her/him self.

Mearns (2011) maintains that although person–centred therapy is about the realization of the 'growthful' dimensions of each individual and the definitions of the conditions of worth and possible social restraints, the objective for person-centred therapists has now slightly altered. Therapists are now called to create the conditions whereby the client becomes aware of his/her own individual actualizing process and how that may have encountered difficulties and possible disruptions. Furthermore, Rennier (2004) explains that Rogers' notion of the person, or the individual, is closely related to ethical evaluations. Furthermore, he emphasizes Rogers' incapability of explicitly distinguishing the ideas of self and self-concept, which results in an obscuring agency. Rennier is in favour of a restructuring of the person-centred approach on the basis of a rather reflexive agent instead of maintaining the unclear understanding of the self, initialled by Rogers.

Self-related Therapeutic Techniques

After discussing the two main schools of psychoanalytic and psychotherapeutic thought (and related approaches), it is time to turn to the therapeutic techniques associated to these tendencies, in order to reveal the ways self is perceived, understood and treated at a more applied level. The uniqueness of any therapeutic technique relates to the fact that unlike any theoretical understanding of the self, these techniques actually intervene into the individual's inner being by following specific ways and purposes. Today, there is a wide variety of psychotherapeutic techniques available. Let me clarify that this chapter is mainly concerned with techniques employed in Western cultures (perhaps more specifically in North America, Great Britain and Australia), which are accredited and approved, by relevant professional associations and governmental authorities.

The first question we need to answer at this point is what psychotherapy is? Counselling and psychotherapy 'are umbrella terms that cover a range of talking therapies. They are delivered by trained practitioners who work with people over a short- or long-term to help them bring about effective change or enhance their wellbeing' (British Association for Counselling and Psychotherapy, 2015). The second question would be: what do psychotherapists do? 'Professional counsellors and psychotherapists work within a clearly contracted, principled relationship that enables individuals to obtain assistance in exploring and resolving issues of an inter-personal, intra-psychic, or personal nature' (Psychotherapy and Counselling Federation of Australia, 2015).

Some popular kinds of psychotherapy include:

- Cognitive therapy

- Behavioural therapy

- Cognitive Behavioural Therapy (CBT)

- Marital or family therapy

- Eye Movement Desensitization and Reprocessing therapy (EMDR)

- Psychoanalytic therapy.

It would be beyond the scope of this chapter to discuss every single kind of psycho-therapeutic technique. Instead, it might be more helpful to explain the psychoanalytic and the person-centred kinds of psychotherapy, as these are the two theoretical approaches that have been considered so far. Still, this chapter is not focused on the exact ways that these techniques operate, rather it is aimed at the notion of self which will be explained through those specific applied therapeutic procedures.

Psychoanalytic psychotherapy

The applicable therapeutic aspect of psychoanalysis as a theory is called psychoana-lytic and psychodynamic psychotherapy and it constitutes a very specific therapeutic method. According to the British Psychoanalytic Council (2015) psychoanalysis, as a therapeutic method, was introduced with the discoveries of Sigmund Freud, a century ago, but its methods have changed and developed a great deal since then. Psychodynamic therapy is primarily associated with Melanie Klein's (1988) tech-niques (which derive from the principles of objects relation theory). The psychoanalytic therapist will seem less socially responsive and will be primarily focused in helping the client to discuss whatever is going through her/his mind by remaining neutral, keeping personal feelings and reactions private. The psychoanalyst will try to pick up hidden patterns and meanings in what the client is saying and will also be interested in the way the client is relating to the therapist. As discussed in the previous sections, psychoanalysis transformed radically after Freud's initial theory resulting in the creation of various psychoanalytic schools of thought. This section will concentrate on the principles of Freudian psychoanalytic therapy associated with the exploration of the self as it would be beyond the scope of this chapter to cover every singly psychotherapeutic technique available.

As already discussed, Freud's firm therapeutic aim (and main reason for introducing psychotherapy as a therapeutic method) was for the individual to gain greater self-knowledge and therefore to make the unconscious, conscious. According to Freud, people experience an inner struggle, as divided selves, between the 'supermoral' superego and the amoral id. People need to follow what is socially acceptable by repressing powerful sexual unconscious drives. Such struggle is experienced according to Freud as a conflict, which in turn becomes anxiety. Overwhelming anxiety is experienced as traumas, which are re-lived throughout a life-time in the hope of eventually resolving them. Freud explains that individuals employ a variety of defences (denial, repression) in order to protect the person from experiencing the pain of self-knowledge (aimed at by the therapy) (Errington and Murdin, 2006).

In order for the individual to achieve self-knowledge and enable the unconscious to become conscious, a sequence of specific steps have to be followed. 'Transference' is one of the most influential psychoanalytic terms, often used by many psychotherapeutic methods. Transference is the situation during which a past trauma is unconsciously repeated during the therapeutic session, or transferred into the present life of the individual. In that instance, usually painful feelings are experienced and therefore can be examined and explored in depth. For example, the client might feel that the therapist is becoming authoritative like her/his parent and this results in experiencing feelings that s/he once felt as a child. Such analysis results in creating liberating potential resolutions to possible or even anticipated difficulties (maybe the client experiences similar feelings on different occasions). The therapist is offering possible 'interpretations' of the links between the past traumas and present situation(s) that may enable the client to let go of some defences (perhaps the therapist might explain why the client would perceive the therapist in such a way). Transference of feelings may usually be projected towards the therapist who should be able to identify such incidents. The experience of the relationship between the client and the therapist is of the utmost importance as the way this relationship is formed aims at helping the client to improve the way s/he experiences all other relationships (Errington and Murdin, 2006). Through such techniques, Freudian psychoanalysis aims at allowing unconscious parts of the self to be relived and eventually resolved. This is the way through which the client is achieving self-knowledge which is an ongoing open-ended therapeutic process.

Person-centred psychotherapy

According to the British Association for the Person-Centred Approach (2015) the person-centred approach developed from the work of the psychologist Dr Carl Rogers. Moving away from psychoanalysis, Rogers (1951) formed a specific approach to psychotherapy and counselling which, at the time, was considered extremely radical. This therapy moved away from the idea that the therapist was the expert and towards a theory that trusted the innate tendency (known as the actualizing tendency) of human beings to find fulfilment of their personal potentials, which includes sociability, the need to be with other human beings and a desire to know and be known by other people. The central truth for Rogers is that the client knows best as he knows what hurts her/him and s/he is the one who is going to discover the way to move forward. For that reason the therapist remains as neutral as possible without revealing her/his expertise or authority. The therapist is taking the role of the companion who can encourage a trustworthy relationship with the client, which in turn will facilitate the client's self-acceptance and self-actualization (Kahn, 1997).

Rogers believed that all individuals strive to grow towards the best possible fulfilment of their potential. This is what he calls 'actualizing tendency'. Mearns and Thorne (2007) explain that some people are fortunate enough to be raised in a loving and caring environment which allowed them to trust themselves and others and be able to make decisions according to their own perceptions and desires. Therefore these individuals are perhaps closer in fulfilling their actualizing tendency. However, those not fortunate enough, who have suffered from the burden of 'many punitive conditions of worth' (p. 13) usually have an irresistible need for positive regard by others. Therefore, the individual is usually unable to trust easily or to make effective decisions. In such cases the actualization tendency can be facilitated by the therapist.

The self-concept (the person's conceptual construction of her/him self) is therefore one of the core concepts in person-centred psychotherapy, as the listener (therapist) is trying to help the client to fully reveal it. The ways each individual perceives her/him self (and thus constructs her/his own self-concept) relate to the ways this person evaluates her/him self. Therefore, if a person believes that he/she is worthless, he/she will probably act in a way that can confirm this belief. Probably, this kind of self-evaluation, derives from '*conditions of worth*' (p. 11, my emphasis) which (significant) others have imposed on them (parents, siblings, peers); consequently, this person will constantly seek to receive positive evaluations by others. In this case the individual, according to Rogers, has moved away from his/her actualizing potential and the therapist (who genuinely believes that all clients have within themselves vast recourses of development) attempts to help the client recover from past deprivation and begin to flourish. The core values of the therapist include being open to experience, being trusting and trustworthy, being curious about the world, being creative and compassionate. Rogers' approach primarily relies on the personal qualities of the therapist/person to build a non-judgemental and empathic relationship (Mearns and Thorne, 2007). Client-centred therapy aims at revealing self-knowledge through enabling the client to experience self-actualization.

Comparison

Psychoanalysis aims to modify personality through introspection and supports that the more aware an individual is of her/his unconscious defences and desires, the freer s/he becomes in dealing with reality. Therefore, psychoanalysis encourages the constant exploration of the unconscious. However, in person-centred psychotherapy, the importance of self-disclosure and self-actualization is central. The therapist is a blank-screen, so that her/his neutrality maximizes the possibility for growth of the individual's resources (Thorne, 1992). Both approaches aim at revealing self-knowledge and enable the client to get to know and accept her/him self. Specific techniques are used (far more complicated and elaborate than those briefly discussed above) in order that the therapist can provide support and understanding towards the client. Psychoanalytic (or even psychodynamic) psychotherapy usually requires a very long period of time to be completed, it has to take place multiple times each week and it is usually open-ended. Person-centred psychotherapy is usually limited in terms of the time required to be completed, it takes place once a week and can be repeated when needed. Admittedly, the self in both psychotherapeutic approaches is not defined through concrete matters, rather it allows space for the individual who is aiming for self-knowledge to reveal what (parts) of his/her self might be, at given times. Therefore, in terms of psychotherapeutic approaches, the idea of self is defined (or perhaps experienced) through the person who is receiving therapy and remains to be explored and revealed by him/her (through the help of the therapist).

Limitations: therapeutic discourse

According to Elliott (2009), both psychoanalytic and psychotherapeutic techniques are characterized as 'talking therapies' since they involve a speaker and a listener (client and therapist) who produce narratives as they tell each other stories (the client tells stories about her/him self and the therapist tells stories that explain the client's narratives about her/him self). Such self-narratives ideally allow emotional exposure and eventualy emotional relief. At the same time, such narratives constitute specific kinds of discourse. Discourse has been defined as the:

> ways of constituting knowledge, together with the social practices, forms of subjectivity and power relations which inhere in such knowledge and relations between them. Discourses are more than ways of thinking and producing meaning. They constitute the 'nature' of the body, unconscious and conscious mind and emotional life of the subjects they seek to govern. (Weedon, 1987: 108)

Psychotherapeutic techniques, but particularly psychoanalytic theory and form of practice, have received extensive criticism as representing a form of theoretical essentialism. Foucault (1979) was one of the first to become critical towards such discourse and he explained that such form of 'expert knowledge' (psychoanalysis, medical narratives, scientific explanations) entail a connection between discourse and power-knowledge (Heaphy, 2007). The reason is, as Elliott (2009) explains, that the language of psychotherapy represents another form of social control, a method of power and policing over the individual's behaviour. Indeed, psychotherapeutic theory and forms of practice imply specific frames of how people should behave or feel or act in order to be or become happy, fulfilled and live meaningful lives.

Interestingly, both person-centred and psychoanalytic practices perceive 'self-knowledge' as the ultimate goal of the therapeutic process; however, in such context, Foucault (1979) characterized self-knowledge as a strategy and effect of power as the client internalizes self-control or monitoring. He believed that any form of categorizations, such as identities, are not pre-given, unified or fixed. Identity (including self-identity) is constantly reconstructed and reinvented. Therefore, self-knowledge constitutes an open-ended and rather vague therapeutic goal, as there is no such thing as an 'ideal self' that the individual is supposed to achieve. As Heaphy (2007) explains, for Foucault psychoanalysis is related to disciplinary power since psychoanalytic discourse aims at judging people's conceptions of normality. He perceives psychotherapeutic discourse as a characteristic form of surveillance as it regulates psycho-somatic norms and primarily deviance.

Foucault's (1979) main concern related to the therapeutic discourse associated to sexuality (primarily related to psychoanalysis and sexology) as experts instruct clients how to discover their 'true self' through following institutional ideas, discourses and practices. For example, a sadomasochistic sexual behaviour would most probably be seen as problematic and in need of therapeutic monitoring. Whereas, as Foucault would argue, the therapist is actually imposing psychological controls while trying to convince the client that s/he is progressing towards emotional liberation. It is thus argued that expert-knowledge and expert-discourse (including psychoanalytic psychotherapy) operate in a way that through discourse (and primarily through the key ideas represented in such discourse), power is exercised and certain forms of control are employed.

For example, Freud had commented on homosexual behaviour numerous times in his writings and had concluded that paranoia and homosexuality were inseparable. Admittedly, sexual behaviour has been highly regulated by expert knowledge up until recently as same-sex desire and relations were considered abnormal and even constituted a crime. According to the American Psychiatric Association, until 1974 homosexuality was a mental illness and homosexuality was decriminalized in the UK in 1967 (Beasley, 2005). Foucault (1969) explains that the way sex is used in language or discourse (and particularly the therapeutic discourse) has changed enormously in recent decades.

At the same time, various forms of criticism have been employed to reveal the limitations of Foucault's thought. Perhaps the most prominent criticism relates to Foucault's reduction of human agency to a social (or rather weak) agency aimed at resisting received identities (Heaphy, 2007). Elliott (2008) explains that Foucault (1985) admitted that surveillance is not imposed on all individuals equally, rather it depends on each person's thoughts and ways of being and he further emphasizes Foucault's suggestion that each individual should know who s/he is by realizing what is happening inside her/him and by acknowledging her/his own limitations (Foucault, 1985). It seems however, that Foucault remains primarily concerned with human sexuality in his attempt to explain subjectivity and what he regards to be the notion of self (without providing a specific definition). His work has undoubtedly offered a powerful and challenging perspective on the culture of modern sexuality and opened the road for even more radical approaches to be evolved (like queer theory). However, such an approach might not be able to answer the questions that psychoanalytic and psychotherapeutic approaches leave unanswered: is the formation of self a result of significant and powerful interpersonal relations like the one between the mother and the child or is it the result of a continuous, eternal struggle between conscious and unconscious powers?

Therapeutic techniques and intra-action

This chapter discussed the aspects of the unconscious as well as conscious self as ways to understand in a more complete manner the idea of self. As already explained in the last chapter the notion of self is indeed rather vague and although the specific conscious and unconscious aspects of it may provide a more insightful exploration of its content, it does not restore any prospect for the re-creation of a universal definition of the self. Still, intra-action remains particularly relevant regarding the therapeutic techniques that could be used as a way to understand oneself. Intra-action concerns any form of exchange of action (including exchange of emotions) within oneself which could be activated internally (i.e. by the individual) or externally (by others) (further discussion follows in Chapter 7). Therapeutic techniques perhaps aim at the activation of such an exchange, which should refer aspects relevant to the context of the therapeutic session. It can therefore be maintained that intra-action might not be at odds with psychotherapeutic techniques; in fact might actually be used as a way to facilitate them, as it concerns a specific way that inner life operates and functions.

Summary

This chapter has been primarily concerned with the exploration of the idea of self through certain psychoanalytic and psychotherapeutic approaches. The notion of the self has been discussed through Freudian psychoanalysis, Neo-Freudian approaches, the Frankfurt School views, post-Freudian ideas and Lacanian-psychoanalytic perceptions. Moving away from the powerful Freudian-related theorizations, the idea of self was then considered in relation to person-centred approaches by defining the self through Rogers' theory. The last section focused on self-related therapeutic techniques by discussing first psychoanalytic and then person-centred applications of therapeutic approaches to the self. Comparisons and contradictions have also been considered whereas limitations are also revealed through the Foucauldian criticism of therapeutic discourse.

• •

Concepts in Context

A young man, in his late twenties is dating a young woman he met while he was a student. They seem a nice couple, sharing loving feelings, able to connect and evolve their relationship. However, the woman often feels unable to control her boyfriend's reactions as he loses his temper easily and he can become very aggressive and extremely controlling. The young woman felt that they both needed therapeutic advice in order to find out what is the cause of their repeated conflicts; she also managed to persuade her partner, although he was extremely reluctant to try therapeutic techniques. After a number of sessions talking about their childhood and their connection to their parents, the counsellor tried to explain to them that possibly the reason for their conflicts has to do with the way each of them were brought up. The girl was raised in a rather spoiled way, allowed to think that she will always be the centre of attention, whereas her partner was raised in a rather abusive way as his father was very violent, aggressive and negative. The therapist explained that neither of them are acting in a conscious way but they both unconsciously try to repeat the behavioural patterns they learned while they were being brought up.

The couple considered the explanation offered by the counsellor and they both wondered what is the truth in his words. Some of what he said could make sense but who is he to judge their loving parents and accuse them for such a damaging upbringing? After all, they are just another couple facing conflicts like many couples do. They both decided that such support was unhelpful and they started making plans for getting married. Unfortunately, this didn't happen as the young man became very abusive one night after realizing that his girlfriend was cheating on him with her ex-boyfriend. Neither of them could tolerate each other so they broke up. The young woman married her ex-boyfriend and the young man is dating periodically various women without being able to form a stable relationship. However, they both still believe that psychotherapy is not a helpful way to resolve personal issues.

• •

──SELF-REFLECTIVE QUESTIONS──

1. How can we study the idea of 'unconscious self' through the cases of these two different people?
2. How can we study the idea of 'conscious self' through the cases of these two different people?
3. How could self-knowledge be revealed through therapeutic techniques?

Possible ways of exploring the questions offered in this chapter and Further Readings:

1. As this example explains, it might be difficult for some people to understand the ways conscious and unconscious patterns of behaviour may affect their lives and the ways they act. And although a therapist (or psychoanalyst) might be able to reveal conscious and unconscious aspects of self, this does not necessarily mean that such explanations will be accepted or will be perceived as accurate. The way these two young people ended up living their lives, has to do with who they are; however, it remains unclear how each individual can find out who s/he really is. A psychoanalytic evaluation of the self, regarding this particular young man and young woman, might have revealed some unrealized behavioural patterns that could explain why these two people find it so difficult to relate to one another. The fact that neither of these two people are willing to adopt such psychoanalytic inter-pretations might be related to the fact that such explanations could become extremely intrusive to each person's privacy, or could become intensively judge-mental and thus discourage potential adaptation of such explanations.

Further Reading:

Elliott, A. (1992) *Social Theory and Psychoanalysis in Transition: Self and Society from Freud to Kristeva*. Oxford: Blackwell.

2. These people's conscious self, or perhaps, the part of the self that they are aware of, relates to the facts that guided them to ask for help (i.e. the young man's aggressive attitude and the young woman's inability to cope with it). Person-centred therapy could possibly emphasize both persons' struggle to cover their own needs (the young man to feel safe and secure and the young woman to feel accepted) through

a self-actualizing tendency which is a separate process for each of them. The needs for these two individuals might actually be contradictory, as the young man while trying to feel safe is becoming controlling and while the young woman is trying to feel special she is becoming insecure. The counsellor would have probably tried to explain these behavioural contradictions to this couple, which of course remain particularly unpleasant if not painful. These parts of each person's selves could be seen as 'responsible' for not allowing their relationship to flourish. Regardless of the question whether this realization might be indeed accurate or not, such evaluation remains rather unsettling regarding the future of this intimate relationship and therefore, this couple would refuse to accept such a prospect easily.

Further Reading:

Rogers, C.R. (1961) *On Becoming a Person.* Boston: Houghton Mifflin.

3.   These particular people could probably learn more about their selves or aspects of themselves through psychotherapeutic processes and techniques. They could probably understand better why they act the way they do and even alter aspects of their behaviour that they consider unhelpful or even damaging. The various versions of psychoanalysis would follow different methods compared to person-centred techniques but both therapeutic forms aim at enabling individuals to understand oneself better. The extent to which this will be achieved will always remain questionable and perhaps the reason is that we still do not have a clear understanding of what the notion of self is or should be or even could be. Psychotherapeutic approaches allow a subjective understanding of the self which is by no means universal or even specific. Thus, whatever the self might mean for each of us could be explored or changed through therapeutic techniques although the idea of self remains abstract and subjectively defined.

Further Reading:

Kahn, M. (1997) *Between Therapist and Client: The New Relationship.* New York: Owl Books.

In conclusion, if this couple would have continued counselling this does not necessarily mean that they would have been able to be together. One might say that they could probably have been able to understand better why they act the way they do, but this of course, cannot be certain for any therapeutic process. There should be some truth in the words of the (or perhaps any) counsellor but can this (or any) explanation of the unconscious and conscious aspect of self determine in such a decisive manner the way these two (or any) people would end up living their lives? Perhaps different approaches on what the individual could be (rather than the self) might be beneficial.

7

Intra-Action

Intra-action includes everything that is happening inside our selves that allows us to be able to interact with everyone including ourselves. (Chalari, 2017)

Why is Intra-action Important?

After discussing a wide range of psychological and sociological approaches regarding the exploration of the individual in relation to society (through the concepts of interaction, socialization, identity and self), it is now time to turn to sociological and psychological theorizations that promote the investigation of inner life. Such views have been able to provide certain forms of explanations about the ways the individual produces intra-action (along with, and separately from, interaction). This chapter aims at explaining the ways individuals exchange action with themselves, in an attempt to get closer to possible understandings of the ways individuals connect to society. Instead of repeating approaches that concentrate on the ways individuals relate to other individuals, structures, institutions and ultimately society, this chapter will explain how the individual relates to oneself. The main way used both by sociologists and psychologists to explore the ways and forms individuals interact with themselves (and thus produce intra-action) is through the examination of the dialogical relationship individuals experience with oneself.

This chapter begins by defining what is intra-action and explains the two main ways that this concept could be approached: as a dualism and as a duality. A brief overview of the origins of intra-action will be discussed by mentioning the contribution of Georg Simmel, American Pragmatism and then the works of Piaget and Vygotsky. The following section explores current theories and applications associated to intra-action. First, the paradigm of dualism will be discussed by including views that may explain intra-action through dialogical terms. Then, the paradigm of duality will follow by discussing views that could explain intra-action through the district concepts of inner speech and internal conversation. Following that, reflexivity will be introduced as an applied approach to intra-action and again, the paradigms of dualism and duality will be discussed separately. Finally, the idea of mediation will be analysed as a way to explain applied intra-action.

EXAMPLE

'And now what?' John thought while waving to his son who left home to begin his studies at university. 'What do I do now?' John silently said to himself. 'Will I spend the rest of my days arguing with my wife, watching TV and waiting for my son's phone call?' John feels sad and proud at the same time. He can't quite put these feeling into words but he gets this mood of unsettlement and discomfort. He doesn't like the fact that his son left although he knew that this would eventually happen. He could talk with his son; not about everything but they were very close. Now John feels that he will have to spend a lot of time on his own, as he is already retired, remembering all the pleasant (and unpleasant) incidents in his life, wondering about how his son is doing, planning his next visit, arranging the next money transfer, getting excited about his first completed year at the university. He thinks that he has to monitor his son's mobile bill as he spends so much time talking to his friends and perhaps call his closest friend to make sure that his son is settling well. John wonders if he is exaggerating or if all parents feel this way when this day comes? All of these thoughts are actually taking place inside John's mind. John is experiencing such conversations with himself very often. Perhaps every single day. He is probably not able to describe them as conversations or dialogues but he can tell for sure that he is talking with himself quite often. Sometimes more than he wants! He can't make himself stop talking to himself! He can get annoyed because of that ... But he doesn't share such concerns with others. He is not sure if other people are actually talking with themselves! So it is better to keep such things quiet and private!

What Do We Mean by Intra-action?

As discussed in the first chapter of this book, intra-action describes the exchange of action within the individual (Chalari, 2009) whereas interaction refers to the exchange of action between individuals; interaction is fundamentally related (if not dependent) upon intra-action. However, interaction and intra-action do not coincide. Following the social theoretical discussion regarding the relationship between structure and agency, there are two main approaches that can be used to explain the connection between intra-action and interaction: a) those who say that individuals/ agency are products of the social circumstances and structure and thus interaction shapes intra-action. This approach perceives interaction and intra-action as a '*dualism*', meaning that intra- and interaction constitute the two sides of the same coin.

Symbolic interactionism would be a characteristic representative of such approach. On the contrary, a different approach would come from b) those who say that the concept of individual/agency is indeed interrelated, interconnected, interdependent with social reality but does not coincide with it. This approach perceives inter-action and intra-action as a '*duality*', namely, as two distinct and at the same time interrelated aspects of social reality. Critical Realism would be considered as a rep-resentative school of such thought.

Interaction and intra-action: a dualism

Charon (2011) explained that human action is not only perceived as interaction between individuals but interaction within the individual. Following the defini-tion of interaction, intra-action concerns the exchange of linguistic, or non-linguistic forms of action between the sender and the receiver who is the same person. Although Vygotsky (1934) was probably the first to introduce the concept of 'intra-psychological' properties, Blumer further explained that the indi-vidual acts towards others but also acts towards oneself (Blumer, 1962). Intra-action refers to human agency and inner life. It refers to thoughts, concerns, dialogues, hopes, anticipations, needs, feelings, plans and intentions that each individual experiences within oneself; others may or may not know about these experiences. Intra-action relates to interaction in the sense that, as individuals are able to exchange action between them (in both verbal and non-verbal manners), similarly, each individual is equally able to experience exchange of action within oneself (in both linguistic or non-linguistic forms). In order for individuals to be able to form connections and relationships with other individuals and therefore produce inter-action, they also need to produce intra-action. As discussed in previous chapters, certain symbolic interactionists made clear that individuals are interacting with others as well as with themselves. Although symbolic interactionism was primarily concentrated on language as a form of symbolic interaction of meaning, intra-action can be perceived in even wider terms. Mead (1934) was one of the first to state that we act towards ourselves as objects in the same way as we act towards others. Following Mead, Blumer (1962) agrees that the individual can act towards oneself like s/he acts towards other people and he explains that as we can judge others, we can judge ourselves and as we can talk to others we can also talk to ourselves. Blumer further explains that as we have feelings towards others, we can also have feelings towards ourselves (being angry, happy or disappointed with ourselves). Blumer clearly states that individuals can act towards themselves as well as towards others. It is thus understood (and it will be further discussed) that although the term intra-action might not be used as such, traces of this human ability are obvious in certain schools of thought that perceive the relationship between structure and agency as a dualism.

Perhaps most of the psychological explanations related to intra-action are not as much concerned with the agential powers of intra-action but they are primarily concerned with the dependence of intra-action upon interaction. For example, Hermans and Hermans-Konoplka (2010: 7), explain that 'actions […] take place between people (conflicts, criticisms, making agreements and consultations) occur also within the self (self-conflicts, self-criticism, self-agreements, and self-consultations). Carrigan (2015) in turn, is focusing on encounters by looking into the connection between interaction and intra-action as he explains that encounters both shape and are shaped by the exercise of our reflexivity. At the same time this term has been occasionally used in current psychological literature primarily involved with intra-communication. Intra-action is then defined as the communication with oneself through the use of external tools like note-taking, annotation, diary-keeping and bookmarking (further discussion follows); such methods involve repeated passing of meaningful messages, both informative and emotional, and hence could be regarded as communication (Hwang et al., 2009). Hermans and Hermans-Konoplka (2010: 6) for example, explain that '[Dialogues] not only take place between different people but, closely intertwined with them, they also take place between different positions or voices in the self' (further discussion follows).

Interaction and intra-action: a duality

Notably, intra-action (as defined in this book) is primarily perceived as a distinct concept, which is indeed interrelated with interaction, but does not coincide with it. In that sense, intra-action is primarily connected with the concept of 'internal conversation' proposed by Archer (2003, 2007), which is defined as a unique aspect of inner life, experienced by all individuals independently from other (verbal or non-verbal) forms of interaction. Although Archer uses the term 'internal conversation' she does not refer exclusively to communicative means of conversation. Rather, she refers to all those ways that individuals use to become reflexive about themselves and about the social world (further discussed in following sections). Such ways include various (if not all) forms of (linguistic and non-linguistic) intra-action. Archer (2007: 2) explains that 'internal conversation' is defined as 'the mental ability of all people to talk to themselves within their own heads, usually silently and usually from an early age'. A wider understanding of this term would include the ability of all individuals to produce intra-action within themselves. As Archer (2007) explains, similar terms used are those of 'self-talk', 'intra-communication', 'amusement', 'inner dialogue' and 'rumination'. Therefore, internal conversation and intra-action may be perceived in similar (if not identical) terms and describe the relationship between structure and agency in terms of duality.

The reason why the term intra-action is used in this book is because this term may be used in a broader way to describe the ability of the individuals to experience exchange of action internally (inside our minds) without necessarily being understood by others. A characteristic example would be that of 'resistance' as individuals can experience internal resistance as something completely different compared to the conventional understanding of resistance as a social act of opposition (Chalari, 2012). In accordance to Archer, Mouzelis (2008: 232) explains that in order for structure to be connected to agency then both intra-action and interaction are needed: 'the self-self internal intra-actions and the self-other interactions which simultaneously takes place in a specific context'. Mouzelis associates intra-action to agentic powers and he explains that discursive processes of intra-action and inter-action link the causal powers of actors with those of structures. In the same vein, additional current sociological approaches, like that of Wiley (2010: 17), promote the dialogical aspect of intra-action as he explains that 'action is the work of the dialogical self conversing with itself'.

Origins of Intra-action

Intra-action has therefore been approached through its connection to inter-action which could be perceived as a dualism or duality. It is not always clear how each theory or theorist define intra-action, given that this term has not been widely used in sociological academic literature. What has been quite explicit, however, has been a tendency of various sociological and psychological perspectives to engage with this idea in various forms and ways. Without attempting to categorize each approach to an exclusive category related to dualism or duality, the following discussion attempts at revealing the origins of this concept by identifying the most relevant views and perspectives.

Georg Simmel

Intra-action might not be a term used frequently by sociologists but it could be argued that it does originate from Simmel's social-theoretical conceptualization of inter-action. As already discussed in previous chapters, Simmel (also discussed in Chapters 1, 3 and 5) very characteristically stated that, if we want to understand how society works, we need to study the people who created society (Simmel, 1950). Simmel is perhaps the first sociologist to introduce the twofold nature of the individual, which derives jointly from the individual's inner existence and external/social environment. Simmel was one of the few scholars to reveal the explicit distinction between the social life of the individual and the individual's inner existence (Spykman, 1965). As Chalari (2009) maintains, for Simmel, society is structured and viewed as the endless combinations of individuals' interactions with each other, but it can also be understood as the endless combinations of individuals' interaction with themselves. Simmel describes the inner life as a process that consists of some elements, like thoughts and moods, which are internal private elements that belong to the inner cosmos of the individual (Simmel, 1950: 385–6). For Simmel, these elements or processes constitute elements of what he construes as inner life. Thus, although for Simmel interaction was coined as the primary reason and form of society's function, some sort of intra-action (although he never used this term) described as 'inner life' remains the source of interaction and consists of thoughts and personal elements. It is thus acknowledged that initial traces of the concept of intra-action are indeed contained in Simmel's explanation of the relationship between structure and agency as a form of duality.

American Pragmatism

The idea of intra-action also originates from the thought of American Pragmatism, as the founding fathers of this school of thought systematically explored the idea of agency (self) in relation to structure (society) and more importantly they introduced a dialogical approach to the exploration of this connection. As discussed in Chapter 5, American Pragmatism is known as a philosophical school of thought (primarily deriving from William James, Georg Herbert Mead and Charles Sanders Peirce), which inspired the analysis of various sociological and psychological approaches regarding the study of self. Each of those pragmatists contributed a dialogical understanding of the ways the individual produces intra-action (although none of the American pragmatists used this term). As the main ideas of each pragmatist, regarding the notion of the self, have been discussed in the previous chapters, this section will concentrate on more recent interpretations regarding how American Pragmatism contributed to the understanding of the idea of intra-action.

The dialogical essence of the self, is related to: a) James' concepts of the self-as-knower (the self as subject, the 'I'), and the self-as-known (the self as object, the 'Me') (James, 1984). At any given moment, the 'I' is conscious, whereas the 'Me' is only one of the things of which the individual is conscious. For James, then, the 'I' is a wider concept, which includes the 'Me' within it. James (1890) describes an interaction between the 'Me' and the 'I' as the 'Me' transports features or elements or experiences from the external world to the 'I', or the internal world (Chalari, 2009). b) Peirce's (1935) views on the twofold essence of the 'ego': the past ('Me', the 'object'), the present ('I', the 'sign') and the future ('You', the 'interpretant'). Wiley (1994, 2010), however, explains that, for Peirce himself, the discussion is not between 'I' and 'Me' (that is, from present to past) but between 'I' and 'You', that is, from present to future. c) Mead's ideas regarding the dialogic interplay between the 'I' (each individual's values and principles and ultimately personality) and the 'Me' (the organized set of others' attitudes, which the individual herself assumes) (Mead, 1934).

Therefore, American Pragmatism introduced some sort of (admittedly quite vague) interplay between two main poles (the I and the Me) and in addition to that, more recently Wiley (1994, 2010) and Colapietro (1989, 2010) incorporated Peirce's idea of the 'You'. The synthesized trialogue 'I-Me-You' introduced by Wiley (1994, 2010) suggests a more complete form of exchange of action (intra-action) within the individual. Wiley (2010) explains that the 'I-Me-You' exchange of action derives from Mead's dialogue between the 'I' and the 'Me' and Peirce's dialogue between the 'I' and the 'You' and describes humans' engagement with temporality (Me = Past, I = Present and You = Future). 'When Mead and Peirce are combined, the dialogical self is the "I" talking directly to the "You" and indirectly or reflexively to the "Me"' (Wiley, 2010: 18). Wiley explains that the 'Me' as the 'past self' consists of various characteristics such as Mead's concept of generalized other (discussed in Chapter 2), memories about the past, an essence or understanding people have about their bodies, the self-concept (discussed in Chapter 5) and habits in the sense of routine action (associated with Bourdieu's (1977, 1990) 'habitus'). The 'You' according to Wiley, gives access to the future, while considering problems that may occur, or opportunities of action or imagined moments of pleasure. The 'Me', through memory, gives access to previous practices of culture, habits of the past and results of previous actions. The 'I' is allowed access to both past and future while composing the present (while dreaming, fantasizing, anticipating, remembering, evaluating, etc.). Such form of exchange of action is taking place in each person's mind through the form of thinking (and the inevitable usage of at least some words). The structure of what is called 'self' is designated according to the exchange of action (or inner speech as he prefers to use this term) between these three poles (I-Me-You) according to Wiley. In addition, Archer (2003: 63) explains that for James, every individual experiences inner life or in different words, 'an intra-active process that consists in moment-by-moment deliberation, evaluation and selection, which is constitutive of thought and is possible because all thinking takes place over time'. It is thus understood, that intra-action in the sense of inner speech or even internal conversation, originates from the school of thought of American Pragmatism.

Vygotsky and Piaget

Developmental psychology has also contributed enormously regarding the formation of the origins of intra-action; particularly the dialogic (linguistic and non-linguistic) forms of exchange of action within individuals of young age. Piaget (1926) (who, along with Vygotsky, are considered the two pioneers of developmental psychology), introduced the term 'egocentric speech' to describe the speech (verbal action) young children produce while they are talking to themselves (namely when they produce intra-action), usually while they are playing. Such speech (or such action) is self-directed and for Piaget, entails egocentrism, a sign of cognitive immaturity and the inability to share the perspective of another child or adult. However, he argues that, as children grow older (around school-age), they increasingly socialize with others and their speech becomes communicative, moving from being self-oriented (intra-action) to other-oriented (interaction), a sign that they are able to appreciate others' perspectives. A child overcomes egocentrism by beginning to think critically and logically, causing egocentric speech to fade away. Piaget perceived this form of intra-action (although he never used this term) as being antisocial since the child prefers to talk to oneself rather than anyone else, forcing others to realize that s/he is ignoring them. This audible form of intra-action, becomes less socially problematic, when the child/adult learns to keep it silent. In the case of an adult talking to her/him self out loud s/he is usually considered as producing antisocial or deviant behaviour; Goffman (1981: 80), used the term 'self-talk' to describe such occurrences. Interestingly, Piaget explains that 'egocentric speech' is visible and audible at a specific age before it 'disappears' or, more accurately, before the social environment contributes to it becoming 'hidden' and internalized (Chalari, 2009). Therefore, egocentric speech in pre-school childhood can be described as an audible form of intra-action as the child exchanges verbal action with her/him self, which includes various forms of experienced action such as: instructions, directions, descriptions, orders, anticipations and perhaps primarily, a wide range of experienced feelings (even though not necessarily verbalized).

Vygotsky (1934) introduced the idea of intra-psychological properties; he explained that a child's cognitive development originates in socialization (and therefore interaction), and then moves through a process of increasing individuality (or else intra-action). In contradiction to Piaget, self-directed speech (vocal action) does not necessarily demonstrate cognitive immaturity but, rather, reveals cognitive development. As a child grows older, self-directed speech changes into silent inner speech (therefore audible intra-action becomes silent intra-action); vocalization becomes unnecessary because the child 'thinks' the words, instead of voicing them. Therefore, inner speech still exists and develops within the child and later on within the adult, but the individual does not externalize it. Thus, silent intra-action remains private and it does not become interaction (Chalari, 2009). Vygotsky (1978: 57) himself states: 'Every function in the child's cultural development appears twice: first, on the social level, and later, on the individual level; first, between people (inter-psychological) and then inside the child (intra-psychological). This applies equally to voluntary attention, to logical memory, and to the formation of concepts. All the higher functions originate as actual relationships between individuals.' Valsiner and Van der Veer (1991: 130) very characteristically explained that Vygotsky as well as Mead revealed the 'dynamic, dialectic nature of the self in its social context'.

Having discussed certain theoretical approaches regarding the origins of intra-action, it becomes understood that both sociology and psychology (philosophy is not excluded) have been repeatedly concerned with the exchange of various forms of action within the individual. The following section will discuss more extensively more recent approaches and theorizations primarily regarding dialogical forms of intra-action.

Current theories and Applications

More recently, psychological and sociological approaches have been concerned with the exploration of inner life by incorporating a wide variety of concepts, terms and

techniques. This section will discuss a plurality of approaches which could be categorized according to the way they perceive the connection between interaction
and intra-action. Intra-action will first be analysed through approaches that derive
from the paradigm of dualism and then, approaches related to the paradigm of duality will be extensively discussed.

Dualism: intra-action in dialogical terms

As discussed, the aspect of the exchange of action (within or between individuals)
in dialogical terms, does not constitute a contemporary realization; still, it has
been recently advanced through current psychological approaches mainly concerned with the aspect of 'voices'. Once again, the concept of intra-action is not
directly used, but a profound and systematic analysis of dialogic forms of intra-
action is revealed. Vocate (1994: 3) introduced the term 'intrapersonal
communication' to describe a form of self-talk (following Vygotsky's term) which
is 'engendered by symbolic interaction and arises from a mental foundation of
inner speech'. Inner speech derives from our own voices or the voices of significant others. Individuals, according to Vocate, are raised as we 'hear voices of others
comforting, chastising, and attempting to persuade us from infancy onward' (p. 3).
Intrapersonal communication concentrates on a single human communicator as
being the sender and receiver or in different words, the source and the object of
interaction.

Hermans (1996, 2001, 2002, 2003, 2004) has been systematically using the concept of 'dialogical self' to describe the realization that each individual (or in this case
self) consists of various voices which are experienced outside as well as inside the
individual/self. 'Dialogue refers not only to productive exchanges between the
voices of individuals but also between collective voices of the groups, communities
and cultures to which the individual person belongs. Collective voices speak through
the mouth of the individual person' (Hermans and Hermans-Konoplka, 2010: 6).
There are external voices that many of us experience internally (our parents) and
there are also internal voices that only the individual concerned can experience
(what one needs, or desires). So as Hermans puts it, the idea of 'other-in-the-self' is
rather inevitable as we need to constantly process the voices of all 'others' who actually have a place in our inner life. 'There is no clear separation between the internal
life of the self and the "outside" world, but rather a gradual transition' (p. 7).
Therefore, the voices the authors refer to, may be also perceived as the various forms
of dialogic interactions (between ourselves and our parents) which are internalized
and therefore have become dialogic forms of intra-actions that we constantly process. Other forms of voices (what we desire) may be experienced as dialogic forms
of intra-action (e.g. visualize sunset and then drive towards the coast to watch the
sun go down). However, there are no clear boundaries between them and therefore
there is no clear separation between the external and the internal voices (inter- and
intra-action): 'the dialogical self is not based on any dualism between self and other:

the other (individual or group) is not outside the self but conceptually included in the self' (Hermans and Hermans-Konoplka, 2010: 7).

Emmanouil (2014), in his narrative-based study of motherhood in multiple sclerosis, approached self/identity utilizing Hermans' notion of subject position or/and voice. Relevant results from the above-mentioned study propose the contribution of participants' voices in the meaning-making process regarding their sense of identity as mothers and MS patients. The author indicates the restrictive potential of the incomplete dialogue between existing fixed – normality based – prevalent or/and silenced subject positions; he also underlines the fruitfulness of the dialogical processes detected in some cases, resulting in a reflexive identity reformation in terms of an ongoing incorporation between motherhood and progressive disability. Such approach shares specific similarities with the view that the self can be perceived as a narrative as Brinthaupt and Lipka (1992: 25) explain: 'on some level we are the stories we tell about ourselves. This is so whether the tales are accurate or inaccurate.' The stories we tell ourselves about ourselves (Ferrara, 1998: 75) but also the stories we tell to others about ourselves (Smith, 2010: 57) have also been defined as 'identity' (discussed in Chapter 5). Ezzy (1998) further argues that narrative identity provides a subjective sense of self-continuity following Ricoeur's (1984, 1986, 1992) premise that both historical action and interpretive imagination shape narrative. Although these stories might be two different kinds of narratives, which are not necessarily consistent (the stories we tell about ourselves at a date, or an interview or to an old friend) each story for one self, deriving from the narratives of significant others. This is an ongoing process which Castoriadis (1975) terms 'social imaginary' and Taylor (1989: 47) would conclude that 'self is a narrative that unifies a life in/over/through time'.

The self (or the individual) in the above cases is perceived as being inseparable from the social world, although the way(s) such connection is formed are not explicit. Lewis (1955: 26) would characteristically add that 'the individual may not control what happens to him, but the meaning he gives to what happens to him is subject to his active selectivity - within limits that are not easily defined'. Admittedly, a degree of subjectivity is indeed recognized, as the 'voices' and the 'narratives' are indeed processed in a subjective manner by the individual concerned. However, the limitation of the individual's agentic power to produce such forms of intra-action (private voice(s), or personal narrative(s)) separately from any given scope of interaction (voices of significant others, context of the narrative) is also profound. Therefore, the dialogic perspective and the narrative explanation of the individual do not allow intra-action to be formed and shaped independently from interaction.

Duality: intra-action through inner speech

'Inner speech' is a term used both by sociological and psychological literature to describe some short of intra-active speech exchange that takes place within the individual. Although this term has been used extensively, there is not a consistent way that it is used by psychological and sociological literature. One of the first definitions comes from Vygotsky who explained that 'inner speech is speech to oneself. External speech is for others' (Vygotsky, 1934: 255); he further explained that inner speech is closer to thought than external speech although inner thought and inner speech do not coincide. According to Morin and Everett (1990) inner speech constitutes one of the most important cognitive processes of introspection, which tries to answer the question: 'how does the self acquire information about itself and form a coherent picture of what it is by talking to itself about itself' (Morin and Everett, 1990: 337). Inner speech consists of: a) *'public self-aspects'*: when the individual is concerned/processes public aspects of oneself and then s/he talks to oneself about public self-aspects; and b) *'private self-aspects'*: when the individual is concerned/processes private aspects of oneself and then s/he talks to oneself about private self-aspects. Consequently, there are two possible sources of self-information: the social world and the self. The first source relates to interpersonal modes of acquisition of self-information, as it is concerned with information we receive about ourselves deriving from the public sphere (significant others, repeated confrontations). This source is primarily related to interaction. The second source relates to intra-personal modes of acquisition of self-information (and thus intra-action) and it refers to information we receive about ourselves when in a state of self-awareness and the individual becomes his/her own source of information. In rather cognitive terms, the second source involves self-directed attention, inner speech and mental self-imagery (Morin and DeBlois, 1989). More recently Morin (2005) re-defined inner speech as a running commentary on any significant aspects of ourselves and our world, that often focuses on the content of one's subjective experience.

Vocate (1994: 6) following further Vygotsky's thought, makes a distinction between two different kinds of intra-personal communication: (i) *'self-talk'*, or the dialogue within oneself which may be internal or external; and (ii) *'inner speech'*, which refers to a process of coding thought into language or decoding perceived language into meaning. Self-talk is then related to dialogues people have with themselves but could be silent or spoken (characterize oneself 'stupid' silently or verbally). Morin and Everett (1990) would use the term *'private-speech'* in this context. However, inner speech is always silent and although it is related to thought and language, it does not coincide with either of these notions. Inner speech is egocentric and private and it is understood only by the individual concerned. Vocate suggests a wider understanding of the individual's need to interact internally with her/him self (and therefore produce intra-action). She also argues that it is the 'inter-action within the self that prevents one's personality from being a compliant recording of input from one's social environment or culture' (1994: 8). It is apparent that she gives 'interaction with the self' a central role in the understanding of the individual and she states that self-talk is the main linkage between the individual and his/her environment. Vocate thus views intra-personal communication as the ability of the individual to interact both with the social environment and with her/ him self (produce intra-action).

Moreover, in 1995, Siegrist suggested that inner speech or self-talk could be an important cognitive process concerning the information about oneself. In line with Vocate's thought, Siegrist distinguishes inner speech from external speech, suggesting that external speech serves interpersonal communication. Moreover, he defines 'inner conversation' as talking to oneself about oneself, and suggests that this can take place either vocally or silently. Siegrist's (1995) study proposes that inner speech is the mediator of self-consciousness (i.e. attention directed towards the private aspects of the self). McGuire and McGuire (1991, 1992) have studied the self as experienced by the person at particularly reflective moments. They note that one is present to oneself in the form of absence, and is most conscious of characteristics perceived as lacking in oneself or others. For example, a woman psychologist, in the company of many women who work at other occupations, thinks of herself as a psychologist; however, when she works with many male psychologists, she thinks of herself as a woman. Morin and Everett (1990: 343–4) explain that it is impossible to know how often people talk to themselves about themselves but they support that there is no question as to whether people actually talk to themselves about themselves. They believe that we all, at some point, have wondered for example, 'how do I feel and why?' and they explain that the extent to which one frequently uses inner speech could explain a person's tendency to direct attention inward. Furthermore, they propose that people having a rich and elaborate self-concept are people that frequently talk to themselves about themselves. According to Morin and Uttl (2013: 3) and Morin (2006), people 'can potentially talk to themselves about a large number of topics related to the self, others and environment' and they also explain that empirical evidence shows that self-reflection is often mediated by one's inner voice (Morin, 2009; Schneider et al., 2005). This argument will be further discussed in the following sections. Table (7.1) describes some indicative measures of inner speech.

In Morin and Uttl's (2013) study, participants (400 students sample) reported that they primarily talk to themselves about themselves and they support that the findings are consistent with the proposed role played by inner speech and self-reflection (Morin and Hamper, 2012). Participants were talking to themselves about private self, aspects (emotions, beliefs) and public self-aspects (physical appearance, behaviour). Table 7.2 describes the most frequently reported inner speech content and functions.

Inner speech serves various important cognitive functions, e.g. planning (Lidstone et al., 2009), self-regulation (Vygotsky, 1934), self-control (Tullett and Inzlicht, 2010) and memory (Buckner et al., 2008). People report talking to themselves mostly about themselves (Morin et al., 2011). Morin and Michaud (2007) explain that inner speech activity is involved during self-information processing and self-reflection tasks. They also explain that more abstract self-aspects need to be verbalized in order to be fully brought to consciousness. According to

Table 7.1   Representative measures of inner speech (Morin and Uttl, 2013: 4)

Measure	Description
Questionnaires	Administrating questionnaires made of self-statements along a variety of domain (e.g. anxious vs non-anxious). Participants rate the frequency of their self-talk using Likert-scale (e.g. from 0 'Never' to 5 'Very often')
Private speech	Recordings of spontaneous speech-for-self emitted by children in social situations
Think out loud method	Recordings of adults' verbalizations as they are working on a given task; participants are explicitly asked to verbalize their thoughts without censoring them
Videotape reconstruction procedure	'Reconstructing' thoughts that participants had during precise situations (e.g. task performance) by showing them video recordings of their behaviour; participants are asked to recall inner speech content as accurately as possible
Thought listing	Retrospectively listing as many thoughts as possible that occurred in specific situations
Thought sampling	Collecting a representative sample of participants' mental experiences in natural settings. Subjects wear beeper that produces audio signals at random intervals throughout the day. They are asked to report the content of their thoughts upon hearing the beep
Electromyographic recordings of tongue movements	Making electromyographic recordings of movements of the lips and tongue during problem-solving tasks. These movements represent an objective external expression of inner speech activity

Table 7.2   Most frequently self-reported inner speech content and functions (Morin and Uttl, 2013: 5)

Inner speech categories	Inner speech content
Self and others – general	• Self-evaluation • Emotions • Physical appearance • Relationships • Problems • Food • Behaviour • Financial situation • Stress • Performance • Future • Education • Beliefs • Others' opinion of self • Hypothetical situations
Functions	• To plan tasks • To remember • To self-motivate • To solve problems

Inner speech categories	Inner speech content
	• To plan when to do specific tasks
	• To think
	• To rehearse upcoming conversations
	• To read, write, calculate
	• To study
	• To control emotions
	• To determine what to wear
	• To self-censor
	• To replay past conversations
Social environment	• Family members
	• Friends
	• People in general
	• Intimate partner
	• Children
Activities	• School and education activities
	• Sports activities
	• Work
	• Leisure activities
	• Chores
	• Music
	• Driving
Physical environment	• Immediate surroundings
Events	• General daily events
	• Future events
	• Past events

Ruby and Legrand (2009) memory recall is directly involved in self-referential processes (like inner speech) and DeSouza et al. (2008) add that inner voice (as discussed above) is directly related to the process of self-reflection (further discussed in the following section). Morin and Hamper (2012), after reviewing a large number of relevant empirical studies, support that speech-for-self is indeed significant when thinking about the self. On the other hand, Williams and Jarrold (2010) as well as Whitehouse et al. (2006) explain that children with autism underuse inner speech whereas Barkley (1997) explains that inner speech is absent if impaired people have a weakened power of agency (ADHD children). Furthermore, people with brain injuries may experience little use of inner speech (Morin, 1993; Rohrer et al., 2008).

Moving away from psychological studies and turning to more sociological conceptualizations Wiley (2006, 2010) attempted a detailed examination of the nature of 'inner speech', on both intra-subjective and dialogical terms. For Wiley, inner speech involves two speakers, but not two persons, for these two speakers are aspects of a single person. Wiley underlines the fact that inner speech employs language but, nevertheless, remains private. This is because 'non-linguistic imagery may also substitute for parts of a (inner) sentence' (Wiley, 2006: 321). Following C.S. Peirce, Wiley states that inner dialogue can be expressed through emotions, sensations, non-linguistic thoughts, speech qualities or even visceral sensations. It is therefore seen that a wide spectrum of intra-active processes are involved. According to Wiley, inner speech (like internal conversation) can be fully understood only by the person within whom it is happening, although that person is capable of giving an account of it to another individual, that is, to an interlocutor. In turn, the interlocutor also chooses which part of each of her/his own inner speech she wishes to share with others and which part to keep private. Wiley states that 'we are little gods in the world of inner speech. We are the only ones, we run the show, we are the boss' (Wiley, 2006: 329) and he explains that we can act because we can think, and the most important thoughts are in the form of inner speech as the pragmatists suggested (already discussed).

The individual uses much the same language format internally as she uses externally but also uses non-linguistic elements. Wiley also explains that 'the inaccessibility [of inner speech] maintains the highly private nature of this language's semantics and syntax' (Wiley, 2006: 337). Although inner speech can and does have linguistic characteristics which would be understood by many individuals, it can also consist of symbols and images which may have meaning for the subject alone; an example might be an individual visualizing the expression on the face of a long dead family member. In this case, the content of inner speech can only be understood directly by the individual who produces it and it is that individual who gives 'permission' to herself about what will be externalized. He further argues that inner speech is partly public or publishable, and partly private, that it is, therefore, a 'semi-private' language. Wiley (2010: 17) further argues that we can act because we can think in this way; action is also exercised through inner speech as we talk our thoughts, options, deliberations and goals. 'Inner speech is the controlling or directing factor in action' but more importantly for Wiley, agency itself seems to be located primarily in inner speech. Inner speech is closely linked to the term 'internal conversation' and according to Wiley (2010) these two terms share common ground.

Duality: intra-action as internal conversation and interaction as external conversation

So far, intra-action has been discussed in relation to dualisms and dualities by incorporating various psychological and certain sociological approaches. The undeniable dialogical structure of intra-action has been revealed through a variety of terms used in current literature: intra-personal communication, dialogical self, voices, self narratives, self talk, egocentric speech and in more detail inner speech. However, this chapter started by emphasizing that intra-action is perceived in this book primarily through the sociological notion of what is called 'internal conversation'. Compared to the previous terms discussed, internal conversation provides a rather explicit understanding regarding the content of intra-action.

'Internal conversation' is a term introduced and advanced by the Critical Realist, Margaret Archer (2000, 2003, 2007) and constitutes an agential property used uniquely by each subject in order to evaluate the social as well as the inner world. Internal conversation refers to the endless dialogues the individual has with her/himself in relation to her/himself and the social environment. In everyday life this dialogue can be about literally anything and may, and often does, incorporate thoughts, dreams, feelings, icons, memories and any other kind of experience that the individual can use in order to deliberate about her/himself and society. Equally important, internal conversation relates to those inner dialogical experiences that the individual may prefer to keep unspoken. Thus, when we refer to 'internal conversation', we refer to personal properties which are known and are experienced only by the individual who produces them. Other individuals are not necessarily aware of them (Chalari, 2009).

Therefore, when we use the term 'internal conversation', we are referring to the dialogical properties of inner life. For Archer (2000, 2003, 2007), internal conversation is 'the personal power that enables us to be the authors of our own projects in society' (Archer, 2003: 34) and Archer maintains that it is 'a personal emergent property' (Archer, 2003: 94). The person is thus understood as an active agent, able to process an external or inner stimulus and then, if appropriate, to externalize a response to it. The individual critically chooses which parts of her internal conversations s/he will share with others, and when s/he will do it, in what way, for what reason, etc. The parts of the internal conversations shared with others are termed 'external conversations' (Chalari, 2009: 1). For example, a student asking her lecturer for an extension might talk in a very polite way to her tutor but, at the same time, might produce a very rude internal (therefore silent) conversation while she is producing the external conversation. 'External conversation refers to the verbal inter-action each person has with one or more individuals, while internal conversation is the non-vocal intra-action the individual has with herself' (Chalari, 2009: 99). External conversation coincides with the normal use of the term conversation. Notably, internal conversation (or parts of it) people produce silently, in their minds, might become external or may remain silent and therefore private and personal. Accordingly, intra-action could potentially become interaction without this being necessary. There are instances between two very close friends or relatives or couples that one part might believe they had said something to the other but actually this had never happened. In such cases, a person is producing internal conversations, which are addressed to somebody else (on an imaginary level), but as these two people are so close and their relationship may be ultimately intimate, the first person genuinely believes that a specific internal conversation was actually external. And of course the reverse may happen, in which case as soon as we say something (perhaps too honest or direct) we immediately regret and realize that what had been said should have remained unspoken. Following Wiley's (2010) views, for any particular individual to produce contributions to external conversation, she first produces internal conversations, since external dialogues originate from internal conversation.

Both Archer and Wiley explain that internal conversation is not understood merely in linguistic terms. Rather, it is described as personal property and as an inner, private and intra-actional process which may involve non-linguistic means and an intra-subjective exchange of actions. Therefore, internal conversation is a broader term that describes 'inner life' and the 'intra-active process [...] of deliberation, evaluation and selection' (Archer, 2003: 63). To be precise, internal conversation consists of 'daydreaming, fantasizing and internal vituperation; rehearsing for some forthcoming encounter, reliving past events, planning for future eventualities, clarifying where one stands or what one understands [...], talking oneself through (or into) a practical activity; to more pointed actions such as issuing internal warnings and making promises to oneself, reaching concrete decisions or coming to a conclusion about a particular problem' (Archer, 2007: 2). Similarly, as Wiley (2006: 321) refers to inner speech, he explains that 'non-linguistic imagery' is involved, as well as 'planning anticipating, rehearsing [...]. This includes both what one will do and how one will do it' (p. 338). In short, external conversation refers to expressed interaction and is associated with conversation *per se*, whereas internal conversation refers to the private, inner cosmos and the ways in which the individual produces intra-action (Chalari, 2012).

However, as already discussed, there are additional forms of intra-action that have already been explored primarily through psychological literature, although some forms are predominantly concerned with dualisms rather than dualities of intra-action. According to Vandenberghe (2005) narration is one of the fundamental characteristics of internal conversation and he explains that narration itself has to be understood as a conversation that is intra-subjectively inter-subjective. Vandenberghe notes that as Mead explains (and as already discussed through Vocate, Hermans and Brinthaupt and Lipka) individuals do not only have conversations with oneself as oneself. We also have conversations with ourselves as others (internal conversations between oneself and our parents, friends, lovers). The author thus explains that in order to properly understand how personal identity is formed, we also need to consider that the internal conversation takes the form of a narration, and it is through an internal conversation with oneself that one communicates with the other. Even in the cases that one narrates to oneself, the (significant) other(s) (friends, partner, family) remain present as an inner witness of the personal identity to which the person is committing her/himself and is responsible about (perhaps our parents are often 'present' while we produce internal conversations about vital decisions, judgements, preferences). Finally, as King (2010) maintains, humans are indeed able to engage eventually in an internal conversation, which takes place between a conscious 'I' who acts and a self-conscious 'Me' who experiences that action. This is how it becomes possible for individuals to consider the society around them, their place in it and their actions. King explains that individuals cannot be merely perceived as parts of social groups as they are able to judge for themselves and adapt their perspectives and practices.

It is therefore understood, that internal conversation is a broader term (not restricted to internalized linguistic forms of interaction), which can provide a specific and complete definition of what intra-action involves. Additionally, the concept of internal conversation promotes the agential properties of the individual by separating inner life from the external/social world. As will be further discussed, internal conversation enables human reflexivity to form the link between individuals with society. As reflexivity has become one of the most popular areas of sociological discussion, various views have been offered; again, the main distinction between diverse views on reflexivity relates with the approaches that perceive structure and agency in terms of dualism or duality.

Reflexivity: applied intra-action

The concept of reflexivity has been employed particularly in current social theory as a way to explain the connection between structure and agency. As reflexivity refers to the ways agency (or the self, the individual or human being) is related to structure (social institutions, social systems or social reality) it might be easy to conclude that reflexivity is about interaction. Indeed, some scholars may further promote such a view. However, reflexivity is primarily perceived as a subjective ability that enables individuals to get in contact with other individuals or aspects of the wider society. Reflexivity therefore, is primarily understood as a subjective process, which is experienced separately by every individual. Accordingly, it is related with inner life and the ways action is exchanged within the individual. Reflexivity is ultimately explained as a specific form of intra-action, which enables individuals to produce interaction if that might be(come) relevant. It is thus described as applied intra-action since, according to relevant literature, it constitutes a separate and distinct human ability, or property, related to subjectivity and agency. Once again, reflexivity as a concept, as well as a form of applied intra-action has been discussed and explained through two main approaches: as a relationship between structure and agency, which is perceived as a dualism (two sides of the same coin) or being perceived as a duality (interdependent but separate concepts).

Reflexivity as dualism

The concept of reflexivity is not new in sociology. However, it has recently received increasing attention as a way to describe the relationship between structure and agency. For the classic social theorists Marx, Weber and Durkheim (with the exception of Simmel as discussed in earlier chapters) have all engaged (through different views) in the examination of this unique relationship by concluding that social reality is investigated as a dualism of structure and agency (perceived as interrelated concepts). In accordance with those views, although using different perspectives, Habermas' theory of communicative action,

Foucault's archaeology, Bourdieu's concept of the habitus and even Alexander's multi-dimensional sociology further promote the analysis and explanation of the relationship of structure and agency as a dualism. Certain contemporary philosophers like Foucault, Baudrillard or Rorty have even concluded that 'the self does not amount to much' (Lyotard, 1984: 15). Taylor (1975: 989) suggests that 'modern self' refers to a particular mode of subjectivity although he believes that self is constructed in the social field. At the same time, he states that human is a 'self interpreting animal' because of the linguistic/communicative forms of interaction followed. As Smith (2010: 49) states 'Taylor is clear that self, like meaning, is always constructed in a (social) field'.

The significance of symbolic meaning as a form of explaining the connection between the social reality and the self has already been extensively discussed. For example, according to Arnason (1989: 28), 'The self can be understood as a magma of imaginary significations constructed by a self-interpreting animal that is condemned to meaning; a magma that is structured and organized in a meaningful way to provide a meaningful orientation in a world that is not intrinsically meaningful.' Such influential interpretation of the relationship between structure and agency constitutes one of the core paradigms regarding the explanation of intra-action as well as reflexivity in terms of dualism. For Smith (2010) individuals are situated in fields of meaning, which are co-constructed with other individuals through inter-action. The self therefore, is constructed both within and from these fields. Such view is a typical perception of the relationship between structure and agency as a dualism.

In accordance to the above-mentioned approaches, reflexivity is defined as 'a very specific mode of self-knowledge (...) it is not a common practice for all human subjects, but it is the capacity to make our "self" the object of "reflexion"' (Smith, 2010: 52). What is important though, is not to just 'do it' but to 'think about how one does it' (p. 53). Taylor explains that 'radical reflexivity' reveals presence to oneself which is inseparable from one's being the agent of experience. He emphasizes the crucial difference between the way that an individual experiences her/his own actions and emotions, and the way other individuals perceive the same actions and emotions. According to Taylor, this is what makes each individual capable of speaking of itself in the first person (Taylor, 1989). Smith (2010) further argues that 'radical reflexivity' refers to the awareness of our awareness and the experience of our experience. Therefore, although reflexivity is indeed related to the individual who experiences it, it is perceived in relation to the interpretations of other individuals as well as the one who experiences it.

Moving away from the emphasis on meaning but remaining in the paradigm of dualism, reflexivity is once again used as the form of explaining the relationship between structure and agency through Giddens' theory of 'structuration'. According to Giddens, reflexivity refers to the 'direct feedback from knowledge to action'; however, reflexivity should not be perceived merely as 'self-consciousness' but as the consistent monitoring of the constant flow of social life (Giddens, 1984: 3).

For Giddens, reflexivity concerns the 'continuous monitoring of action which human beings display and expect others to display. The reflexive monitoring of action depends upon rationalization, understood here as a process rather than a state and as inherently involved in the competence of agents' (Giddens, 1984: 3). In this context, Giddens describes reflexivity as a form of monitoring everyday life through means of rationalization. Furthermore, Beck et al. (1994: 154) argue that self-reflection is strongly related to modernization and the increase of knowledge and scientization. They distinguish reflexivity from reflection by saying that reflexivity pertains to the undesired transition from industrial to risk society (Beck et al., 1994). In this sense, reflexivity is inevitably related to structures, rules, knowledge and modernization.

Donati (2011: 21) further clarifies that 'reflexive modernization' as used by Ulrich Beck (1992, 1995) refers to the ways through which modernity 'becomes its own issue'. However, Donatti explains that for Beck et al. (2003: 3) reflexivity is not about enabling individuals to lead a more conscious life. Elder-Vass (2007a, 2007b, 2007c) further supports the view that Beck et al. do not distinguish between the different types of reflexivity as they do not explain the difference between the role of socio-cultural structures and the role of personal and social reflexivity. Donati (following Latour, 2003) clarifies that reflexivity (as discussed above), does not signify an increase in mastery and consciousness. The reason is that structure and agency are perceived as a dualism and therefore reflexivity (as the relationship between the two) is not about promoting the significance of agency and the role of individuals within society, but rather to emphasize the interdependence between these two concepts. It is thus understood that through this approach, reflexivity is defined in diverse manners, which are not in accordance to the usage of the term intra-action (as defined in this book). However, approaches that promote the concept of reflexivity through duality offer a more specific interpretation of reflexivity as an applied form of intra-action.

Reflexivity as duality

The most concrete explanation of reflexivity is offered by Archer (2007: 4); she defines reflexivity as 'the regular exercise of the mental ability, shared by all normal people, to consider themselves in relation to their (social) contexts and vice versa'. Donati (2011) emphasizes that reflexivity is synonymous with internal conversation, and therefore is perceived as a human ability rather than a characteristic of social networks and organizations. It can, however, be extended to social groups, given that they can express a collective mode of reflexivity. Archer's work on reflexivity has become a central reference in the sociological study of the interplay between structure and agency (King, 2010; Caetano, 2015). Archer's main contribution refers to the clarity of what reflexivity stands for, and more importantly to the fact that reflexivity is defined through internal conversation(s) which activates the causal powers of structures and allows individuals to form their actions based on the interplay between their own personal concerns and the social conditions (restrictions and enablements) that make it possible to accomplish them. Reflexivity, exercised by internal dialogues, not only mediates the impact that structures have on agents, it also conditions individual responses to particular social situations (Caetano, 2015).

A key element of Archer's proposal is that even though reflexivity is perceived as an ability that all individuals can potentially exercise, different people exercise it differently. Based on qualitative research carried out by means of biographical interviews, Archer (2012) proposes a typology of four modes of reflexivity: a) communicative; b) autonomous; c) meta; and d) fractured (see Table 7.3). All individuals are potentially able or already have exercised each of the modes of reflexivity to varying degrees on different occasions and in different situations but, Archer explains that, the majority of people exhibit a dominant mode at any particular point in time.

The question, however, one might ask is: in what way(s) is reflexivity perceived as applied intra-action? The answer relates primarily through the ways that internal conversation is used. Archer explains that the mode of reflexivity helps us to conceptually 'open up' many everyday mental activities and ultimately 'make our way through the world': 'mulling-over' (a problem, situation or relationship), 'planning' (the day, the week or further ahead), 'imagining' (as in 'what would happen if …?'), 'deciding' (debating what to do or what is for the best), 'rehearsing' (practising what to say or do), 'reliving' (some event, episode or relationship), 'prioritizing' (working out what matters to you most), 'imaginary conversations' (with people you know, have known or have known about), 'budgeting' (working out if you can afford to do something, in terms of money, time or effort) and 'clarifying' (sorting out what you think about some issue, person or problem) (Archer, 2012: 13). All these very specific intra-active practices are fully experienced only by the individual concerned and some or the entire internal conversation associated to such deliberations may or may not be revealed. Although this typology is very specific, Archer explains that the way reflexivity is practised does not derive from homogeneous processes of internal deliberation; rather, it is exercised in diverse ways

Table 7.3　Reflexivity modes as defined by Archer (2012: 13)

Communicative Reflexivity	Internal Conversations need to be confirmed and completed by others before they lead to action
Autonomous Reflexivity	Internal Conversations are self-contained, leading directly to action
Meta-Reflexivity	Internal Conversations critically evaluate previous inner dialogues and are critical about effective action in society
Fractured Reflexivity	Internal Conversations cannot lead to purposeful courses of action, but intensify personal distress and disorientation resulting in expressive action

depending on the relations people establish with their social contexts and their main concerns. Intra-action is involved precisely in this process, which is indeed distinct for each individual.

Applied intra-action through mediation

Such process has been termed 'mediation' by Chalari (2009) and refers to: 'the deliberative process that enables the individual to achieve a subjectively-defined degree of "inner balance" between her inner and external world which is satisfactory to her' (Chalari, 2009: 1–2). Individuals produce internal conversations in order to deliberate reflexively upon themselves and society; then, they may externalize their internal conversations, notably in different ways, although their reasons for doing so might be similar. As Archer maintains, each individual evaluates external situations in different ways and responds accordingly. External conversation (and therefore interaction in wider terms) derives from internal conversation and is connected with internal conversation in a particular way, which may differ dramatically between different individuals.

As I have discussed elsewhere (Chalari, 2009, 2012), every individual tries to find the best way to externalize what s/he internally may consider appropriate. However, there is no standardized method that all individuals use in order to interact with themselves (and thus produce intra-action) and others. Some individuals might maintain a stable and satisfactory relationship with themselves and others, whereas for other people it may be extremely difficult to find peace of mind. It is profound, of course, that there is no such thing as 'permanent happiness', but it seems that all individuals try to achieve dialogically a subjectively defined degree of (most of the time ephemeral) balance between their inner concerns and their outer social environment, whatever that might mean for each one of us. And indeed, it is unimaginable what human beings are capable of doing (or not doing), in order to get as close as it might be possible to their own 'inner peace of mind'. 'Mediation' therefore, is the process that enables the constant exercise of intra-action and constitutes the process that provides individuals with the means to exercise reflexivity as defined by Archer. The exact way that mediation operates (and possible combinations with reflexivity) can be found in Figure 7.1.

This diagram describes possible ways that intra-action may be experienced, associated to internal conversation as well as external conversation (namely interaction). Here it is argued that external conversation (or any form of interaction or a stimulus associated to interaction) can be internalized by the individual and further processed in a form of interplay between what we care about (personal concerns) and what we have to be concerned about (social expectations). An example could be of a young girl who wants to spend the night with her boyfriend but her parents prohibit such an option; the girl wants to stay out late but she also considers her parents' prohibitions. She therefore struggles between what she wants to do and what she has to do. This interplay is experienced in the form of internal conversation

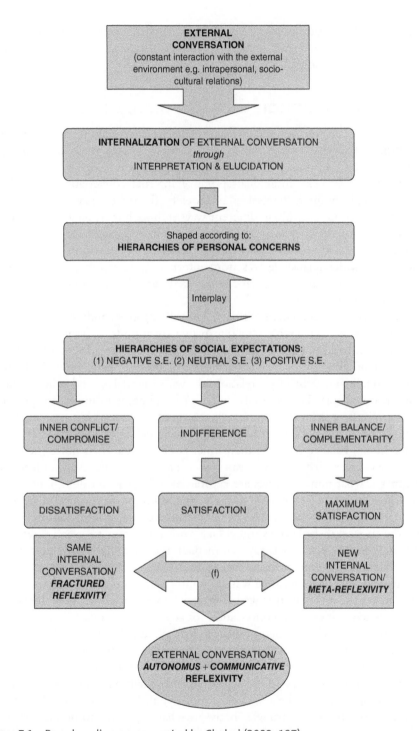

Figure 7.1   Based on diagram presented by Chalari (2009: 197)

(as defined by Archer) and constitutes an intra-active process, which involves personal as well as social qualities. This interplay may result in: a) inner conflict, which probably involves some level of compromise (the young girl going back home in time but being dissatisfied, annoyed and disappointed); b) indifference (the girl doesn't really care about what her parents tell her and she is therefore doing whatever she wants to do); and c) inner balance (in the case that her parents actually allow her to spend the night out) and therefore the girl can do what she wants to do and her parents approve of her concerns. In each of the above-mentioned cases, the young girl (or any individual) may follow three options: i) keep on reproducing the same internal conversations (could be related to Fractured Reflexivity); ii) externalize the whole aspect of the internal conversation(s) (could be associated with Communicative and Autonomous Reflexivity); and iii) begin new internal conversation(s) (could be referred to Meta-Reflexivity).

This is an applied way of perceiving intra-action by utilizing Archer's theory of internal conversation and reflexivity as well as Chalari's process of mediation. What has to remain clear is that in each case, the interplay between the personal 'wants' and the 'social shoulds' each individual experiences within oneself, constitutes a subjective, personal and therefore intra-active experience which may or may not be externalized. For each individual such interplay is unique and the outcome of such a process can be fully experienced, monitored, controlled, evaluated and ultimately explained, only by the individual concerned. The central role of the sociological and psychological empirical investigation of internal conversation (or even inner speech) is profound. Still, the theoretical foundations of this exploration are now in place and the initial attempts for such investigations have already been discussed. Intra-action is therefore discussed as a process equally important with that of interaction as they constitute interdependent and interconnected concepts although they do not coincide. The exploration of the one concept, definitely promotes the understanding of the other.

Summary

This chapter offered a definition of what intra-action is by incorporating the two main ways that this concept could be approached: as a dualism and as a duality. A brief overview of the origins of intra-action has been discussed by including the works of Georg Simmel, American Pragmatism, as well as Piaget and Vygotsky. Certain theories and applications associated to intra-action have been discussed; first, through the paradigm of dualism which has been related with views that may explain intra-action through dialogical terms; second, through the paradigm of duality which has been associated with views that could explain intra-action through the district concepts of inner speech and internal conversation. Following that, the notion of reflexivity has be introduced as an applied approach to intra-action and again, the paradigms of dualism and duality have been discussed separately. Finally, the idea of mediation has been analysed as a way to explain applied intra–action.

• •

Concepts in Context

A gay couple have lived together for the last ten years. After a serious car accident one of them (Richard) lost his ability to walk and the other (Chris) managed to start using his feet again after one year. Richard is Canadian and Chris is Greek-Canadian. They spend most of their time in Vancouver and visit Athens occasionally. They feel that their life is easier in Canada, as perhaps certain social structures are more open and supportive. In one of their visits to Greece, Richard got closer and spent some time with a Greek family with a child in a wheel chair. This experience made him realize even more intensively that he wanted to be a father. When he told Chris about his plan, Chris immediately turned down the idea and explained that for as long as they are in Greece, adopting a child is just not an option for gay couples as society is not ready to accept such a thing. Although Richard was surprised he insisted that they would both be wonderful fathers and that they should consider this decision more seriously. They could go back and start the adoption procedures in Canada. Chris was distressed. He knew that Richard would have been a very good parent but Chris also knew that deep down he didn't want to take the responsibility of raising a child on his own. He was afraid that Richard's condition will not allow him to always be there for the child and therefore, Chris would have to give up everything for this child to be raised. Chris also knew that it would have been very difficult for his Greek family to accept the possibility that he will adopt a child. He thinks to himself 'It was already dramatic for them to accept that I am gay, how could I ever tell them that I will now be a gay father raising an adopted child with my disabled partner?' and he was considering that 'such an idea is not only against my family's views, or against Greek society's stereotypes … such idea would be against common sense!' He lost sleep, as he couldn't stop considering what he would do. He refused to talk to Richard about it. What could he tell Richard? He would hurt Richard so much! He could hear so many voices in his head and they were so 'noisy' that after a point he couldn't even understand what all these voices in his mind were telling him. But he knew that he was distressed and unsettled and on bad terms with his partner whom he didn't want to lose.

• •

——— SELF-REFLECTIVE QUESTIONS ———————————

1. How can we study this person's 'intra-active' experiences?
2. In what forms is intra-action experienced?
3. Why is this specific intra-active experience complex?

Possible ways of exploring the questions offered in this chapter and Further Readings:

1. In this (quite extreme and complex) example, Chris is struggling to figure out how he should respond to a clear conflict between: a) social expectations (deriving primarily from family and also social stereotypes); b) how he could make his partner happy (through raising a child with him); and c) what he really wants (to make his partner happy but without having to raise a child on his own and without provoking his family any further). Is there a realistically achievable solution to such a struggle? Perhaps there is (adopting a child in Vancouver, where this opportunity could be offered to gay couples and receive support if needed to raise the child). But this is not necessarily what Chris is trying to figure out. In fact, he is trying to find a way to cope with what is happening inside his mind.

Further Reading:

Chalari, A. (2009) *Approaches to the Individual: The Relationship between Internal and External Conversation*. London: Palgrave Macmillan.

2. Chris is experiencing endless internal conversations inside his mind with Richard, with his family, his friends, the social services, the homophobes who might attack him, even with the child that they may adopt. He is experiencing various versions of inner speeches between himself and all these 'others'. He hears voices, he is involved in dialogues, arguments, disagreements. He is experiencing endless emotions and he is trying to find the right responses to potential external conversations that he might share with others about his thoughts, his feelings, his needs and his own desires. He is involved in a multi-level battle of endless parallel inner conversations, dialogues, speeches, talks with himself and other 'voices' (talks), or other feelings (fear), structures (stereotypes) or even future possibilities. Such an intense exchange of action within oneself, inevitably keeps Chris' mind quite busy.

Further Reading:

Hermans, H.J.M. and Hermans-Konoplka, A. (2010) *Dialogical Self Theory: Positioning and Counter Positioning in a Globalizing Society*. Cambridge: Cambridge University Press.

Morin, A. and Hamper, B. (2012) 'Self-reflection and the inner-voice: activation of the left inferior frontal gyrus during perceptual and conceptual self-referential thinking'. *The Open Neuroimaging Journal*, 6: 78–89.

3.   Chris is producing reflexive deliberations as he tries to consider himself in relation to what he wants to do and what social reality expects him to do. He is producing endless circles of new and old internal conversations with himself about what he really wants and how prepared he is to fight against everyone and everything for it. Chris is not talking to anyone about his thoughts, his fears, his needs or his anxieties. Perhaps, because he was raised in a family unwilling to hear his concerns. Then again, it might be the right time to talk to a professional psychotherapist, as the frustration is so intense that his everyday life is affected. But even if this is what he is going to do he would still have to make a decision and then he would have to deal with the consequences of this decision on a personal and interpersonal level. But then again, there are already consequences he needs to deal with, for as long as he is keeping all these internal conversations unspoken.

Further Reading:

Archer, M.S. (2007) *Making Our Way Through the World: Human Reflexivity and Social Mobility*. Cambridge: Cambridge University Press.

Such complex and intense experience of various forms of intra-action including voices, inner speeches and dialogues, internal conversations, social prohibitions and even enablements, endless emotions and also the need to maintain a functional everyday life, do not constitute a rare or extreme state of inner life. Actually, such intra-active processes (and perhaps even more) may be experienced by any individual on an everyday basis, for an unimaginable number of reasons, within an endless combination of social circumstances and interactions. And every single individual needs to find a way to move on in life and remain able to co-exist with others. *This is why intra-action may be perceived as the centre of the human existence; it includes everything that is happening inside our selves that allows us to interact with everyone including ourselves.*

Conclusion

This book explored, through the eyes of a sociologist, a wide variety of sociological and psychological literature associated with the sociological exploration of the individual. To do that, specific concepts were examined which are often (if not always) involved in the discussion about the ways agency is related to structure. Such concepts include interaction (and symbolic interaction), socialization, identity, self, conscious and unconscious self. Finally the concept of intra-action was discussed as a possible synthesized sociological explanation of the notion of the individual. Every chapter was designed in a way that could reveal the crucial relevance of each (of the above-mentioned) concepts to the exploration of the individual along with the inevitable limitations of each perspective to actually provide a specific, explicit and clear definition of what the individual is.

This book tried to explore areas that probably any sociologist (and even psychologist) would consider appropriate or relevant in the investigation of a specific understanding of the individual (in relation to society). Admittedly, a plurality of related views has been discussed but unsurprisingly, each of them were offering either over-generalized or over-specialized or even vague or complex explanations, which could not be easily employed in this book's attempt to provide a synthesized sociological explanation of the individual. At the same time, it would have been impossible to exclude any of these views as they all contributed towards the construction of a blended sociological evaluation of the concept of intra-action as a potential way of explaining the essence of the individual. Regrettably, although even more views and approaches could have been included, it would have been beyond the purpose of this book to include every single perspective and interpretation associated to the sociological and psychological investigation of the individual.

Over the years that I have been engaged with the sociological exploration of the notion of the individual, I have been driven by the inevitable realization that the individual can only be studied in relation to society. Indeed, this unquestionable principle has been followed extensively in such a plurality of psychological and sociological attempts to explain concepts related to the individual. Many of those approaches employ the extraordinary conceptualization of interaction, to describe, analyse and explain the meaning of the individual (or self) in relation to society. And indeed, as Simmel very correctly stated, interaction between individuals constitutes the basis of society. Therefore, if we are able to explore the ways individuals exchange action between them then we could potentially understand society as a whole.

But, surprisingly enough, the exchange of action was primarily investigated while taking place between individuals. Still, such exchange of action derived by individuals themselves, therefore, inevitably leads to some short of exchange of action taking place within the individual. Such realization was mainly explained again in terms of interaction, as whatever is happening within the individual has been perceived as a 'replicate' of what is happening outside and around the individual. And this is a conceptualization of the relationship between structure and agency that is perceived as a dualism. The individual can only be studied, analysed and explained through its connection to society.

For many years, this realization seemed to me enormously inspiring and indeed it was. But I was not able to understand the cases that certain individuals managed to operate 'outside the social/cultural box', the cases of those who tried and some succeeded in moving away from family anticipations and community expectations; and cases of other individuals who enabled their selves to lead a fulfilling and meaningful life. This was perhaps the reason why I became passionate with the idea of intra-action.

Probably because it helped me understand that inter-action is taking place because individuals themselves allow such structured exchanges of action to be formed within specific social circumstances. And individuals are able to produce interaction because we are able to produce and experience intra-action first. We are able to experience exchange of action within ourselves, within our minds, and we are able to do (or not do) something with and about it. Intra-action may explain why individuals may think, act and behave in different ways and ultimately why individuals are different even on the occasions of social environments that operate under extremely restricted authorities. Views that are able to explain and support such approaches are mainly related with duality as a way to explain the relationship between structure and agency.

But after the realization that perhaps intra-action might be a rather simplified way to understand the individual in a synthesized manner, it remained pivotal to recognise that intra-action can be fully explored in relation to interaction, as it is because of the sociological exploration of interaction that intra-action was revealed as a missing sociological area of exploration. Still, as it was repeatedly emphasized throughout this book, intra-action and interaction constitute a duality rather than a dualism, as they can be studied, analysed and explained distinctly. Still the interconnected form of their relation has to be explicitly recognized and emphatically promoted.

Therefore, intra-action had to be examined through the overview of related concepts, terms, notions, theorizations and ideas, which either disclosed the multiple interactional aspects of the relationship between structure and agency or concentrated on the agentic properties of this eternal association. In either case, intra-action has been promoted as an additional way that supports the connection between the individual and society in terms of duality.

While approaching the completion of this project, I am hoping that the main targets of this attempt have been met:

- This book offered a thorough, critical and simplified overview of key sociological and psychological concepts related to the sociological exploration of the individual.

- It has been able to explain the limitations related to each conceptualization regarding its ability to provide a concrete definition of what the individual is.

- It has tried to combine in a balanced way, sociological and psychological explanations of the approaches that have been employed, in a complementary rather than contradictory way.

- It has offered a rather simplified opportunity to a wider public to get engaged with fairly complex sociological and psychological intellectual discussions regarding the ways the individual is connected to society.

- It has inspired, through everyday examples, a more comprehensive understanding of applicable sociological and psychological theorizations related to the individual.

- It has combined, in a critical and synthesized manner, sociological and psychological views towards the construction of a meaningful, comprehensible and applicable sociological theorization of intra-action.

- Finally, it has made clear that the relationship between the individual and society or between structure and agency can be approached through the combined as well as distinct examination of the concepts of interaction and intra-action.

The exciting exploration of the relationship between structure and agency remains an eternal enterprise which hopefully will keep on inspiring even more sociologists (and hopefully psychologists) who might be willing to further promote and expand such a fundamental and inspirational exploration of knowledge. This book aimed at offering an additional view or perspective associated to intra-action and its connection to interaction, as a synthesized way to approach the relationship between the individual and society.

Bibliography

Introduction

Adams, M. (2007) *Self and Social Change*. London: Sage.

Apter, T. and Garnsey, E. (1994) 'Enacting inequality: structure, agency and gender'. *Women's Studies International Forum*, 17(1): 19–31.

Archer, M.S. (2003) *Structure, Agency and the Internal Conversation*. Cambridge: Cambridge University Press.

Archer, M.S. (2007) *Making Our Way Through the World: Human Reflexivity and Social Mobility*. Cambridge: Cambridge University Press.

Bratman, M.E. (2007) *Structures of Agency: Essays*. Oxford: Oxford University Press.

Burkitt, I. (2008) *Social Selves: Theories of Self and Society*. London: Sage.

Elder-Vass, D. (2010) *The Causal Powers of Social Structures: Emergence, Structure and Agency*. Cambridge: Cambridge University Press.

Elliott, A. (2009) *Concepts of Self*. Cambridge: Polity.

Fleetwood, S. (2008) 'Structure, institution, agency, habit and reflexive deliberation'. *Journal of Institutional Economics*, 4(2): 183–203.

Harre, R. and Moghaddam, F. (2003) *The Self and Others: Positioning Individuals and Groups in Personal, Political and Cultural Contexts*. London: Praeger.

Hewitt, J.P. (1997) *Self and Society: A Symbolic Interactionist Social Psychology*. Boston, MA: Allyn and Bacon.

Hitlin, S. and Elder, G.H. (2007) 'Time, self and the curiously abstract concept of agency'. *Sociological Theory*, 25(2): 170–91.

Kogler, H.H. (2012) 'Agency and the other: on the intersubjective roots of self-identity'. *New Ideas in Psychology*, 30: 47–64.

May, V. (2013) *Connecting Self and Society: Belonging in a Changing World*. London: Palgrave Macmillan.

Wang, Y. (2008) 'Agency: the internal split of structure'. *Sociological Forum*, 23(3): 481–502.

Chapter 1

Abrams, D., Hopthrow, T., Frings, D. and Hulbert, L.G. (2006) 'Groupthink? The effect of alcohol on risk attraction among groups versus individuals'. *Journal of Studies on Alcohol*, 67(4): 628–36.

Agger, B. (1998) *Critical Social Theories: An Introduction*. Boulder, CO: Westview.

Aiello, J.R. and Douthitt, E.Z. (2001) 'Social facilitation from Triplett to electronic performance monitoring'. *Group Dynamics: Theory, Research and Practice*, 5: 163–80.

Ajrouch, K.A. (2007) 'Reference groups', in G. Ritzer (ed.), *The Blackwell Encyclopaedia of Sociology*. Malden, MA: Blackwell, 3828–9.

Archer, M.S. (2003) *Structure, Agency and Internal Conversation*. Cambridge: Cambridge University Press.

Archer, M.S. (2007) *Making Our Way Through the World: Human Reflexivity and Social Mobility*. Cambridge: Cambridge University Press.

Asch, S.E. (1952) *Social Psychology*. New York: Prentice-Hall.

Blau, P. (1964) *Exchange and Power in Social Life*. New York: Wiley.

Blau, P. (1994) *Structural Contexts of Opportunities*. Chicago: University of Chicago Press.

Bougle, C. (1905) 'Review of soziologie'. *L'Année Sociologique*, vol. xi, 1906–9: 18.

Brandstatter, H., Davis, J.H. and Stocker-Kreichgauer, G. (1982) *Group Decision Making*. New York: Academic Press.

Carrigan, M. (2015) 'Between interaction and intra-action' available at: http://markcarrigan.net/2014/10/13/between-interaction-and-intra-action/ (visited in July 2015).

Chalari, A. (2009) *Approaches to the Individual: The Relationship between Internal and External Conversation*. London: Palgrave Macmillan.

Chalari, A. (2012) 'The causal impact of resistance: mediating between resistance and internal conversation about resistance'. *Journal for the Theory of Social Behaviour*, 43(1): 66–86.

Charon, J.M. (2011) *Symbolic Interactionism: An Introduction, an Interpretation, an Integration* (10th ed.). New Delhi: PHI Learning Private Limited.

Chen, L.H., Baker, S.P., Braver, E.R. and Li, G. (2000) 'Carrying passengers as a risk factor for crashes fatal to 16- and 17-year-old drivers'. *Journal of the American Medical Association*, 283: 1578–82.

Chriss, J.J. (2007) 'Networks', in G. Ritzer (ed.), *The Blackwell Encyclopaedia of Sociology*. Malden, MA: Blackwell, 3182–5.

Cicourel, A. (1981) 'Notes on the integration of micro- and macro-levels of analysis', in K. Knorr-Cetina and A. Cicourel (eds), *Advances in Social Theory and Methodology*. New York: Methuen, 51–79.

Collins, R. (1975) *Conflict Sociology: Toward an Explanatory Science*. New York: Academic Press.

Collins, R. (1981) 'On the microfoundations of macrosociology'. *American Journal of Sociology*, 86: 984–1014.

Cooley, C.H. (1909) *Social Organization: A Study of the Larger Mind*. New York: Charles Scribner's Sons.

Craib, I. (1997) *Classic Social Theory: An Introduction to the Thought of Marx, Weber, Durkheim and Simmel*. Oxford: Oxford University Press.

Davies, B. (2014) 'Reading anger in early childhood intra-actions: a diffractive analysis'. *Qualitative Inquiry*, 20(6): 734–41.

Habermas, J. (1970) *Towards a Rational Society*. Boston: Beacon Press.

Habermas, J. (1971) *Knowledge and Human Interests*. Boston: Beacon Press.

Habermas, J. (1984) *The Theory of Communicative Action*. Vol. 1, *Reason and the Rationalization of Society*. Boston: Beacon Press.

Hardy, C. and Latane, B. (1986) 'Social loafing in a cheering task'. *Social Science*, 71: 165–72.

Harkins, S.G. (1981) 'Effects of Task Difficulty and Task Responsibility on Social Loafing'. Presentation of the *First International Conference on Social Process in Small Groups*. North Carolina: Kill Devil Hills.

Hoigaard, R., Safvenbom, R. and Tonnessen, F.E. (2006) 'The relationship between group cohesion, group norms and perceived social loafing in soccer teams'. *Small Group Research*, 37(3): 217–32.

Hwang, W.-Y., Hsu, J.-L., Tretiakov, A., Chou, H.-W. and Lee, C.-Y. (2009) 'Intra-action, interaction and outeraction in blended learning environments'. *Educational Technology & Society*, 12(2): 222–39.

Janis, I.L. (1971) 'Groupthink'. *Psychology Today*, November: 43–6.

Janis, I.L. (1982) 'Counteracting the adverse effects of concurrence-seeking in policy-planning groups: theory and research perspectives', in H. Brandstatter, J.H. Davis and G. Stocker-Kreichgauer (eds), *Group Decision Making*. New York: Academic Press.

Jerolmack, C. (2009) 'Humans, animals and play: theorising interaction when inter-subjectivity is problematic'. *Sociological Theory*, 27(4): 371–89.

Kadushin, C. (2012) *Understanding Social Networks: Theories, Concepts and Findings*. New York: Oxford University Press.

Karau, S.J. and Williams, K.D. (1993) 'Social loafing: a meta-analytic review and theoretical integration'. *Journal of Personality and Social Psychology*, 65: 681–706.

Kinney, W.J. (2007) 'Asch experiments', in G. Ritzer (ed.), *The Blackwell Encyclopaedia of Sociology*. Malden, MA: Blackwell: 189–91.

Kugihara, N. (1999) 'Gender and social loafing in Japan'. *Journal of Social Psychology*, 139: 516–26.

Martin, R., Hewstone, M. and Martin, P.Y. (2008) 'Majority versus minority: the role of message processing in determining resistance to counter-persuasion'. *European Journal of Social Psychology*, 38: 16–34.

McGrath, J.E. (1984) *Interaction and Performance*. Englewood Cliff, NJ: Prentice-Hall.

Merton, R. and Kitt, A.S. (1950) 'Contributions to the theory of reference group behaviour', in R.K. Merton and P.F. Lazarsfeld (eds), *Continuities in Social Research*. Glencoe, IL: Free Press.

Milgram, S. (1974) *Obedience to Authority: An Experimental View*. New York: Harper & Row.

Mouzelis, N. (2008) *Modern and Postmodern Social Theorising: Bridging and Divide.* Cambridge: Cambridge University Press.

Mullen, B., Bryant, B. and Driskell, J.E. (1997) 'Presence of others and arousal: an integration'. *Group Dynamics: Theory, Research and Practice*, 1: 52–64.

Nehring, D. (2013) *Sociology: An Introductory Textbook to the Reader.* London: Routledge.

Nemeth, C.J., Personnaz, B., Personnaz, M. and Goncalo, J.A. (2004) 'The liberating role of conflict in group creativity: a study in two countries'. *European Journal of Social Psychology*, 34: 365–74.

Pampel, F.C. (2000) *Sociological Lives and Ideas: An Introduction to the Classical Theorists.* New York: Worth.

Parsons, T. (1951) *The Social System.* Glencoe, IL: Free Press.

Pfeffer, M.J. and Parra, P.A. (2009) 'Strong ties, weak ties and human capital: Latino immigrant employment outside the enclave'. *Rural Sociology*, 74(2): 241–69.

Poggi, G. (2005) 'Max Weber and Georg Simmel', in A. Harrington (ed.), *Modern Social Theory: An Introduction.* Oxford: Oxford University Press, 64–86.

Rietzschel, E.F., Nijstad, B.A. and Stroebe, W. (2006) 'Productivity is not enough: a comparison of interactive and nominal brainstorming groups on idea generation and selection'. *Journal of Experimental Social Psychology*, 42: 244–51.

Ritzer, G. and Stepnisky, J. (2014) *Sociological Theory* (9th ed.). New York: McGraw-Hill.

Shaw, M. (1981) *Group Dynamics: The Psychology of Small Group Behaviour.* New York: McGraw-Hill.

Shepperd, J.A. and Taylor, K.M. (1999) 'Ascribing advantages to social comparison targets'. *Basic and Applied Social Psychology*, 21: 103–17.

Siebold, G.L. (2007) 'The essence of military cohesion'. *Armed Forces and Society*, 33(2): 286–95.

Simmel, G. (1908a) *Soziologie*, repr as *The Sociology of Georg Simmel*, K.H. Wolff (ed.). New York: Free Press, 1950 (original in German).

Simmel, G. (1908b) 'Conflict', repr in *Conflict and the Web of Group Affiliations*, K. Wolff (ed.). New York: Free Press, 1955 (original in German).

Simmel, G. (1908c) 'The significance of numbers in social life', in *Soziologie*, repr as *The Sociology of Georg Simmel*, K.H. Wolff (ed.). New York: Free Press, 1950 (original in German).

Simmel, G. (1950) *The Sociology of Georg Simmel.* Translated, edited and with an introduction by K. H. Wolff. New York: Free Press.

Smith, D. (1979) 'A sociology for women', in J.A. Sherman and E.T. Beck (eds), *The Prism of Sex: Essays in Sociology of Knowledge.* Madison, WI: University of Wisconsin Press.

Stryker, S. (1998) 'Communicative action in the new social movements: the experience of the students for a democratic society'. *Current Perspective in Social Theory*, 18: 79–98.

Vom Lehn, D. (2007) *The Young and the Digital: What the Migration to Social Network Sites, Games and Anytime, Anywhere Media Means for Our Future.* Boston: Beacon Press.

Watier, W. (2008) 'Georg Simmel', in R. Stones (ed.), *Key Sociological Thinkers.* London: Palgrave Macmillan, 90–105.

Webster, M. and Sell, J. (2012) 'Groups and Institutions, Structures and Processes', in G. Ritzer (ed.), *The Wiley-Blackwell Companion to Sociology.* Malden, MA: Wiley-Blackwell, 139–63.

Wolfson, A. (2005) 'A hoax most cruel'. *The Courier Journal,* 9 October.

Wortham, J. (2013) 'A growing app lets you see it, then you don't'. *New York Times,* 9 February, A1, A3.

Zajonc, R.B. (1965) 'Social facilitation'. *Science,* 149: 269–74.

Zimbardo, P. (1973) 'On the ethics of intervention in human psychological research: with special reference to the Stanford Prison Experiment'. *Cognition,* 2: 243–56.

Chapter 2

Archer, M.S. (2000) *Being Human: The Problem of Agency.* Cambridge: Cambridge University Press.

Archer, M.S. (2003) *Structure, Agency and the Internal Conversation.* Cambridge: Cambridge University Press.

Berger, P.L. and Luckman, T. (1967) *The Social Construction of Reality: A Treatise on the Sociology of Knowledge.* Garden City, NY: Doubleday.

Blumer, H. (1962) 'Society as symbolic interaction', in A. Rose (ed.), *Human Behaviour and Social Processes.* Boston: Houghton Miffin Co.: 179–92.

Blumer, H. (1966) 'Social implications of the thought of George Herbert Mead'. *American Journal of Sociology,* 71: 535–44.

Blumer, H. (1969) 'Society as symbolic interaction', in H. Blummer, *Symbolic Interaction.* Englewood Cliffs, NJ: Prentice-Hall.

Chalari, A. (2009) *Approaches to the Individual: The Relationship between Internal and External Conversation.* London: Palgrave Macmillan.

Chalari, A. (2012) *Why Greeks Interrupt Each Other? The Phenomenon of 'Overlaps' in Everyday Greek Conversations.* Saarbucken, Germany: Lap Lambert Academic Publishing.

Charon, J.M. (2011) *Symbolic Interactionism: An Introduction, an Interpretation, an Integration* (10th ed.). New Delhi: PHI Learning Private Limited.

Cooley, C.H. (1902/1964) *Human Nature and the Social Order.* New York: Scribner's.

Cooley, C.H. (ed.) (1909/1962) *Social Organization.* New York: Schocken Books.

Cooley, C.H. (1970) *Human Nature and the Social Order.* New York: Schocken Books.

Dennis, A., Philburn, R. and Smith, G. (2013) *Sociologies of Interaction.* Cambridge: Polity.

Dewey, J. (1940) *Human Nature and Conduct.* New York: Modern Library.

Fine, G.A. (ed.) (1995) *A Second Chicago School? The Development of a Post-war American Sociology.* Chicago: University of Chicago Press.

Garfinkel, H. (1967/1984) *Studies in Ethnomethodology*. Cambridge: Polity Press.

Garfinkel, H. (ed.) (1986) *Ethnomethodological Studies of Work*. London: Routledge and Kegan Paul.

Goffman, E. (1959) *Presentation of Self in Everyday Life*. Garden City, NY: Anchor.

Goffman, E. (1961a) *Encounters: Two Studies in the Sociology of Interaction*. Indianapolis: Bobbs-Merrill.

Goffman, E. (1961b) *Asylums: Essays on the Social Situation of Mental Patients and Other Inmates*. New York: Doubleday.

Heritage, J. (1984) *Garfinkel and Ethnomethodology*. Cambridge: Polity Press.

Hewitt, J.P. (2003) *Self and Society: A Symbolic Interactionist Perspective*. Boston: Allyn and Bacon.

Hochschild, A. (1983/2003) *The Managed Heart: Commercialization of Human Feeling*, 20th Anniversary Edition. Berkeley, CA: University of California Press.

Jacobsen, M.H. (2009) *Encountering the Everyday*. New York: Palgrave.

James, W. (1890/1950) *The Principles of Psychology*. New York: Dover.

James, W. (1909/1977) 'Radical empiricism', in J. J. McDermott (ed.), *The Writings of William James: A Comprehensive Edition*. New York: Random House, 136.

Kailoglou, L. (2010) *Style and sociolinguistic variation in Athens*. Unpublished PhD Thesis, University of Essex, UK.

Kuhn, M. (1964) 'Major trends in symbolic interaction theory in the past twenty-five years'. *Sociological Quarterly*, 5: 61–84.

Manning, P. (2005) 'Erving Goffman', in G. Ritzer (ed.), *Encyclopedia of Social Theory*. Thousand Oaks, CA: Sage, 333–9.

Mead, G.H. (1932) *The Philosophy of the Present*. Chicago: Chicago University Press.

Mead, G.H. (1934) *Mind, Self and Society from the Standpoint of a Social Behaviourist*. Chicago: Chicago University Press.

Mead, G.H. (1956/1964) *On Social Psychology: Selected Papers*, Strauss, A. (ed.). Chicago: Chicago University Press.

Mead, G.H. (1982) *The Individual and the Social Self: Unpublished Work of George Herbert Mead*. Chicago: University of Chicago Press.

Meltzer, B. (1964/1978) 'Mead's social psychology', in J. Manis and B. Meltzer (eds), *Symbolic Interaction: A Reader in Social Psychology*, 3rd ed. Boston: Allyn and Bacon, 15–27.

Meltzer, B., Petras, J. and Reynolds, L. (1975) *Symbolic Interactionsim: Genesis, Varieties and Criticism*. London: Routledge and Kegan Paul.

Miller, D.E. (2011) 'Toward theory of interaction: the Iowa School'. *Symbolic Interaction*, 34(4): 340–8.

Myers, D., Abell, J., Kolstad, A. and Sani, F. (2010) *Social Psychology*. London: McGraw-Hill.

Orbuch, T.L. (1997) 'People's accounts count: the sociology of accounts', in J. Hagan and Karen S. Cook (eds), *Annual Review of Sociology*, vol. 23. Palo Alto, CA: Annual Reviews, 455–78.

Pollner, M. (1987) *Mundane Reason: Reality in Everyday and Sociological Discourse*. Cambridge: Cambridge University Press.

Ritzer, G. and Stepnisky, J. (2014) *Sociological Theory* (9th ed.). New York: McGraw-Hill.

Rock, P. (1979) *The Making of Symbolic Interactionism*. Totowa, NJ: Rowman and Littlefield.

Rohall, D.E., Milkie, M.A. and Lucas, J.W. (2007) *Social Psychology: Sociological Perspectives*. Boston: Pearson.

Sacks, H. (1992) *Lectures in Conversation*. Oxford: Basil Blackwell.

Sacks, H., Schegloff, E. and Jefferson, G. (1978) 'A simplest systematics for the organization of turn-taking for conversation', in J. Schenkein (ed.), *Studies in the Organization of Conversational Interaction*. New York: Academic Press, 7–55.

Schegloff, E. (1996) 'Turn organization: the interaction of grammar and interaction', in E. Ochs, E. Schegloff and S. Thompson (eds), *Interaction and Grammar*. Cambridge: Cambridge University Press.

Simmel, G. (1950) *The Sociology of Georg Simmel*. Translated, edited and with an introduction by K.H. Wolff. New York: Free Press.

Stryker, S. (1980) *Symbolic Interactionism: A Social Structural Version*. Menlo Park, CA: Benjamin/Cummings.

Stryker, S. (1990) 'Symbolic interactionism: themes and variations', in M. Rosenberg and R.H. Turner (eds), *Social Psychology: Sociological Perspectives*. New Brunswick, NJ: Transaction.

Taylor, C. (1985) *Human Agency and Language*. Cambridge: Cambridge University Press.

Turner, J.H. and Stets, J.E. (2005) *The Sociology of Emotions*. Cambridge: Cambridge University Press.

Waskul, D.D. (2009) 'Symbolic interactionism: the play and fate of meanings in everyday life', in M.H. Jacobsen, *Encountering the Everyday: An Introduction to the Sociologies of the Unnoticed*. London: Palgrave Macmillan.

Weigert, A.J. and Gecas, V. (2003) 'Self', in L.T. Reynolds and N. Herman-Kinney (eds), *Handbook of Symbolic Interactionism*. New York: Rowman and Littlefield.

Williams, R. (1998) 'Erving Goffman', in R. Stoned (ed.), *Key Sociological Thinkers*. New York: Palgrave Macmillan, 151–62.

Chapter 3

Archer, M.S. (2003) *Structure, Agency and the Internal Conversation*. Cambridge: CUP.

Archer, M.S. (2007) *Making Our Way Through the World: Human Reflexivity and Social Mobility*. Cambridge: CUP.

Bandura, A. (1969) *Principles of Behaviour Modification*. New York: Holt, Rinehart and Winston.

Bandura, A. (1977) *Social Learning Theory*. Englewood Cliffs, NJ: Prentice Hall.

Beasley, C. (2005) *Gender and Sexuality: Critical Theories, Critical Thinkers*. London: Sage.

Bennett, M.D. and Fraser, M.W. (2000) 'Urban violence among African American males: intergrating family, neighborhood, and peer perspectives'. *Journal of Sociology and Social Welfare*, 27: 93–117.

Bernstein, B. (1981) 'Codes, moralities and the process of child reproduction: a model'. *Language in Society*, 10: 327–63.

Bourdieu, P. and Passeron, J.C. (1977) *Reproduction in Education, Society, and Culture.* London: Sage.

Bowie, B.H., Carrère, S., Cooke, C., Valdivia, G., Mcallister, B. and Doohan, E.A. (2013) 'The role of culture in parents' socialization of children's emotional development'. *Western Journal of Nursing Research*, 35(4): 514–33.

Bruner, J. (1990) *Acts of Meaning.* Cambridge, MA: Harvard University Press.

Buckinghan, D. (ed.) (2008) *Youth Identity and Digital Media.* Cambridge, MA: MIT Press.

Chalari, A. (2009) *Approaches to the Individual: The Relationship between Internal and External Conversation.* London: Palgrave Macmillan.

Comstock, G. and Scharrer, E. (2007) *Media and American Child.* Burlington, MA: Academic Press.

Cooley, C.H. (1902/1964) *Human Nature and the Social Order.* New York: Scribner.

Corsaro, E.A. (2011) *The Sociology of Childhood.* Thousand Oaks, CA: Pine Forge Press.

Craib, I. (1997) *Classic Social Theory: An Introduction to the Thought of Marx, Weber, Durkheim and Simmel.* Oxford: OUP.

DeSuza, V. (2011) *Group Psychotherapy: Exercise at Hand: Practical Guide to Group Coping Skills, Stress Management Skills, Anger Management Skills, Communication Skills and Relapse Prevention Skills.* Bloomington, IN: iUniverse.

Dobbs-Oates, J., Kaderavek, J.N., Guo, Y. and Justice, L.M. (2011) 'Effective behavior management in preschool classrooms and children's task orientation: enhancing emergent literacy and language development'. *Early Childhood Research Quarterly*, 26(4): 420–9.

Durkheim, E. (1912/1995) *The Elementary Firms of Religious Life* (tr. K. Fields). New York: Free Press.

Erikson, E.H. (1950/1963) *Childhood and Society.* (2nd ed.). New York: Norton.

Fairlie, A.M., Wood, M.D. and Laird, R.D. (2012) 'Prospective protective effect of parents on peer influences and college alcohol involvement'. *Journal of the Society of Psychologists in Addictive Behaviors*, 26(1): 30–41.

Fine, G. (1987) *With the Boys: Little League Baseball and Preadolescent Culture.* Chicago: University of Chicago Press.

Freud, S. (1961/2004) *Civilization and its Discontents.* London: Penguin.

Giddens, A. (2009) *Sociology* (6th ed.). Cambridge: Polity.

Gambino, M. (2013) 'Erving Goffman's asylums and institutional culture in the mid-twentieth-century United States'. *Harvard Review of Psychiatry*, 21: 52–7.

Goffman, E. (1959) *Presentation of Self in Everyday Life.* Garden City, NY: Anchor.

Goffman, E. (1961a) *Encounters: Two Studies in the Sociology of Interaction.* Indianapolis: Bobbs-Merrill.

Goffman, E. (1961b) *Asylums: Essays on the Social Situations of Mental Patients and Other Inmates.* Garden City, NY: Anchor.

Goode, W.J. (1977) *Principles of Sociology.* New York: McGraw-Hill.

Harris, J.R. (1998) *The Nurture Assumption: Why Children Turn Out the Way They Do.* New York: Free Press.

Inkeles, A. (1968) 'Society, social structure and child socialization', in J.A. Clausen (ed.), *Socialization in Society.* Boston: Little, Brown.

Kendall, S.P. (1974) 'Preference for intermittent reinforcement'. *Journal of the Experimental Analysis of Behaviour*, 21: 463–73.

Krosnick, J.A. and Judd, C.M. (1982) 'Transitions in social influence at adolescence: who induces cigarette smoking?' *Developmental Psychology*, 18: 359–68.

Lorber, J. (2000) 'Using gender to undo gender: a feminist degendering movement'. *Feminist Theory*, 1(1): 79–95.

Luborsky, L. (1984) *Principles of Psychoanalytic Psychotherapy: A Manual for Supportive, Expressive Treatment.* New York: Basic Books.

Maccody, E.E. (1992) 'The role of parents in the socialization of children: an historical overview'. *Developmental Psychology* 28(6): 1006–17.

Mackay, R.W. (1974) 'Words, utterances and activities', in R. Turner (ed.), *Ethnomethodology: Selected Readings.* Harmondsworth: Penguin, 197–215.

McHale, S., Crouter, A.C. and Whiteman, S.D. (2003) 'The family contexts of gender development in childhood and adolescence social development'. *Social Development*, 12: 125–48.

Mead, G.H. (1934) *Mind, Self and Society.* Chicago: University of Chicago Press.

Naouri, A. (2005) *Mothers and Fathers.* London: Free Association Books.

Naouri, A. (2008) *Éduquer ses enfants. L'urgence aujourd'hui.* France: Odile Jacob.

Parsons, T. (1937) *The Structure of Social Action.* New York: McGraw-Hill.

Parsons, T. (1951) *The Social System.* Glencoe: Free Press.

Persell, C.H. (1990) 'Becoming a member of society through socialization', in *Understanding Society: An Introduction to Sociology* (3rd ed.). New York: Harper & Row, 98–107.

Phelps, J.L., Belsky, J. and Crnic, K. (1998) 'Earned security, daily stress, and parenting: a comparison of five alternative models'. *Development and Psychopathology*, 10(1): 21–38.

Piaget, J. (1926) *Play, Dreams and Imitation in Childhood* (trans. from French by C. Gattegno and F.M. Hodgson). London: Routledge & Kegan Paul.

Pugliese, J.A. and Okun, M.A. (2014) 'Social control and strenuous exercise among late adolescent college students: parents versus peers as influence agents'. *Journal of Adolescence*, 37(5): 543–54.

Rideout, V.J., Foehr, U.G. and Roberts, D.F. (2010) *Generation M2: Media in the Lives of 8-to-18-Year-Olds.* Menlo Park, CA: Kaiser Family Foundation.

Ritzer, G. (2015) *Essentials of Sociology.* Thousand Oaks, CA: Sage.

Rogers, C. (1951) *Client-centered Therapy: Its Current Practice, Implications and Theory.* London: Constable.

Rogers, C. (1959) 'A theory of therapy, personality and interpersonal relationships as developed in the client-centered framework', in S. Koch (ed.), *Psychology: A Study of a Science. Vol. 3: Formulations of the Person and the Social Context.* New York: McGraw-Hill.

Rogers, C. (1974) 'Empathic: an unappreciated way of being'. *The Counseling Psychologist*, 5(2): 2–10.

Rogers, C. (1986) 'Carl Rogers on the development of the person-centered approach'. *Person-Centered Review*, 1(3): 257–9.

Rohlinger, D.A. (2007a) 'Socialization, gender', in G. Ritzer (ed.), *The Blackwell Encyclopaedia of Sociology*. Malden, MA: Blackwell: 4571–4.

Rohlinger, D.A. (2007b) 'American media and deliberative democratic processes'. *Sociological Theory*, 25(2): 122–48.

Sagi-Schwartz, A. (2012) 'Children of war and peace'. *Journal of Conflict Resolution*, 56(5): 933–51.

Simmel, G. (1950) *The Sociology of Georg Simmel*. Translated, edited and with an introduction by K.H. Wolff. New York: Free Press.

Skinner, B.F. (1989) *The Origins of Cognitive Thought, Recent Issues in the Analysis of Behavior*. Princeton, NJ: Merrill Publishing Company.

Slaughter-Defoe, D. (1994) *Revisiting the Concept of Socialization: Caregiving and Teaching in the 90s – A Personal Perspective*. Center for Urban Affairs and Policy Research, Northwestern University, Evanston, IL.

Speier, M. (1970) 'The everyday world of the child', in J. Douglas (ed.), *Understanding Everyday Life*. Chicago: Aldine.

Steinberg L. and Monahan, K.C. (2007) 'Age differences in resistance to peer difference'. *Developmental Psychology*, 43: 1531–43.

Stern, D. (1977) *The First Relationship: Infant and Mother*. Cambridge, MA: Harvard University Press.

Turner, B.S. (2006) *The Cambridge Dictionary of Sociology*. Cambridge: CUP.

Vygotsky, L.S. ([1934] 1962) *Thought and Language*. (12th ed., 2000). Cambridge, MA: MIT Press.

Vygotsky, L.S. (1978) *Mind in Society: The Development of Higher Psychological Processes*. Cambridge, MA: Harvard University Press.

Watkins, S.C. (2009) *The Young and the Digital: What the Migration to Social Network Sites, Games, and Anytime, Anywhere Means for Our Future*. Boston: Beacon Press.

Watson, J. (1928) *The Ways of Behaviorism*. New York: Harper & Brothers.

Wentworth, W.M. (1980) *Context and Understanding: An Inquiry into Socialization Theory*. New York: Elsevier.

White, G. (1977) *Aspects of Modern Sociology: Social Processes, Socialization*. New York: Longman.

Wunder, D.F. (2007) 'The agents of socialization', in G. Ritzer (ed.), *Blackwell Encyclopaedia of Sociology*. London: Blackwell.

Zigler, E., Lamb, M. and Child, I. (1982) *Socialization and Personality Development*. Oxford: Oxford University Press.

Chapter 4

Allen-Collinson, J. and Hockey, J. (2007) 'Working out identity: distance runners and the management of disrupted identity'. *Leisure Studies*, 26(4): 381–98.

Atkins, R., Hart, D. and Donnelly, T.M. (2005) 'The association of childhood personality type with volunteering during adolescence'. *Merrill-Palmer Quarterly*,
51: 145–62.

Berger, P. (1963) *Invitation to Sociology*. New York: Doubleday.

Boulu-Reshef, B. (2015) 'Toward a personal identity argument to combine potentially conflicting social identities'. *Review of Social Economy*, 73(1): 1–18.

Burke, P.J. (1991) 'Identity processes and social stress'. *American Sociological Review*,
56: 836–49.

Burke, P.J. and Tully, J.T. (1977) 'The measurement of role/identity'. *Social Forces*,
55: 880–97.

Burkitt, I. (1999) *Bodies of Thought: Social Relations, Activity and Embodiment*. London:
Sage.

Burkitt, I. (2008) *Social Selves: Theories of Self and Society*. London: Sage.

Butler, J. (2004) *Undoing Gender*. New York: Routledge.

Chávez, A.F. and Guido-DiBrito, F. (1999) 'Racial and ethnic identity and development'. *New Directions for Adult and Continuing Education*, 84: 39–47.

Côté, J.E. and Levine, C.G. (2002) *Identity Formation, Agency, and Culture: A Social
Psychological Synthesis*. Mahwah, NJ: Lawrence Erlbaum Associates.

Davis, J.B. (2009) 'Identity and individual economic agents: a narrative approach'.
Review of Social Economy, 67(1): 71–94.

Dennis, A., Philburn, R. and Smith, G. (2013) *Sociologies of Interaction*. Cambridge: Polity.

Edwards, J. (2009) *Language and Identity*. Cambridge: Cambridge University Press.

Elliott, A. (2009) *Concepts of the Self*. Cambridge: Polity.

Emmanouil, S. (2014) *Narratives and identity in chronic-illness: the example of motherhood
in multiple sclerosis*. Unpublished PhD Thesis, Panteion University of Athens.

Erikson, E. (1946) 'Ego development and historical change'. *The Psychoanalytic Study
of the Child*, 2: 359–96.

Erikson, E.H. (1950) *Childhood and Society*. New York: Norton.

Ervin, L. and Stryker, S. (2000) 'Theorising the relationship between self-esteem and
identity', in T.J. Owens, S. Stryker and N. Goodman (eds), *Extending Self-Esteem
Theory and Research: Sociological and Psychological Currents*. New York: Cambridge
University Press, 29–55.

Foucault, M. (1978) *The History of Sexuality: Volume 1, An Introduction*. New York: Vintage.

Geertz, C. (1973) *The Interpretation of Culture*. New York: Basic Books.

Giffney, N. (2004) 'Denormatising queer theory: more than (simply) gay and lesbian
studies'. *Feminist Theory* 5(1): 73–8.

Goffman, E. (1963) *Stigma: Notes on the Management of Spoiled Identity*. Englewood
Cliffs, NJ: Prentice Hall.

Goffman, E. (1979) *Gender Advertisements*. London: Macmillan.

Heckert, D.M. and Best, A. (1997) 'Ugly duckling to swan: labelling theory and the
stigmatization of red'. *Symbolic Interaction* 20: 365–84.

Heise, D.R. (1977) 'Social action as the control of affect'. *Behavioural Science*,
22: 163–77.

Helms, J.E.N. (1993) 'Introduction: review of racial identity terminology', in J.E. Helms (ed.), *Black and White Racial Identity: Theory, Research and Practice.* Westport, CT: Praeger.

James, W. (1890/1950) *The Principles of Psychology.* New York: Dover.

Jenkins, R. (2007) 'Ethnicity', in G. Ritzer (ed.), *Blackwell Encyclopaedia of Sociology* Available at: http://www.sociologyencyclopedia.com.gate2.library.lse.ac.uk/subscriber/uid=28/tocnode?query=personal+identity+&widen=1&resultnumber=2&from=search&id=g9781405124331_yr2014_chunk_g978140512433115_ss1-6&type=std&fuzzy=0&slop=1. (last visited on 30 August 2015)

Jenkins, R. (2008) *Social Identity* (3rd ed.). London: Routledge.

Kelly, J.R. (1983) *Leisure Identities and Interactions.* London: George Allen and Unwin.

Kim, E. (2011) 'Asexuality in disability narratives'. *Sexualities*, 24: 479–93.

Marcia, J.E. (1966) 'Development and validation of ego identity status'. *Journal of Personality and Social Psychology*, 5: 551–8.

Marcia, J.E. (1993) 'The relational roots of identity', in J. Kroger (ed.), *Discussions on Ego Identity.* Hillsdale, NJ: Lawrence Erlbaum Associates, 101–20.

McCall, G.J. and Simmons, J.L. (1966) *Identities and Interaction.* New York: Free Press.

Melucci, A. (1989) *Nomads of the Present.* Philodelphia: Temple University Press.

Owens, T.J. (2013) 'Self and Identity' in J. Delamater (ed.), *Handbook of Social Psychology.* New York: Plenum Publishers.

Polletta, F. and Jasper, J. (2001) 'Collective identity and social movements'. *Annual Review of Sociology* 27(1): 283–305.

Rapaport, D. (1958) 'A historical survey of psychoanalytic ego psychology'. *Bulletin of the Philadelphia Association of Psychoanalysis*, 8: 105–20.

Ritzer, G. and Stepnisky, J. (2014) *Sociological Theory* (9th ed.). New York: McGraw-Hill.

Rohall, D.E., Milkie, M.A. and Lucas, J.W. (2007) *Social Psychology: Sociological Pespectives.* Boston: Allyn and Bacon.

Schur, E.M. (1971) *Labelling Deviant Behaviour: Its Sociological Implications.* New York: Harper & Row.

Schwartz, S.J. (2001) 'The evolution of Eriksonian and neo-Eriksonian identity theory and research: a review and integration'. *Identity: An International Journal of Theory and Research*, 1(1): 7–58.

Scott, B.M. and Schwartz M.A.A. (2008) *Sociology: Making Sense of the Social World.* New York: Allyn and Bacon.

Sedikides, C. and Gregg, A.P. (2008) 'Self-enhancement: food for thought'. *Perspectives on Psychological Science*, 3: 102–16.

Segal, L. (2010) 'Genders: deconstructed, reconstructed, still on the move', in M. Wetherell and C.T. Mohanty (eds), *The Sage Handbook of Identities.* London: Sage, 321–38.

Stets, J.E. and Tsushima, T.M. (2001) 'Negative emotion and coping responses within identity control theory'. *Social Psychology Quarterly*, 64: 283–95.

Stone, G.P. (1981) 'Appearance and the self: a slightly revised version', in G.P. Stone and H.A. Farberman (eds), *Social Psychology Through Symbolic Interaction.* New York: Wiley, 188.

Stryker, S. (1968) 'Identity theory and role performance'. *Journal of Marriage and the Family*, 30: 558–64.

Stryker, S. (1980) *Symbolic Interactionism: A Social Structural Version*. Menlo Park, CA: Benjamin Cummings.

Stryker, S. (1987) 'The vitalisation of symbolic interactionism'. *Social Psychology Quarterly*, 50: 83–94.

Stryker, S. (1991) 'Exploring the relevance of social cognition for the relationship of self and society: linking the cognitive perspectives and identity theory', in J.A. Howard and P.L. Collero (eds), *The Self–Society Dynamic: Cognition, Emotion and Action*. New York: Cambridge University Press, 19–54.

Tajfel, H. (1981) *Human Groups and Social Categories: Studies in Social Psychology*. Cambridge: Cambridge University Press.

Tajfel, H. and Turner, J.C. (1986) 'The social identity theory of intergroup behavior', in S. Worchel and W.G. Austin (eds), *Psychology of Intergroup Relations*. Chicago: Nelson-Hall, 7–24.

Taylor, C. (1990) *Sources of the Self*. Cambridge, MA: Harvard University Press.

Thoits, P.A. and Virshup, L.K. (1997) 'Me and we's: forms and functions of social identities', in R.D. Ashmore and L. Jussim (eds), *Self and Identity: Fundamental Issues* (vol. 1). New York: Oxford University Press, 106–33.

Turner, J.C. and Onorato, R.S. (1999) 'Social identity, personality, and the self-concept', in T.R. Tyler, R.M. Kramer and O.P. John (eds), *The Psychology of the Social Self*. Mahwah, NJ: Lawrence Erlbaum Associates, 11–46.

Vignoles, V.L., Schwartz, S.J. and Luyckx, K. (2011) 'Introduction: toward an integrative view of identity', in S.J. Schwartz, K. Luyckx and V.L. Vignoles (eds), *Handbook of Identity Theory and Research* (Vol. 1). New York: Springer, 1–30.

Vryan, K.D. (2007) 'Identity: social psychological aspects', in G. Ritzer (ed.), *Blackwell Encyclopaedia of Sociology Online*. Available at: http://www.sociology encyclopedia.com.gate2.library.lse.ac.uk/subscriber/uid=28/tocnode?query=person al+identity+&widen=1&resultnumber=2&from=search&id=g9781405124331_ yr2014_chunk_g978140512433115_ss1-6&type=std&fuzzy=0&slop=1. (last visited on 30 August 2015).

Weigert, A.J. (1983) 'Identity: its emergence within sociological social psychology'. *Symbolic Interaction*, 6(2): 183–206.

Wetherell, M. (2010) 'The field of identity studies', in M. Wetherell and C.T. Mohanty (eds), *The Sage Handbook of Identities*. London: Sage, 3–2.

Whooley, O. (2007) 'Collective identity', in G. Ritzer (ed.), *Blackwell Encyclopaedia of Sociology Online*. Available at: http://www.sociologyencyclopedia. com.gate2.library.lse.ac.uk/subscriber/uid=28/tocnode?query=personal+ide ntity+&widen=1&resultnumber=2&from=search&id=g9781405124331_ yr2014_chunk_g978140512433115_ss1-6&type=std&fuzzy=0&slop=1. (last visited on 30 August 2015

Yinger, J.M. (1976) 'Ethnicity in complex societies', in L.A. Coser and O.N. Larsen (eds), *The Uses of Controversy in Sociology*. New York: Free Press.

Chapter 5

Adams, M. (2007) *Self and Social Change*. London: Sage.

Archer, M.S. (2000) *Being Human: The Problem of Agency*. Cambridge: Cambridge University Press.

Benson, P.L. (2003) 'Developmental assets and asset-building community: conceptual and empirical foundations', in R.M. Lerner and P.L. Benson (eds), *Developmental Assets and Asset-Building Communities: Implications for Research, Policy, and Practice*. New York: Kluwer Academic/Plenum Publishers, 19–43.

Blumstein, P.W. (1975) 'Identity bargaining and self conception'. *Social Forces*, 53: 476–85.

Blumstein, P. (2001) 'The production of selves in personal relationships', in A. Branaman (ed.), *Self and Society*, Oxford: Blackwell, 183–97.

Brinthaupt, T.M. and Erwin, L.J. (1992) 'Reporting about the self: issues and implications', in T.M. Brinthaupt and R.P. Lipka (eds), *The Self: Definitional and Methodological Issues*. New York: State University of New York Press, 137–71.

Burkitt, I. (2008) *Social Selves: Theories of Self and Society* (2nd ed.). London: Sage.

Burns, R.B. (1979) *The Self Concept: Theory, Measurement, Development and Behaviour*. London: Longman.

Buss, A. (1980) *Self Consciousness and Social Anxiety*. San Francisco: W.H. Freeman.

Byrne, B. M., Shavelson, R. J. and Marsh, H. W. (1992) Multigroup comparisons in self-concept research: Reexamining the assumption of equivalent structure and measurement. In T. M. Brinthaupt and R.P. Lipka (eds), *The Self: Definitional and Methodological Issues*. Albany: State University of New York Press. pp. 172–203.

Carver, C.S. (1979) 'A cybernetic model of self-attention processes'. *Journal of Personality and Social Psychology*, 37: 1251–81.

Carver, C.S. and Scheier, M.F. (1981) *Attention and Self-regulation: A Control-theory Approach to Human Behaviour*. New York: Spinger-Verlag.

Carver, C.S. and Scheier, M.F. (1985) 'A control-systems approach to the self-regulation of action', in J. Kuhl and J. Beckman (eds), *Action Control: From Cognition to Behaviour*. New York: Springer-Verlag.

Chalari, A. (2009) *Approaching the Individual: The Relationship Between Internal and External Conversation*. London: Palgrave Macmillan.

Charon, J.M. (2011) *Symbolic Interactionism: An Introduction, an Interpretation, an Integration* (10th ed.). New Delhi: PHI Learning Private Limited.

Colvin, C.R., Block, J. and Funder, D.C. (1995) 'Overly positive self-evaluations and personality: negative implications for mental health'. *Journal of Personality and Social Psychology*, 68: 1152–62.

Cooley, C.H. (1902/1964) *Human Nature and the Social Order*. New York: Scribner's.

Crocker, J. and Park, L.E. (2004) 'The costly pursuit of self-esteem'. *Psychological Bulletin*, 116: 3–10.

Dewey, J. (1940) *Freedom and Culture*. London: George Allen and Unwin.

Dewey, J. (1971) *The Early Works (1882–1898)*. Vol. 4 (1893–1894). Carbondale: Southern Illinois University Press.

Durkheim, E. (1952) *Suicide: A Study in Sociology* (tr. J.A. Spalding and G. Simpson). London: Routledge and Kegan Paul.

Durkheim, E. (1969) 'Individualism and the intellectuals' (tr. S. and J. Lukes). *Political Studies*, XVII (1): 14–30.

Durkheim, E. (1984) *The Division of Labour in Society* (tr. W.D. Halls). London: Macmillan.

Duval, T.S. and Wicklund, R.A. (1972) *A Theory of Objective Self-Awareness*. New York: Academic Press.

Elliott, A. (2002) *Psychoanalytic Theory: An Introduction*. London: Palgrave.

Elliott, A. (2009) *Concepts of Self*. Cambridge: Polity.

Epstein, S. (1973) 'The self-concept revisited: or a theory of a theory'. *American Psychologist*, 28: 404–16.

Epstein, S. and O'Brien, E.J. (1985) 'The person-situation debate in historical and current perspective'. *Psychological Bulletin*, 98: 513–37.

Fenigstein, A., Scheier, M.F. and Buss, A.H. (1975) 'Public and private self-consciousness: assessment and theory'. *Journal of Consulting and Clinical Psychology*, 36: 1241–50.

Fiske, S.T. and Taylor, S.E. (1984) *Social Cognition*. Reading, MA: Addison-Wesley.

Geertz, C. (1973) *The Interpretation of Cultures: Selected Essays*. New York: Basic Books.

Gekas, V. and Burke, P.J. (1995) 'Self and identity', in K.S. Cook, G.A. Fine and J.S. House (eds), *Sociological Perspectives on Social Psychology*. Boston, MA: Allyn and Bacon, 41–67.

Gergen, K.J. (1968) 'Personal consistency and the presentation of self', in C. Gordon and K.J. Gergen (eds), *The Self in Social Interaction*. New York: Wiley, 299–308.

Gergen, K.J. (1991) *The Saturated Self: Dilemmas of Identity in Contemporary Life*. New York: Basic Books.

Gibbons, F.X. (1990) 'Self attention and behaviour: a review and theoretical update, in M.P. Zanna (ed.), *Advances in Experimental Social Psychology*. 23: 249–303. New York: Academic Press.

Glăveanu, V. (2010) 'The self in social psychology: towards new perspectives'. *Revista de Psihologie*, 56(3–4): 269–83.

Goffman, E. (1956) *The Presentation of Self in Everyday Life*. London: Allen Lane.

Goffman, E. (1961) *Encounters: Two Studies in Sociology of Interaction*. London: Allen Lane.

Greenwald, A.G. and Banaji, M.R. (1989) 'The self as a memory system: powerful but ordinary'. *Journal of Personality and Social Psychology*, 57: 41–5.

Harre, R. (1998) *The Singular Self*. London: Sage.

Heider, F. (1958) *The Psychology of Interpersonal Relations*. New York: Wiley.

Hewitt, J.P. (2003) *Self and Society: A Symbolic Interactionist Perspective*. Boston: Allyn and Bacon.

Howard, J.A. (2001) 'A sociological framework cognition', in A. Branaman (ed.), (2001) *Self and Society*. Oxford: Blackwell, 97–120.

Hull, J.G., Slone, L.B., Meteyer, K.B. and Matthews, A.R. (2002) 'The non-consciousness of self-consciousness'. *Journal of Personality and Social Psychology*, 83(2): 406–24.

Huntington, M.J. (1957) 'The development of a professional self image', in R.K. Merton, G.G. Reeder and P. Kendall (eds), *The Student Physician*. Cambridge, MA: Harvard University Press, 179–87.

James, W. (1890) *The Principles of Psychology. Vol. 1*. London: Macmillan.

Jenkins, R. (1996) *Social Identities*. London: Routledge.

John, O.P. (1990) 'The "Big Five" factor taxonomy: dimensions of personality in the natural language and in questionnaires', in L. A. Pervin (ed.), *Handbook of Personality: Theory and Research*. New York: Guilford Press, 66–100.

John, O.P. and Srivastava, S. (1999) 'The big five trait taxonomy: History, measurement, and theoretical perspectives', in L.A. Pervin and O.P. John (eds), *Handbook of Personality: Theory and research* (2nd ed.). New York: Guilford Press, 102–38.

Joireman, J.A., Parrott, L. and Hammersla, J. (2002) 'Empathy and the self-absorption paradox: support for the distinction between self-rumination and self-reflection'. *Self and Identity*, 1: 53–65.

Jones, E.E. and Davis, K.E. (1965) 'From acts to dispositions', in L. Berkowitz (ed.), *Advances in Experimental Social Psychology. Vol. 2*. New York: Academic.

Jones, E.E. and McGillis, D. (1976) 'Correspondent inferences and the attribution cube: a comparative reappraisal', in J.H. Harvey, W. Ickes and R.F. Kidd (eds), *New Directions in Attribution Research. Vol. 1*. Hillsdale, NJ: Erlbaum.

Kadushin, C. (1969) 'The professional self-concept of music students'. *American Journal of Sociology*, 84: 427–36.

Kelley, H.H. (1967) 'Attribution theory in social psychology', in D. Levine (ed.), *Nebraska Symposium on Motivation, Vol. 15*. Lincoln: University of Nebraska Press.

Kelley, H.H. (1973) 'The processes of causal attribution'. *American Psychologist*, 28: 107–28.

Langer, E.J. (1975) 'The illusion of control'. *Journal of Personality and Social Psychology*, 32: 311–28.

Leary, M.R. and Tangney, J.P. (2003) 'The self as an organizing construct in the behavioral and social', in M.R. Leary and J.P. Tangney (eds), *Handbook of Self and Identity*. New York: Guildford Press, 3–14.

Levine, D.N. (1971) *Georg Simmel: On Individuality and Social Forms*. Chicago: University of Chicago Press.

Linville, P.W. and Carlston, D.E. (1994) 'Social cognition perspective on self', in P.C. Devine, D.L. Hamilton and T.M. Ostrom (eds), *Social Cognition: Contributions to Classic Issues in Social Psychology*. New York: Springer-Verlag, 143–93.

Markus, H.R. and Wurf, E. (1987) 'The dynamic self-concept: a social psychological perspective'. *Annual Review of Psychology*, 38: 299–337.

Marsh, H.W., Byrne, B.M. and Shavelson, R. (1988) 'A multifaceted academic self-concept: its hierarchical structure and its relation to academic achievement'. *Journal of Educational Psychology*, 80: 366–80.

THE SOCIOLOGY OF THE INDIVIDUAL

Marsh, H.W., Byrne, B.A. and Shavelson, R. J. (1992) 'A multidimentional hierar-
    chical self-concept', in T.M Brinthaupt and R.P Lipka (eds) *The Self: Definitional
    and Methodological Issues*. New York: State University of New York Press, 44–95.
Marx, K. and Engels, F. (1970) *The German Ideology: Part One*. London: Lawrence and
    Wishart.
McCall, G.J. and Simmons, L.J. (1966) *Identities and Interactions*. New York: Free
    Press.
McConnel, A.R. and Strain, L.M. (2007) 'Content and structure of the self concept',
    in C. Sedikides and S.J. Spencer (eds), *The Self*. New York: Psychology Press,
    Taylor and Francis Group, 51–73.
McCrae, R.R. and Costa, P.T. (1999) 'A five-factory theory of personality', in
    L. A. Pervin and O. P. John (eds), *Handbook of Personality: Theory and Research*
    (2nd ed.). New York: Guilford Press, 139–53.
McCrae, R.R. and John, O.P. (1992) 'An introduction to the five-factor model and
    its applications'. *Journal of Personality*, 54: 430–46.
Mead, G.H. (1934) *Mind, Self, and Society*. Chicago: University of Chicago Press.
Menand, L. (2002) *American Studies*. New York: Farrar, Straus, and Giroux.
Morin, A. (2002) 'Do you self-reflect or self-ruminate?' Available at: http://www.
    sci-con.org/articles/20021201.html (visited on 10 November 2015).
Morin, A. (2005) 'Possible links between self-awareness and inner speech: theoretical
    background, underlying mechanisms, and empirical evidence'. *Journal of
    Consciousness Studies*, 12(4–5): 114–34.
Morin, A. and Everett, J. (1990) 'Inner speech as a mediator of self-awareness, self
    consciousness, and self-knowledge: a hypothesis'. *New Ideas in Psychology*, 8(3):
    337–56.
Owens, T.J. (2013) 'Self and identity', in J. Delamater (ed.), *Handbook of Social
    Psychology*. New York: Plenum Publishers.
Peirce, C.S. (1935) *Collected Papers on Charles Sanders Peirce. Vol. 6*. Cambridge:
    Cambridge University Press.
Peirce, C.S. (1940) *The Philosophy of Peirce – Selected Writings*. J. Buchler (ed.).
    London: Routledge.
Peirce, C.S. (1958) *Collected Papers on Charles Sanders Peirce. Vol. 7: Science and
    Philosophy*. Cambridge: Cambridge University Press.
Piaget, J. (1952) *The Origins of Intelligence*. New York: International Universities Press.
Rime, B. and LeBon, C. (1984) 'Le concept de conscience de soi et ses operation-
    nalisations (The concept of self-awareness and its operations)'. *L'Année
    Psychologique*, 84: 535–55.
Rogers, C.R. (1951) *Client-centered Therapy*. New York: Houghton-Mifflin.
Rohall, D.E., Milkie, M.A. and Lucas, J.W. (2007) *Social Psychology: Sociological
    Perspectives*. Boston: Pearson.
Rosenberg, M. (1979) *Conceiving the Self*. New York: Basic Books.
Scheier, M.F. and Carver, C.S. (1983) 'Two sides of the self: one for you and one for
    me', in J. Suls and A.G. Greenwalt (eds), *Psychological Perspectives on the Self*.
    London: Lawrence Erlbaum Associates.

Shavelson, R.J., Hubner, J.J. and Stanton, G.C. (1976) 'Self-concept: validation of construct interpretations'. *Review of Educational Research*, 45: 407–41.

Simmel, G. (1950) *The Sociology of Georg Simmel*. Translated, edited and with an introduction by K.H. Wolff. New York: Free Press.

Smith, M.B. (1991) *Values, Self and Society: Toward a Humanist Social Psychology*. New Brunswick, NJ: Transaction Publishers.

Spykman, N.J. (1965) *The Social Theory of Georg Simmel*. New York: Atherton Press.

Swann, W.B. (1997) 'The trouble with change: self-verification and allegiance to the self'. *Psychological Science*, 8: 177–80.

Swann, W.B. Jr. and Read, S.J. (1981) 'Self-verification process: how we sustain our self-conceptions'. *Journal of Experimental Social Psychology*, 17: 351–72.

Tan, S.-L. and Moghaddam, F.M. (1995) 'Reflective positioning and culture'. *Journal for the Theory of Social Behaviour*, 25(4): 387–400.

Taylor, S.E. and Brown, J.D. (1988) 'Illusion and well-being: a social psychological perspective on mental health'. *Psychological Bulletin*, 103: 193–210.

Taylor, S.E. and Brown, J.D. (1994) 'Positive illusions and well-being revisited: separating fact from fiction'. *Psychological Bulletin*, 116: 21–7.

Taylor, S.E., Lerner, J.S., Sherman, D.K., Sage, R.M. and McDowell, N.K. (2003) 'Portrait of the self-enhancer: well adjusted and well liked or maladjusted and friendless?' *Journal of Personality and Social Psychology*, 84: 165–76.

Trapnell, P.D. and Campbell, J.D. (1999) 'Private self-consciousness and the five factor model of personality: distinguishing rumination from reflection'. *Journal of Personality and Social Psychology*, 76: 284–304.

Turner, R. (1978) 'The role and the person'. *American Journal of Sociology*, 84: 1–23.

Vignoles, V.L., Schwartz, S.J. and Luyckx, K. (2011) 'Introduction: toward an integrative view of identity', in S.J. Schwartz, K. Luyckx and V.L. Vignoles (eds), *Handbook of Identity Theory and Research. Vol. 1*. New York: Springer, 1–30.

Weber, M. (1930) *The Protestant Ethic and the Spirit of Capitalism*. (tr. T. Parsons) (1985). London: Counterpoint.

Wetherell, M. and Maybin, J. (1996) 'The distributed self: a social constructionist perspective', in R. Stevens (ed.), *Understanding the Self*. London: Sage, 219–79.

Wicklund, R.A. (1975) 'Objective self awareness', in L. Erkowitz (ed.), *Advances in Experimental Social Psychology*, 8: 233–75.

Wiley, M.G. and Alexander, N.C. (1987) 'From situated activity to self-attribution: the impact of social structure schemata', in K. Yardley and T. Honess (eds), *Self and Identity: Psychological Perspectives*. Chichester: Wiley, 105–17.

Wiley, N. (1994) *The Semiotic Self*. Cambridge: Polity Press.

Chapter 6

Adler, A. (1927) *The Practice and Theory of Individual Psychology*. New York: Harcourt Press.

Adorno, T. (1966/1973) *Negative Dialectics* (tr. E.B. Ashton). New York: Continuum.

Beasley, C. (2005) *Gender and Sexuality: Critical Theories, Critical Thinkers*. London: Sage.

British Association for Counselling and Psychotherapy (2015) https://www.bacp. co.uk/crs/Training/whatiscounselling.php (visited on 30 October 2015).

British Association for the Person-Centred Approach (2015) http://www.bapca. org.uk/about/what-is-it.html (visited on 30 October 2015).

British Psychoanalytic Council (2015) http://www.bpc.org.uk/psychoanalysis-and-psychotherapy (visited on 30 October 2015).

Burns, R.B. (1979) *The Self Concept: Theory, Measurement, Development and Behaviour*. London: Longman.

Carver, C.S. and Scheier, M.F. (1996) *Perspectives on Personality* (3rd ed.). London: Allyn and Bacon.

Elliott, A. (1992) *Social Theory and Psychoanalysis in Transition: Self and Society from Freud to Kristeva*. Oxford: Blackwell.

Elliott, A. (2002) *Psychoanalytic Theory: An Introduction*. London: Palgrave.

Elliott, A. (2008) *Contemporary Social Theory: An Introduction*. London: Routledge.

Elliott, A. (2009) *Concepts of Self*. Cambridge: Polity.

Erikson, E.H. (1965) *Childhood and Society*. London: Hogarth Press.

Errington, M. and Murdin, L. (2006) 'Psychoanalytic Therapy: Sigmund Freud: 1856–1939', in C. Feltham and I. Horton (eds), *The Sage Handbook of Counselling and Psychotherapy*. London: Sage, 250–3.

Fink, B. (1995) *The Lacanian Subject: Between Language and Jouissance*. Princeton, NJ: Princeton University Press.

Foucault, M. (1969) *The Archaeology of Knowledge and the Discourse on Language*. New York: Harper Colophon.

Foucault, M. (1979) *The History of Sexuality, Vol. 1: An Introduction*. Harmondsworth: Penguin.

Foucault, M. (1985) *The History of Sexuality, Vol. 2: The Use of Pleasure*. New York: Pantheon.

Freud, A. (1937) *The Ego and the Mechanism of Defence*. London: Hogarth Press and Institute of Psycho-Analysis.

Freud, S. (1900/1954) *The Interpretation of Dreams*. London: George Allen & Unwin.

Freud, S. (1901/1975) *The Psychopathology of Everyday Life*. Harmondsworth: Penguin.

Freud, S. (1905/1977) 'Three essays on sexuality', in id., '*On Sexuality*'. Harmondsworth.

Freud, S. (1915–17/1922) *Introductory Lectures on Psychoanalysis*. London: George Allen & Unwin.

Freud, S. (1953–74) 'A difficulty in the path of psychoanalysis'. *Standard Edition of the Complete Psychological Works, Vol. 17*. J. Strachey (ed.). London: Hogarth.

Harre, R. (1979) *Social Being*. Oxford: Blackwell.

Heaphy, B. (2007) *Late Modernity and Social Change: Reconstructing Social and Personal Life*. London: Routledge.

Horney, K. (1945) *Our Inner Conflicts*. New York: Norton.

James, W. (1890/1950) *The Principles of Psychology*. New York: Dover.

Jung, C. (1960) *Collected Works* (14 Volumes). Princeton, NJ: Princeton University Press.

Kahn, M. (1997) *Between Therapist and Client: The New Relationship*. New York: Owl Books.

Klein, M. (1988) *Love Guild and Reparation and Other Works: 1921–1945*. London: Virago.

Lacan, J. (1949/2006) 'The mirror stage as formative of the I function as revealed in psychoanalytic experience', in *Écrits: The First Complete Edition in English* (tr. B. Fink). New York: W.W. Norton and Company.

Marcuse, H. (1956) *Eros and Civilization: A Philosophical Inquiry into Freud*. London: Ark.

Mearns, D. (2011) 'Further theoretical propositions in regard to self theory within person-centered therapy'. *Person-Centered and Experiential Psychotherapies*, 1(1/2): 14–27.

Mearns, D. and Thorne, B. (2007) *Person Centred Counselling in Action*. London: Sage.

Psychotherapy and Counselling Federation of Australia (2015) http://www.pacfa.org.au/practitioner-resources/counselling-psychotherapy-definitions/ (visited on 30 October 2105).

Rennier, D.L. (2004) 'Reflexivity and person-centered counseling'. *Journal of Humanistic Psychology,* 44(2): 182–203.

Rhawn, J. (1980) 'Awareness, the origin of thought, and the role of conscious self-deception in resistance and repression'. *Psychological Reports*, 46: 767–81.

Rogers, C.R. (1951) *Client-centered Therapy: Its Current Practice, Implications and Theory*. Boston, MA: Houghton Mifflin.

Rogers, C.R. (1959) 'A theory of therapy, personality and interpersonal relationships, as developed in the client-centered framework', in S. Koch (ed.), *Psychology: A Study of Science*. New York: McGraw Hill, 184–256.

Rogers, C.R. (1961) *On Becoming a Person*. Boston, MA: Houghton Mifflin.

Ryckman, R.M. (1993) *Theories of Personality* (5th ed.) Pacific Grove, CA: Brooks/Cole Publishing Co.

Searle, J.R. (1998) *The Rediscovery of the Mind*. Boston, MA: MIT Press.

Stanford Encyclopedia of Philosophy (2015) http://plato.stanford.edu/entries/lacan/ (visited on 31 October 2015).

Sullivan, H.S. (1953) *Interpersonal Theory of Psychiatry*. New York: Norton.

Thorne, B. (1992) *Carl Rogers: Key Figures in Counselling and Psychotherapy*. London: Sage.

Weedon, C. (1987) *Feminist Practice and Poststructuralist Theory*. Oxford: Blackwell.

Winnicott, D.W. (1965) *The Maturation Process and the Facilitating Environment*. London: Hogarth.

Winnicott, D.W. (1974) *Playing and Reality*. Harmondsworth: Penguin.

Chapter 7

Archer, M.S. (2000) *Being Human: The Problem of Agency*. Cambridge: Cambridge University Press.

Archer, M.S. (2003) *Structure, Agency and Internal Conversation*. Cambridge: Cambridge University Press.

Archer, M.S. (2007) *Making Our Way Through the World: Human Reflexivity and Social Mobility*. Cambridge: Cambridge University Press.

Archer, M.S. (2012) *The Reflexive Imperative in Late Modernity*. Cambridge: Cambridge University Press.

Arnason, J.P. (1989) 'Culture and imaginary specifications'. *Thesis Eleven*, 22: 24–45.

Barkley, R.A. (1997) *ADHD and the Nature of Self-Control*. New York: The Guilford Press.

Beck, U. (1992) *Risk Society: Towards a New Modernity*. London: Sage.

Beck, U. (1995) *Ecological Politics in an Age of Risk*. Cambridge: Polity Press.

Beck, U., Giddens, A. and Lash, S. (1994) *Reflective Modernization*. Cambridge: Polity Press.

Beck, U., Bonss, W. and Lau, C. (2003) 'The theory of reflexive modernization. Problematic, hypotheses and research program'. *Theory, Culture and Society*, 20(2): 1–33.

Blumer, H. (1962) 'Society as symbolic interaction', in A. Rose (ed.), *Human Behaviour and Social Processes*. Boston: Houghton Miffin Co., 179–92.

Bourdieu, P. (1977) *Outline of a Theory of Practice* (tr. R. Nice). Cambridge; New York: Cambridge University Press.

Bourdieu, P. (1990) *In Other Words: Essays Towards a Reflexive Sociology* (tr. M. Adamson). Cambridge: Polity.

Brinthaupt, T.M. and Lipka, R.P. (eds) (1992) *The Self: Definitional and Methodological Issues*. New York: State University of New York Press.

Buckner, R.L., Andrews-Hanna, J.R. and Schacter, D.L. (2008) 'The brain's default network: anatomy, function, and relevance to disease'. *Annals of the New York Academy of Sciences*, 1124: 1–38.

Caetano, A. (2015) 'Defining personal reflexivity: a critical reading of Archer's Approach'. *European Journal of Social Theory*, 18(1): 60–75.

Carrigan, M. (2015) 'Reflexivity'. Available at: http://markcarrigan.net/tag/reflexivity/ (visited on 8 February 2016).

Castoriadis, C. (1975) *The Imaginary Institution of Society*. Boston, MA: MIT Press.

Chalari, A. (2009) *Approaches to the Individual: The Relationship between Internal and External Conversation*. London: Palgrave Macmillan.

Chalari, A. (2012) 'The causal impact of resistance: mediating between resistance and internal conversation about resistance'. *Journal for the Theory of Social Behavior*, 43(1): 66–86.

Chalari, A. (2017) *The Sociology of the Individual*. London: Sage.

Charon, J.M. (2011) *Symbolic Interactionism: An Introduction, an Interpretation, an Integration* (10th ed.). New Delhi: PHI Learning Private Limited.

Colapietro, V. (1989) *Peirce's Approach to the Self.* Albany, NY: SUNY Press.

Colapietro, V. (2010) 'Cartesian privacy and Peircean interiority', in M.S. Archer (ed.), *Conversations About Reflexivity*. London: Routledge, 39–54.

DeSouza, M., DaSilveira, A. and Gomes, W. (2008) 'Verbalized inner speech and the expressiveness of self-consciousness'. *Qualitative Research in Psychology*, 5(2): 154–70.

Donati, P. (2011) 'Modernization and relational reflexivity'. *International Review of Sociology*, 21(1): 21–39.

Elder-Vass, D. (2007a) 'Searching for realism, structure, and agency in Actor Network Theory'. Paper presented to BSA Realism Study Group, London, 18 January.

Elder-Vass, D. (2007b) 'Luhmann and emergentism. Competing paradigms for social systems theory?' *Philosophy of the Social Sciences*, 37(4): 408–32.

Elder-Vass, D. (2007c) 'For emergence: refining Archer's account of social structure'. *Journal for the Theory of Social Behaviour*, 37(1): 25–44.

Emmanouil, S. (2014) 'Narrative and identity in chronic illness: the example of motherhood in Multiple Sclerosis'. Unpublished Doctoral Thesis, Panteion University of Social and Political Sciences, Athens, Greece.

Ezzy, D. (1998) 'Theorizing narrative identity: symbolic interactionism and hermeneutics'. *The Sociological Quarterly*, 39(2): 239–52.

Ferrara, A. (1998) *Reflexive Authenticity: Rethinking the Project of Modernity*. London: Routledge.

Giddens, A. (1984) *The Constitution of Society*. Berkeley, CA: University of California Press.

Goffman, E. (1981) *Forms of Talk*. Oxford: Oxford University Press.

Hermans, H.J. (1996) 'Voicing the self: from information processing to dialogical inter-change'. *Psychological Bulletin*, 119: 31–50.

Hermans, H.J. (2001) 'The dialogical self: toward a theory of personal and cultural positioning'. *Culture and Psychology*, 7: 243–81.

Hermans, H.J. (2002) 'The dialogical self as a society of mind: introduction'. *Theory and Psychology*, 12: 147–60.

Hermans, H.J. (2003) 'The construction and reconstruction of a dialogical self'. *Journal of Constructivist Psychology*, 16: 89–130.

Hermans, H.J. (2004) 'The dialogical self: between exchange and power', in H.J.M. Hermans and G. Dimaggio (eds), *The Dialogical Self in Psychotherapy*. New York: Brunner-Routledge, 13–28.

Hermans, H.J.M. and Hermans-Konoplka, A. (2010) *Dialogical Self Theory: Positioning and Counter Positioning in a Globalizing Society*. Cambridge: Cambridge University Press.

Hwang, G.-J., Yang, T.-C., Tsai, C.-C. and Yang, S. J. (2009) 'A context-aware ubiquitous learning environment for conducting complex science experiments', *Computers & Education*, 53(2): 402–13.

James, W. (1890) *The Principles of Psychology, vol. 1*. London: Macmillan.

James, W. (1984) *Psychology: Brief Course*. Cambridge: Harvard University Press.

King, A. (2010) 'The odd couple: Margaret Archer, Anthony Giddens and British social theory'. *The British Journal of Sociology*, 61(supp 1): 253–9.

Latour, B. (2003) 'Is re-modernization occurring and if so, how to prove it?' *Theory, Culture and Society*, 20(2): 35–48.

Lewis, C.I. (1955) *The Ground and Nature of the Right*. New York: Columbia University Press.

Lidstone, J.S.M., Fernyhough, C., Meins, E. and Whitehouse, A.J.O. (2009) 'Brief report: inner-speech impairment in children with autism is associated with greater nonverbal than verbal skills'. *Journal of Autism and Developmental Disorders*, 39(8): 1222–5.

Lyotard, J.F. (1984) *The Postmodern Condition: A Report on Knowledge* (tr. G. Bennington and B. Massumi). Minneapolis, MN: University of Minnesota Press (*La Condition postmoderne: Rapport sur le savoir*. Paris: Éditions de Minuit, 1979).

Mead, G.H. ([1934] 1962) *Mind, Self and the Society: From the Standpoint of a Social Behaviourist*. Chicago, IL: University of Chicago Press.

McGuire, W.J. and McGuire, C.V. (1991) 'The content, structure, and operation of thought systems', in R.S. Wyer, Jr. and T.K. Srull (eds), *Advances in Social Cognition, vol. IV*. Hillsdale, NJ: Erlbaum, 1–78.

McGuire, W.J. and McGuire, C.V. (1992) 'Cognitive-versus-affective positivity asymmetries in thought systems'. *European Journal of Social Psychology*, 22: 571–91.

Morin, A. (1993) 'Self-talk and self-awareness: on the nature of the relation'. *The Journal for Mind and Behavior*, 14: 223–34.

Morin, A. (2005) 'Possible links between self-awareness and inner speech: theoretical background, underlying mechanisms, and empirical evidence'. *Journal of Consciousness Studies* 12(4–5): 115–34.

Morin, A. (2006) 'Levels of consciousness and self-awareness: a comparison and integration of various neuro-cognitive views'. *Consciousness and Cognition*, 15(2): 358–471.

Morin, A. (2009) 'Self-awareness deficits following loss of inner speech: Dr Jill Bolte Taylor's study'. *Consciousness and Cognition*, 18(2): 524–9.

Morin, A. and DeBlois, S. (1989) 'Gallup's Mirrors: more that an operationalization of self-awareness in primates?' *Psychological Reports*, 65: 289–91.

Morin, A. and Everett, J. (1990) 'Inner speech as a mediator of self awareness, self consciousness and self knowledge: an hypothesis'. *New Ideas in Psychology*, 2: 337–56.

Morin, A. and Hamper, B. (2012) 'Self-reflection and the inner-voice: activation of the left inferior frontal gyrus during perceptual and conceptual self-referential thinking'. *The Open Neuroimaging Journal*, 6: 78–89.

Morin, A. and Michaud, J. (2007) 'Self-awareness and the left inferior frontal gyrus: inner speech use during self-related processing'. *Brain Research Bulletin*, 74: 387–96.

Morin, A. and Uttl, B. (2013) 'Inner speech: a window into consciousness' *Neuropsychotherapist.com* Available at: http://www2.mtroyal.ab.ca/~amorin/Neuropsychotherapist.pdf (visited on 13 February 2106.

Morin, A., Uttl, B. and Hamper, B. (2011) Self-reported frequency, content, and functions of inner speech. *Procedia-Social and Behavioral Journal*, 30: 1714–18.

Mouzelis, N. (2008) *Modern and Postmodern Social Theorizing: Bridging and Divide.* Cambridge: Cambridge University Press.

Peirce, C.S. (1935) *Collected Papers on Charles Sanders Peirce, vol. 6.* Cambridge, MA: Belknap Press.

Piaget, J. (1926) *Play, Dreams and Imitation in Childhood* (transated from French by C. Gattegno and F.M. Hodgson). London: Routledge & Kegan Paul.

Ricoeur, P. (1984) *Time and Narrative (Temps et Récit), vol. 1.* (tr. K. McLaughlin and D. Pellauer). Chicago, IL: University of Chicago Press.

Ricoeur, P. (1986) *From Text to Action: Essays in Hermeneutics II* (tr. K. Blamey and J.B. Thompson). Evanston, IL: Northwestern University Press.

Ricoeur, P. (1992) *Oneself as Another (Soi-même comme un autre)* (tr. K. Blamey). Chicago, IL: University of Chicago Press.

Rohrer, J.D., Knight, W.D., Warren, J.E., Fox, N.C., Rossor, M.N., Warren, J.D. (2008) 'Word-finding difficulty: a clinical analysis of the progressive aphasias'. *Brain*, 131(1): 8–38.

Ruby, D. and Legrand, P. (2009) 'What is self-specific? Theoretical investigation and critical review of neuroimaging results'. *Psychological Review*, 116(1): 252–82.

Schneider, J.F., Pospeschill, M. and Ranger, J. (2005) 'Self-consciousness as mediator between self-talk and self-knowledge'. *Psychological Reports*, 96: 387–96.

Siegrist, M. (1995) 'Inner speech as a cognitive process mediating self-consciousness and inhibiting self deception'. *Psychological Reports*, 76: 259–65.

Simmel, G. (1950) *The Sociology of Georg Simmel.* Translated, edited and with an introduction by K.H. Wolff. Glencoe, IL: The Free Press.

Smith, K.E. (2010) *Meaning, Subjectivity, Society: Making Sense of Modernity.* Boston, MA: Brill.

Spykman, N.J. (1965) *The Social Theory of Georg Simmel.* New York: Atherton Press.

Taylor, C. (1975) *Hegel.* Cambridge: Cambridge University Press.

Taylor, C. (1989) *Sources of the Self.* Cambridge: Cambridge University Press.

Tullett, A.M. and Inzlicht, M. (2010) 'The voice of self-control: blocking the inner voice increases impulsive responding'. *Acta Psychologica (Amsterdam)*, 135(2): 252–6.

Valsiner, J. and Van der Veer, R. (1991) *Understanding Vygotsky: A Guest of Synthesis.* Oxford: Basil Blackwell.

Vandenberghe, F. (2005) 'Book review: The Archers: a tale of folk (final episode?)'. *European Journal of Social Theory*, 8: 227–37.

Vocate, D.R. (1994) 'Self-talk and inner speech: understanding the uniquely human aspects of intrapersonal communication', in D.R. Vocate (ed.), *Intrapersonal Communication: Different Voices, Different Minds.* Mahwah, NJ: Lawrence Erlbaum.

Vygotsky, L.S. ([1934] 1962) *Thought and Language* (12th ed., 2000). Cambridge, MA: MIT Press.

Vygotsky, L.S. (1978) *Mind in Society*. Cambridge, MA: Harvard University Press.

Whitehouse, A.J.O., Murray, T.M. and Durkin, K. (2006) 'Inner speech impairment in autism'. *Journal of Child Psychology and Psychiatry*, 47: 847–65.

Wiley, N. (1994) *The Semiotic Self*. Cambridge: Polity Press.

Wiley, N. (2006) Inner speech as a language: a Saussurean inquiry'. *Journal for the Theory of Social Behaviour*, 36(3): 319–41.

Wiley, N. (2010) 'Inner speech and agency', in M.S. Archer (ed.), *Conversations about Reflexivity*. London: Routledge, 17–38.

Williams, D.M. and Jarrold, C. (2010) 'Brief report: predicting inner speech use among children with Autism Spectrum Disorder (ASD): the roles of verbal ability and cognitive profile'. *Journal of Autism Developmental Disorders*, 40: 907–13.

Index

Note: italics denote highlighted terms